# Probation Officer/ Parole Officer Exam

## 6th Edition

Jeffrey P. Rush, DPA

**THOMSON**

**PETERSON'S**

Australia • Canada • Mexico • Singapore • Spain • United Kingdom • United States

## About Thomson Peterson's

Thomson Peterson's (www.petersons.com) is a leading provider of education information and advice, with books and online resources focusing on education search, test preparation, and financial aid. Its Web site offers searchable databases and interactive tools for contacting educational institutions, online practice tests and instruction, and planning tools for securing financial aid. Peterson's serves 110 million education consumers annually.

**Petersons.com/publishing**

Check out our Web site at www.petersons.com/publishing to see if there is any new information regarding the test and any revisions or corrections to the content of this book. We've made sure the information in this book is accurate and up-to-date; however, the test format or content may have changed since the time of publication.

For more information, contact Peterson's, 2000 Lenox Drive, Lawrenceville, NJ 08648; 800-338-3282; or find us on the World Wide Web at www.petersons.com/about.

An American BookWorks Corporation Project

ISBN: 0-7689-0702-0

Printed in the United States of America

10  9  8  7  6  5  4          06  05  04

Sixth Edition

# CONTENTS

# WHAT THIS BOOK WILL DO FOR YOU

Arco Publishing has followed testing trends and methods ever since the firm was founded in 1937. We *specialize* in books that prepare people for tests. Based on this experience, we have prepared the best possible book to help *you* score high.

To write this book we carefully analyzed every detail surrounding the forthcoming examinations. Since there is such variation in exams, we cannot predict exactly what your exam will be like. *However*, after studying many announcements and many exams, we have written this book to prepare you for the most probable question types. The instructional chapters will prepare you for questions that you are likely to face. The model exams, while they are not actual exams, will give you excellent practice and preparation for your civil service exam. Other features of this book include details about:

- the job itself

- official and unofficial announcements concerning the examination

- all the previous examinations, although many not available to the public

- related examinations

- technical literature that explains and forecasts the examination

## CAN YOU PREPARE YOURSELF FOR YOUR TEST?

You want to pass this test. That's why you bought this book. Used correctly, your "self-tutor" will show you what to expect and will give you a speedy brush-up on the subjects tested in your exam. Some of these are subjects not taught in schools at all. Even if your study time is very limited, you should:

- become familiar with the type of examination you will have

- improve your general examination-taking skill

- improve your skill in analyzing and answering questions involving reasoning, judgment, comparison, and evaluation

- improve your speed and skill in reading and understanding what you read — an important part of your ability to learn and an important part of most tests

This book will help you in the following ways:

**Present every type of question you will get on the actual test.** This will make you at ease with the test format.

**Find your weaknesses.** Once you know what subjects you're weak in, you can get right to work and concentrate on those areas. This kind of selective study yields maximum test results.

**Give you confidence** *now.* It will build your self-confidence while you are preparing for the test. As you proceed, it will prevent the kind of test anxiety that causes low test scores.

**Stress the multiple-choice type of question because that's the kind you'll have on your test.** You must not be satisfied with merely knowing the correct answer for each question. You must find out why the other choices are incorrect. This will help you remember a lot you thought you had forgotten.

After testing yourself, you may find that you are weak in a particular area. You should concentrate on improving your skills by using the specific practice sections in this book that apply to you.

## HOW DO I USE THIS BOOK?

If you already know what type of career you wish to pursue, this book will help you prepare for any of the major exams. If you don't know what type of job you'd like to apply for, this book will also help you. Not only will you be able to prepare for your exam, but you will also find information here about various types of careers, and perhaps it will narrow down your choices. This book offers you an overview of the world of civil service, a brief introduction to federal, state, and city employers and their hiring requirements, and in-depth descriptions of a number of widely used examinations.

## PART ONE

There are five parts to this book. Part One covers the major employment sectors: federal, state, municipal (city), and private industry careers. There's more than enough for everyone here. Each sector has its own requirements and tests. However, as you will see, there are certain types of questions that will appear on most of these exams, regardless of the type of test you will take.

Also in this section is important information on test-taking techniques. This will give you guidelines to help you prepare for the actual test. Feeling anxious before you take a test is a normal reaction. We provide you with tips on feeling relaxed and comfortable with your exam so you can get a great test score.

## PART TWO

Part Two is an overview of the various types of careers available. If you haven't already been in the field, you will be surprised by the number of different job opportunities there are as well as the varied jobs within an area. For example, did you know that there are almost 2,000 different job titles just within the United States Postal Service? This is just *one* federal agency.

If you are beginning your career or job shopping at this time, you should read this section carefully. It will help introduce you to the different jobs and the many opportunities that await you. We hope you will be inspired and excited and will be motivated to apply for, study for, and land one of those jobs. If this section helps you narrow your area of interest, you can then concentrate on the exams that will help you prepare for the job you want. If you are still wide open, give equal attention to each exam.

## PART THREE

That leads us into Part Three of this book. In this section, we detail test-types and requirements. We've also given you a review section so that you can practice on a variety of different question types. We suggest you go through this chapter to get an idea of where your strengths lie and what weaknesses you'll have to deal with on the actual test.

We've also provided you with a variety of different types of tests that you will encounter in almost any job you apply for in the civil service, since there are certain basics that need to be covered. For example, in most tests, you will be asked to understand vocabulary and the use of grammar. Some tests will test your memory abilities and your ability for recall. Can you alphabetize easily and quickly? That's an area also covered on many of these tests.

## PART FOUR

In Part Four, there are either real examinations, (official sample examinations) or others are model examinations closely patterned on the actual exams. Timing, level of difficulty, question styles, and scoring methods all conform closely to the examinations for which they are meant to prepare. And a special feature of this book is that all the correct answers are explained.

When you do take the sample exams, try to set aside the full measure of time to take the exam at one sitting. Time yourself accurately (a stopwatch or a kitchen timer will work well) and stop working when the time is up. If you have not completed all of the questions when the time expires, stop anyway. Check your answers against the provided correct answers and score your paper. Then continue with the remaining questions to get in all the practice you can. Carefully study all the answer explanations, even those for questions that you answered correctly. By reading all of the explanations, you can gain greater insight into methods of answering questions and the reasoning behind the correct choices.

One very important suggestion: We strongly believe that regardless of the test that you think you're planning to take—or the career path you want to follow—try to take *all* of the exams in this book. It may seem like a lot of extra work, but you never know where you may end up. You may think you're interested in a job with the local city government, and end up instead in a private company. Or the exam you were hoping to take is not being given for another year, but some other test is being given next month. It is always better to be prepared.

## PART FIVE

Finally, Part Five contains civil service career information resources. Here you will find out how to go about looking for available jobs, as well as important addresses, phone numbers, and Internet websites that will help you pursue your career in civil service.

The most important thing is to *use* this book. By going through all of the sections and reading them, reviewing question types, and taking the practice exams, you will be using what you learned here to the best of your ability to succeed in your intended career path.

**PART ONE**

# So You Want to Work for The Government

Government service is one of the nation's largest sources of employment. About one in every six employed persons in the United States is in some form of civilian government service. Of those government employees, five out of six workers are employed by state or local governments, and the remainder work for the federal government.

As you can see, government employees represent a significant portion of the nation's work force. They work in large cities, small towns, and remote and isolated places such as lighthouses and forest ranger stations, and a small number of federal employees work overseas. In this chapter, we will outline the various types of careers that are available in the federal, state, and local governments.

# WHERE THE JOBS ARE: FEDERAL CIVILIAN EMPLOYMENT

The federal government is the nation's largest employer. It employs almost 3 million civilian workers in the United States and an additional 130,000 civilian workers—half of them U.S. citizens—in U.S. territories and foreign countries. The headquarters of most government departments and agencies are in the Washington, D.C., area, but only one out of eight federal employees works there.

Federal employees work in occupations that represent nearly every kind of job in private employment as well as some unique to the federal government such as regulatory inspectors, foreign service officers, and Internal Revenue agents. Most federal employees work for the executive branch of the government.

The executive branch includes the Office of the President, the cabinet departments, and about 100 independent agencies, commissions, and boards. This branch is responsible for activities such as administering federal laws, handling international relations, conserving natural resources, treating and rehabilitating disabled veterans, delivering the mail, conducting scientific research, maintaining the flow of supplies to the armed forces, and administering other programs to promote the health and welfare of the people of the United States.

The Department of Defense, which includes the Departments of the Army, Navy, and Air Force, is the largest department. It employs about one million civilian workers. The Departments of Agriculture, Health and Human Services, and the Treasury are also big employers. The two largest independent agencies are the U.S. Postal Service and the Veterans Administration.

There is also federal civilian employment available in the legislative branch, which includes Congress, the Government Printing Office, the General Accounting Office, and the Library of Congress. The judicial branch, the smallest employer, hires people for work within the court system.

## WHITE-COLLAR OCCUPATIONS

Because of its wide range of responsibilities, the federal government employs white-collar workers in a great many occupational fields. About one of four of these are administrative and clerical workers.

General clerical workers are employed in all federal departments and agencies. These include office machine operators, secretaries, stenographers, clerk-typists, mail- and file-clerks, telephone operators, and workers in computer and related occupations. In addition, there are the half million postal clerks and mail carriers.

Many government workers are employed in engineering and related fields. The engineers represent virtually every branch and specialty of engineering. There are large numbers of technicians in areas such as engineering, electronics, surveying, and drafting. Nearly two-thirds of all engineers are in the Department of Defense.

Of the more than 120,000 workers employed in accounting and budgeting work, 35,000 are professional accountants or Internal Revenue officers. Among technician and administrative occupations are accounting technicians, tax accounting technicians, and budget administrators. There are also large numbers of clerks in specialized accounting work. Accounting workers are employed throughout the government, particularly in the Departments of Defense and the Treasury and in the General Accounting Office.

Many federal employees work in hospitals or in medical, dental, and public health activities. Three out of five are either professional nurses or nursing assistants. Other professional occupations in this field include physicians, dieticians, technologists, and physical therapists. Technician and aide jobs include medical technicians, medical laboratory aides, and dental assistants. Employees in this field work primarily for the Veterans Administration; others work for the Departments of Defense and Health and Human Services.

Other government workers are engaged in administrative work related to private business and industry. They arrange and monitor contracts with the private sector and purchase goods and services needed by the federal government. Administrative occupations include contract and procurement specialists, production control specialists, and Internal Revenue officers. Two out of three of these workers are employed by the Departments of Defense and Treasury.

Another large group works in jobs concerned with the purchase, cataloging, storage, and distribution of supplies for the federal government. This field includes many managerial and administrative positions such as supply management officers, purchasing officers, and inventory management specialists, as well as large numbers of specialized clerical positions. Most of these jobs are in the Department of Defense.

Throughout the federal government, many people are employed in the field of law. They fill professional positions, such as attorneys or law clerks, and administrative positions, such as passport and visa examiners or tax law specialists. There also are many clerical positions that involve examining claims.

The social sciences also employ many government employees. Economists are employed throughout the government; psychologists and social workers work primarily for the Veterans Administration; and foreign affairs and international relations specialists, for the Department of State. One third of the workers in this field are social insurance administrators employed largely in the Department of Health and Human Services.

About 50,000 biological and agricultural science workers are employed by the federal government, mostly in the Departments of Agriculture and Interior. Many of these work in forestry and soil conservation activities. Others administer farm assistance programs. The largest number are employed as biologists, forest and range fire controllers, soil conservationists, and forestry technicians.

The federal government employs another 50,000 people in investigative and inspection work. Large numbers of these are engaged in criminal investigation and health regulatory inspections, mostly in the Departments of Treasury, Justice, and Agriculture.

Physical sciences is another area of government employment. Three out of four workers in the physical sciences are employed by the Departments of Defense, Interior, and Commerce. Professional workers include chemists, physicists, meteorologists, cartographers, and geologists. Aides and technicians include physical science technicians, meteorological technicians, and cartography technicians.

And in the mathematics field are professional mathematicians and statisticians and mathematics technicians and statistical clerks. They are employed primarily by the Departments of Defense, Agriculture, Commerce, and Health and Human Services.

Entrance requirements for white-collar jobs vary widely. A college degree in a specified field or equivalent work experience is usually required for professional occupations such as physicists and engineers.

Entrants into administrative and managerial occupations usually are not required to have knowledge of a specialized field, but must instead indicate a potential for future development by having a degree from a 4-year college or responsible job experience. They usually begin as trainees and learn their duties on the job. Typical jobs in this group are budget analysts, claims examiners, purchasing specialists, administrative assistants, and personnel specialists.

Technician, clerical, and aide-assistant jobs have entry-level positions for people with a high school education or the equivalent. For many of these positions, no previous experience or training is required. The entry level position is usually that of trainee. Persons who have junior college or technical school training or those who have specialized skills may enter these occupations at higher levels. Typical jobs are engineering technicians, supply clerks, clerk-typists, and nursing assistants.

## BLUE-COLLAR OCCUPATIONS

Blue-collar occupations—craft, operative, laborer, and some service jobs—provide full-time employment for more than half a million federal workers. The Department of Defense employs about three fourths of these workers in establishments such as naval shipyards, arsenals, the Air or Army depots, as well as on construction, harbor, flood control, irrigation, or reclamation projects. Others work for the Veterans Administration, U.S. Postal Service, General Services Administration, Department of the Interior, and Tennessee Valley Authority.

The largest single blue-collar group consists of manual laborers. Large numbers also are employed in machine tool and metal work, motor vehicle operation, warehousing, and food preparation and serving. The federal government employs a wide variety of individuals in maintenance and repair work, such as electrical and electronic equipment installation and repair, and in vehicle and industrial equipment maintenance and repair. All these fields require a range of skill levels and include a variety of occupations comparable to the private sector.

Although the federal government employs blue-collar workers in many different fields, about half are concentrated in a small number of occupations. The largest group, the skilled mechanics, works as air-conditioning, aircraft, automobile, truck, electronics, sheet-metal, and general maintenance mechanics. Another large number of craft workers is employed as painters, pipefitters, carpenters, electricians, and machinists. A similar number serves as warehouse workers, truck drivers, and general laborers. An additional group of workers is employed as janitors and food service workers.

## ENTRANCE REQUIREMENTS

Persons with previous training in a skilled trade may apply for a position with the federal government at the journey level. Those with no previous training may apply for appointment to one of several apprenticeship programs. Apprenticeship programs generally last four years; trainees receive both classroom and on-the-job training. After completing this training, a person is eligible for a position at the journey level. There are also a number of positions which require little or no prior training or experience, including janitors, maintenance workers, messengers, and many others.

## THE MERIT SYSTEM

More than nine out of ten jobs in the federal government are under a merit system. The Civil Service Act, administered by the U.S. Office of Personnel Management, covers six out of ten federal titles. This act was passed by Congress to ensure that federal employees are hired on the basis of individual merit and fitness. It provides for competitive examinations and the selection of new employees from among the most qualified applicants.

Some federal jobs are exempt from civil service requirements either by law or by action of the Office of Personnel Management. However, most of these positions are covered by separate merit systems of other agencies such as the Foreign Service of the Department of State, the Federal Bureau of Investigation, the Nuclear Regulatory Commission, and the Tennessee Valley Authority.

## EARNINGS, ADVANCEMENT, AND WORKING CONDITIONS

Most federal civilian employees are paid according to one of three major pay systems: the **General Pay Schedule,** the **Wage System**, or the **Postal Service Schedule.**

## GENERAL PAY SCHEDULE

More than half of all federal workers are paid under the General Schedule (GS), a pay scale for workers in professional, administrative, technical, and clerical jobs, and for workers such as guards and messengers. General Schedule jobs are classified by the U.S. Office of Personnel Management in one of fifteen grades, according to the difficulty of duties and responsibilities and the knowledge, experience, and skills required of the workers. GS pay rates are set by Congress and apply to government workers nationwide. They are reviewed annually to see whether they are comparable with salaries in private industry. They are generally subject to upwards adjustment for very high-cost-of-living regions. In low-cost areas, the GS pay scale may exceed that of most private-sector workers.

Most employees receive within-grade pay increases at one-, two-, or three-year intervals if their work is acceptable. Within-grade increases may also be given in recognition of high-quality service. Some managers and supervisors receive increases based on their job performance rather than on time in grade.

High school graduates who have no related work experience usually start in GS-2 jobs, but some who have special skills begin at grade GS-3. Graduates of 2-year colleges and technical schools often can begin at the GS-4 level. Most people with bachelor's degrees appointed to professional and administrative jobs such as statisticians, economists, writers and editors, budget analysts, accountants, and physicists, can enter at grades GS-5 or GS-7, depending on experience and academic record. Those who have a master's degree or Ph.D. or the equivalent education or experience may enter at the GS-9 or GS-11 level. Advancement to higher grades generally depends upon ability, work performance, and openings in jobs at higher grade levels.

## FEDERAL WAGE SYSTEM

About one quarter of federal civilian workers are paid according to the Federal Wage System. Under this system, craft, service, and manual workers are paid hourly rates established on the basis of "prevailing" rates paid by private employers for similar work in the same locations. As a result, the federal government wage rate for an occupation varies by locality. This commitment to meeting the local wage scale allows the federal wage earner to bring home a weekly paycheck comparable to that which he or she would earn in the private sector and to enjoy the benefits and security of a government job at the same time. The federal wage earner has the best of all possible worlds in this regard.

Federal government employees work a standard 40-hour week. Employees who are required to work overtime may receive premium rates for the additional time or compensatory time off at a later date. Most employees work eight hours a day, five days a week, Monday through Friday, but in some cases, the nature of the work requires a different workweek. Annual earnings for most full-time federal workers are not affected by seasonal factors.

Federal employees earn 13 days of annual (vacation) leave each year during their first three years of service; 20 days each year until the end of 15 years; after 15 years, 26 days each year. Workers who are members of military reserve organizations also are granted up to 15 days of paid military leave a year for training purposes. A federal worker who is laid off, though federal layoffs are uncommon, is entitled to unemployment compensation similar to that provided for employees in private industry.

Other benefits available to most federal employees include: a contributory retirement system, optional participation in low-cost group life and health insurance programs which are partly supported by the government (as the employer), and training programs to develop maximum job proficiency and help workers achieve their highest potential. These training programs may be conducted in government facilities or in private educational facilities at government expense.

## GENERAL SCHEDULE
### (Range of Salaries)

Effective as of January 1, 2001

| GS Rating | Low | High |
|---|---|---|
| 1 | $14,244 | $17,819 |
| 2 | 16,015 | 20,156 |
| 3 | 17,474 | 22,712 |
| 4 | 19,616 | 25,502 |
| 5 | 21,957 | 28,535 |
| 6 | 24,463 | 31,798 |
| 7 | 27,185 | 35,339 |
| 8 | 30,107 | 39,143 |
| 9 | 33,254 | 43,226 |
| 10 | 36,621 | 47,610 |
| 11 | 40,236 | 52,305 |
| 12 | 48,223 | 62,686 |
| 13 | 57,345 | 74,553 |
| 14 | 67,765 | 88,096 |
| 15 | 79,710 | 103,623 |

# WHERE THE JOBS ARE: STATE AND LOCAL GOVERNMENTS

State and local governments provide a very large and expanding source of job opportunities in a wide variety of occupational fields. About fifteen million people work for state and local government agencies; nearly three fourths of these work in units of local government such as counties, municipalities, towns, and school districts. The job distribution varies greatly from that in federal government service. Defense, international relations and commerce, immigration, and mail delivery are virtually non-existent in state and local governments. On the other hand, there is great emphasis on education, health, social services, transportation, construction, and sanitation.

## EDUCATIONAL SERVICES

About one half of all jobs in state and local government are in educational services. Educational employees work in public schools, colleges, and various extension services. About half of all education workers are instructional personnel. School systems, colleges, and universities also employ administrative personnel, librarians, guidance counselors, nurses, dieticians, clerks, and maintenance workers.

## HEALTH SERVICES

The next largest field of state and local government employment is health services. Those employed in health and hospital work include physicians, nurses, medical laboratory technicians, dieticians, kitchen and laundry workers, and hospital attendants. Social services make up another aspect of health and welfare. Unfortunately, the need for welfare and human services has been increasing greatly. As the need grows, the opportunities for social workers and their affiliated administrative and support staff also grows.

## GOVERNMENT CONTROL/FINANCIAL ACTIVITIES

Another million workers work in the areas of general governmental control and financial activities. These include chief executives and their staffs, legislative representatives, and persons employed in the administration of justice, tax enforcement and other financial work, and general administration. These functions require the services of individuals such as lawyers, judges and other court officers, city managers, property assessors, budget analysts, stenographers, and clerks.

## STREETS AND HIGHWAYS

The movement of people is of great concern to both state and local governments. Street and highway construction and maintenance are of major importance. Highway workers include civil engineers, surveyors, operators of construction machinery and equipment, truck drivers, concrete finishers, carpenters, construction laborers, and, where appropriate, snow removers. Toll collectors are relatively few in number, but they too are state or county employees or employees of independent authorities of the states or counties. Mass transportation within municipalities and between the cities and their outlying suburbs is also the province of local government. Maintaining vehicles, roadbeds and signaling systems, and staffing the vehicles themselves, requires a large and varied work force.

## POLICE AND FIRE PROTECTION SERVICES

Police and fire protection is another large field of employment. Along with uniformed officers, these services include extensive administrative, clerical, maintenance, and custodial personnel.

## MISCELLANEOUS STATE AND LOCAL OCCUPATIONS

Other state and local government employees work in a wide variety of activities, including local utilities (water in most areas, electricity in some); natural resources; parks and recreation; sanitation; corrections; local libraries; sewage disposal; and housing and urban renewal. These activities require workers in diverse occupations such as economists, electrical engineers, electricians, pipefitters, clerks, foresters, and bus drivers.

## CLERICAL, ADMINISTRATIVE, MAINTENANCE, AND CUSTODIAL WORKERS

A large percentage of employment in most government agencies is made up of clerical, administrative, maintenance, and custodial workers. Among the workers involved in these activities are word processors, secretaries, data processors, computer specialists, office managers, fiscal and budget administrators, bookkeepers, accountants, carpenters, painters, plumbers, guards, and janitors. The list is endless.

Most positions in state and local governments are filled by residents of the state or locality. Many localities have residency requirements. Exceptions are generally made for persons with skills that are in special demand.

## EARNINGS

Job conditions and earnings of state and local government employees vary widely, depending upon occupation and locality. Salary differences from state to state and even within some states tend to reflect differences in the general wage level and cost of living in the various localities.

As with the federal government, a majority of state and local government positions are filled through some type of formal civil service test; that is, personnel are hired and promoted on the basis of merit. State and local government workers have the same protections as federal government workers: they cannot be refused employment because of their race; they cannot be denied promotion because someone else made a greater political contribution; and they cannot be fired because the boss's son needs a job. Jobs tend to be classified according to job description and pegged to a salary schedule that is based upon the job classifications. Periodic performance reviews also are standard expectations. Nearly every group of employees has some sort of union or organization, but the functions and powers of these units vary greatly.

Since states and local entities are independent, the benefits packages they offer their employees can be quite different. Most state and local government employees are covered by retirement systems or by the federal social security program. Most have some sort of health coverage. They usually work a standard week of 40 hours or less with overtime pay or compensatory time benefits for additional hours of work.

# PREPARING YOURSELF FOR THE CIVIL SERVICE EXAMINATION

Most federal, state, and municipal units have recruitment procedures for filling civil service positions. They have developed a number, of methods to make job opportunities known. Places where such information may be obtained include:

1. The offices of the State Employment Services. There are almost two thousand throughout the country. These offices are administered by the state in which they are located, with the financial assistance of the federal government. You will find the address of the one nearest you in your telephone book.

2. Your state Civil Service Commission. Address your inquiry to the capital city of your state.

3. Your city Civil Service Commission. It is sometimes called by another name, such as the Department of Personnel, but you will be able to identify it in your telephone directory under the listing of city departments.

4. Your municipal building and your local library.

5. Complete listings are carried by such newspapers as *The Chief-Leader* (published in New York City), as well as by other city and state-wide publications devoted to civil service employees. Many local newspapers run a section on regional civil service news.

6. State and local agencies looking for competent employees will contact schools, professional societies, veterans organizations, unions, and trade associations.

7. School boards and boards of education, which employ the greatest proportion of all state and local personnel, should be asked directly for information about job openings.

You will find more in-depth information at the end of this book.

## THE FORMAT OF THE JOB ANNOUNCEMENT

When a position is open and a civil service examination is to be given for it, a job announcement is drawn up. This generally contains everything an applicant has to know about the job.

The announcement begins with the job title and salary. A typical announcement then describes the work, the location of the position, the education and experience requirements, the kind of examination to be given, and the system of rating. It may also have something to say about veteran preference and the age limit. It tells which application form is to be filled out, where to get the form, and where and when to file it.

Study the job announcement carefully. It will answer many of your questions and help you decide whether you like the position and are qualified for it. We have included sample job announcements in a later chapter.

There is no point in applying for a position and taking the examination if you do not want to work where the job is. The job may be in your community or hundreds of miles away at the other end of the state. If you are not willing to work where the job is, study other announcements that will give you an opportunity to work in a place of your choice. A civil service job close to your home has an additional advantage since local residents usually receive preference in appointments.

The words **Optional Fields**—sometimes just the word **Options**—may appear on the front page of the announcement. You then have a choice to apply for that particular position in which you are especially interested. This is because the duties of various positions are quite different even though they bear the same broad title. A public relations clerk, for example, does different work from a payroll clerk, although they are considered broadly in the same general area.

Not every announcement has options. But whether or not it has them, the precise duties are described in detail, usually under the heading, **Description of Work.** Make sure that these duties come within the range of your experience and ability.

Most job requirements give a **deadline for filing** an application. Others bear the words, **No Closing Date** at the top of the first page; this means that applications will be accepted until the needs of the agency are met. In some cases a public notice is issued when a certain number of applications has been received. No application mailed past the deadline date will be considered.

Every announcement has a detailed section on **education and experience requirements** for the particular job and for the optional fields. Make sure that in both education and experience you meet the minimum qualifications. If you do not meet the given standards for one job, there may be others open where you stand a better chance of making the grade.

If the job announcement does not mention **veteran preference,** it would be wise to inquire if there is such a provision in your state or municipality. There may be none or it may be limited to disabled veterans. In some jurisdictions, surviving spouses of disabled veterans are given preference. All such information can be obtained through the agency that issues the job announcement.

Applicants may be denied examinations and eligible candidates may be denied appointments for any of the following reasons:

- intentional false statements

- deception or fraud in examination or appointment

- use of intoxicating beverages to the extent that ability to perform the duties of the position is impaired

- criminal, infamous, dishonest, immoral, or notoriously disgraceful conduct

The announcement describes the **kind of test** given for the particular position. Please pay special attention to this section. It tells what areas are to be covered in the written test and lists the specific subjects on which questions will be asked. Sometimes sample questions are given.

Usually the announcement states whether the examination is to be **assembled** or **unassembled.** In an assembled examination applicants assemble in the same place at the same time to take a written or performance test. The unassembled examination is one where an applicant does not take a test; instead, he or she is rated on his or her education and experience and whatever records of past achievement the applicant is asked to provide.

In the competitive examination all applicants for a position compete with each other; the better the mark, the better the chance of being appointed. Also, competitive examinations are given to determine desirability for promotion among employees.

Civil service written tests are rated on a scale of 100, with 70 usually as the passing mark.

# FILLING OUT THE APPLICATION FORM

Having studied the job announcement and having decided that you want the position and are qualified for it, your next step is to get an application form. The job announcement tells you where to send for it.

On the whole, civil service application forms differ little from state to state and locality to locality. The questions that have been worked out after years of experimentation are simple and direct, designed to elicit a maximal amount of information about you.

Many prospective civil service employees have failed to get a job because of slipshod, erroneous, incomplete, misleading, or untruthful answers. Give the application serious attention, for it is the first important step toward getting the job you want.

Here, along with some helpful comments, are the questions usually asked on the average application form, although not necessarily in this order.

- **Name of examination or kind of position applied for.** This information appears in large type on the first page of the job announcement.

- **Optional job** (if mentioned in the announcement). If you wish to apply for an option, simply copy the title from the announcement. If you are not interested in an option, write *None*.

- **Primary place of employment applied for.** The location of the position was probably contained in the announcement. You must consider whether you want to work there. The announcement may list more than one location where the job is open. If you would accept employment in any of the places, list them all; otherwise list the specific place or places where you would be willing to work.

- **Name and address.** Give in full, including your middle name if you have one, and your maiden name as well if you are a married woman.

- **Home and office phones.** If none, write *None*.

- **Legal or voting residence.** The state in which you vote is the one you list here.

- **Height without shoes, weight, sex.** Answer accurately.

- **Date of birth.** Give the exact day, month, and year.

- **Lowest grade or pay you will accept.** Although the salary is clearly stated in the job announcement, there may be a quicker opening in the same occupation but carrying less responsibility and thus a lower basic entrance salary. You will not be considered for a job paying less than the amount you give in answer to this question.

- **Will you accept temporary employment if offered you for (a) one month or less, (b) one to four months, (c) four to twelve months?** Temporary positions come up frequently and it is important to know whether you are available.

- **Will you accept less than full-time employment?** Part-time work comes up now and then. Consider whether you want to accept such a position while waiting for a full-time appointment.

- **Were you in active military service in the Armed Forces of the United States?** Veterans' preference, if given, is usually limited to active service during the following periods: 12/7/41–12/31/46; 6/27/50–1/31/55; 6/1/63–5/7/75; 6/1/83–12/1/87; 10/23/83–11/21/83; 12/20/89–1/3/90; 8/2/90 to end of Persian Gulf hostilities.

- **Do you claim disabled veterans credit?** If you do, you have to show proof of a war-incurred disability compensable by at least 10 percent. This is done through certification by the Veterans Administration.

- **Special qualifications and skills.** Even though not directly related to the position for which you are applying, information about licenses and certificates obtained for teacher, pilot, registered nurse, and so on, is requested. List your experience in the use of machines and equipment and whatever other skills you have acquired. Also list published writings, public speaking experience, membership in professional societies, and honors and fellowships received.

- **Education.** List your entire educational history, including all diplomas, degrees, and special courses taken in any accredited or armed forces school. Also give your credits toward a college or a graduate degree.

- **References.** The names of people who can give information about you, with their occupations and business and home address, are often requested.

- **Your health.** Questions are asked concerning your medical record. You are expected to have the physical and psychological capacity to perform the job for which you are applying. Standards vary, of course, depending on the requirements of the position. A physical handicap usually will not bar an applicant from a job he can perform adequately unless the safety of the public is involved.

- **Work history.** Considerable space is allotted on the form for the applicant to tell about all his past employment. Examiners check all such answers closely. Do not embellish or falsify your record. If you were ever fired, say so. It is better for you to state this openly than for the examiners to find out the truth from your former employer.

On the following pages are samples of a New York City Application for Examination and a state application from Louisiana.

## WHY PEOPLE CHOOSE GOVERNMENT SERVICE

There are many similarities between work in the private sector and work for the government. Within each occupation, the similarities of the daily duties far outweigh the differences in employers. Regardless of the nature of the employer—government, private business, nonprofit organization—typists type; doctors heal, teachers teach; electricians install wiring.

As was mentioned at the beginning of this chapter, one in six of employed persons in the United States is in government service. The five in six persons who are employed by nongovernmental employers all hope for just compensation for their work, for promotions when merited, and for fair and equal treatment with reference to their co-workers. They all hope that they will not be discriminated against for any non-job-related reasons, that they will not be fired capriciously, and that their opinions and suggestions will be taken seriously. In the great majority of cases, these expectations will be met.

But, in the private sector, there are no guarantees of employment practices. In government service these guarantees are a matter of policy and law. Each governmental jurisdiction has its own body of rules and procedures. In other words, not all government service is alike. The Federal Civil Service does serve as a model for all other governmental units.

# NEW YORK CITY APPLICATION FOR EXAMINATION

**DEPARTMENT OF CITYWIDE ADMINISTRATIVE SERVICES**
**DIVISION OF CITYWIDE PERSONNEL SERVICES**
1 Centre Street, 14th floor
New York, NY 10007

## APPLICATION FOR EXAMINATION

(Directions for completing this application are on the *back* of this form. Additional information is on the Special Circumstances Sheet)

Download this form on-line: nyc.gov/html/dcas

**FOLLOW DIRECTIONS ON BACK**
Fill in all requested information clearly, accurately, and completely.

*The City will only process applications with complete, correct, legible information which are accompanied by correct payment or waiver documentation.*

*All unprocessed applications will be returned to the applicant.*

1. EXAM #:

2. EXAM TITLE:

Check One:
☐ Open Competitive
☐ Promotion

4. LAST NAME:

5. FIRST NAME:

6. MIDDLE INITIAL:

3. SOCIAL SECURITY NUMBER: — —

7. MAILING ADDRESS:

8. APT. #:

9. CITY OR TOWN:

10. STATE:

11. ZIP CODE: —

12. PHONE: — —

13. OTHER NAMES USED IN CITY SERVICE:

14. RACE/ETHNICITY (Check One):
☐ White
☐ American Indian/ Alaskan Native
☐ Black
☐ Asian/Pacific Islander
☐ Hispanic

15. SEX (Check One):
☐ Male
☐ Female

16. ARE YOU EMPLOYED BY THE HEALTH AND HOSPITALS CORPORATION? (Check One)   ☐ YES   ☐ NO

17. CHECK ALL BOXES THAT APPLY TO YOU: (Directions for this section are found on the "Special Circumstances" Sheet)
☐ I AM A SABBATH OBSERVER AND WILL REQUEST AN ALTERNATE TEST DATE (Verification required. See Item A on Special Circumstances Sheet).
☐ I HAVE A DISABILITY AND WILL REQUEST SPECIAL ACCOMMODATIONS (Verification required. See item B on Special Circumstances Sheet).
☐ I CLAIM VETERANS' CREDIT (For qualifications see item C on Special Circumstances Sheet)
☐ I CLAIM DISABLED VETERANS CREDIT (For qualifications see item C on Special Circumstances Sheet)

Questions 14 & 15:
Discrimination on the basis of sex, sexual orientation, race, creed, color, age, disability status, veteran status or religious observance is prohibited by law. The City of New York is an equal opportunity employer. The identifying information requested on this form is to be used to determine the representation of protected groups among applicants. This information is voluntary and will not be made available to individuals making hiring decisions.

18. Your Signature: _____   Date: _____

## STATE OF LOUISIANA APPLICATION—page 1

SF 10
(Page 1)
REV. 1/97

**STATE PRE-EMPLOYMENT APPLICATION**

**STATE OF LOUISIANA
DEPARTMENT OF CIVIL SERVICE**
P.O. Box 94111, Capitol Station
Baton Rouge, Louisiana 70804-9111

AN EQUAL OPPORTUNITY EMPLOYER

**FOR OFFICE USE**

Special _____
Promo _____
Action(s) _____

Session _____

Data Entry Completed _____

**1. TEST LOCATION-Check only one.**

| Baton Rouge (3) (Weekday) ☐ | New Orleans (6) (Weekday) ☐ | Lafayette (4) (Sat. only) ☐ | Shreveport (7) (Sat. only) ☐ |
|---|---|---|---|
| | New Orleans (12) (Saturday) ☐ | Lake Charles (5) (Sat. only) ☐ | West Monroe (8) (Sat. only) ☐ |

**2. Enter Name and Complete Address below.**

**3. Parish of Residence**

**4. Are you 18 or older?** ☐ Yes ☐ No

**5. Other names ever used on SF-10**

NAME - First    Middle    Last

Mailing Address

City    State    Zip Code

**6. Social Security Number**
(For identification purpose)

Work Telephone No.

Home Telephone No.

L A S T → P R I N T

F I R S T

M I D D L E →

JS No.

V.P.

S.R.

| 7. REGISTER TITLE(S) APPLIED FOR | FOR OFFICE USE | | | | | ADDITIONAL TITLES | FOR OFFICE USE | | | | |
|---|---|---|---|---|---|---|---|---|---|---|---|
| | SER | CD | REJ | GRD | TR | | SER | CD | REJ | GRD | TR |
| | | | | | | | | | | | |
| | | | | | | | | | | | |
| | | | | | | | | | | | |
| | | | | | | | | | | | |

**ALL TITLES LISTED ABOVE MUST HAVE THE SAME SERIES NO.**

**8. JOB LOCATION AVAILABILITY - IMPORTANT:** Read Item 9 on the Instruction Page before completing this item. Mark at least one (1), but no more than twenty (20) parishes.

| | | | | | | | |
|---|---|---|---|---|---|---|---|
| 01 Acadia | 09 Caddo | 17 E. Baton Rouge | 25 Jackson | 33 Madison | 41 Red River | 49 St. Landry | 57 Vermillion |
| 02 Allen | 10 Calcasieu | 18 E. Carroll | 26 Jefferson | 34 Morehouse | 42 Richland | 50 St. Martin | 58 Vernon |
| 03 Ascension | 11 Caldwell | 19 E. Feliciana | 27 Jeff Davis | 35 Natchitoches | 43 Sabine | 51 St. Mary | 59 Washington |
| 04 | 12 Cameron | 20 Evangeline | 28 Lafayette | 36 Orleans | 44 St. Bernard | 52 St. Tammany | 60 Webster |
| 05 Avoyelles | 13 Catahoula | 21 Franklin | 29 Lafourche | 37 Ouachita | 45 St. Charles | 53 Tangipahoa | 61 W. Baton Rouge |
| 06 Beauregard | 14 Claiborne | 22 Grant | 30 LaSalle | 38 Plaquemines | 46 St. Helena | 54 Tensas | 62 W. Carroll |
| 07 Bienville | 15 Concordia | 23 Iberia | 31 Lincoln | 39 Pte. Coupee | 47 St. James | 55 Terrebonne | 63 W. Feliciana |
| 08 Bossier | 16 DeSoto | 24 Iberville | 32 Livingston | 40 Rapides | 48 St. John | 56 Union | 64 Winn |

9. ☐ Permanent ☐ Temporary—Type of employment you will accept
NOTE: Most Temporary Appointments are 3 - 12 months

10. ☐ YES ☐ NO  Do you possess a valid driver's license?

11. ☐ YES ☐ NO  Do you possess a valid commercial driver's license?

12. ☐ YES ☐ NO  Are you currently holding or running for an elective public office?

13. ☐ YES ☐ NO  Have you ever been on probation or sentenced to jail/prison as a result of a felony conviction or guilty plea?

14. ☐ YES ☐ NO  Have you ever been fired from a job or resigned to avoid dismissal?

NOTE: If answers to Items 13 and/or 14 are "YES", you MUST complete Item 24 on Page 2 of this application

15. ☐ YES ☐ NO  Are you claiming Veteran's Preference points on this application? (If "YES", see Item 20 on Page 2.)

The following information is collected to complete Equal Opportunity Reports required by law. You ARE NOT LEGALLY OBLIGATED to provide this information.

16. RACIAL/ETHNIC GROUP    16A. DATE OF BIRTH    17. SEX    ☐ Male ☐ Female

**I HAVE READ THE FOLLOWING STATEMENTS CAREFULLY BEFORE SIGNING THIS APPLICATION:**

18. Date    Social Security No. (for verification)

19. Signature of Applicant

**AUTHORITY TO RELEASE INFORMATION:** I consent to the release of information concerning my capacity and/or all aspects of prior job performance by employers, educational institutions, law enforcement agencies, and other individuals and agencies to duly accredited investigators, personnel technicians, and other authorized employees of the state government for the purpose of determining my eligibility and suitability for employment.

I certify that all statements made on this application and any attached papers are true and complete to the best of my knowledge. I understand that information on this application may be subject to investigation and verification and that any misrepresentation or material omission may cause my application to be rejected, my name to be removed from the eligible register and/or subject me to dismissal from state service.

## STATE OF LOUISIANA APPLICATION—page 2

**20. ACTIVE MILITARY SERVICE/VETERAN'S PREFERENCE**

See Item 10 on the Instruction Page to determine your eligibility for Veteran's Preference. If you are a first-time applicant or if you are claiming Veteran's Preference for the first time, required PROOF MUST BE ATTACHED to this application to have preference points added to your score.

List the dates (month and year) and branch for all ACTIVE DUTY military service. Was this service performed on an active, full-time basis with full pay and allowances? (Check YES or NO for each period of service.)

| FROM | TO | BRANCH OF SERVICE | YES | NO |
|---|---|---|---|---|
|  |  |  |  |  |
|  |  |  |  |  |

List all GRADES held and dates of each grade. Begin with the highest grade. IMPORTANT: Use E-, O-, or WO-grade.

| FROM | TO | GRADE HELD | FROM | TO | GRADE HELD |
|---|---|---|---|---|---|
|  |  |  |  |  |  |
|  |  |  |  |  |  |

**21. TRAINING AND EDUCATION**

Have you received a high school diploma or equivalency certificate?

☐ YES   Date received _____

☐ NO   Highest grade completed _____

| A. LIST BUSINESS OR TECHNICAL COLLEGES ATTENDED | NAME/LOCATION OF SCHOOL | Dates Attended (Month & Year) FROM — TO | Did You Graduate? YES — NO | TITLE OF PROGRAM | CLOCK HOURS PER WEEK |
|---|---|---|---|---|---|
|  |  |  |  |  |  |
|  |  |  |  |  |  |
|  |  |  |  |  |  |

List any accounting practice sets completed: _____

| B. LIST COLLEGES OR UNIVERSITIES ATTENDED (Include graduate or professional schools) | NAME OF COLLEGE OR UNIVERSITY/ CITY AND STATE | Dates Attended (Month & Year) FROM — TO | Total Credit Hours Earned Semester — Quarter | Type of Degree Earned | Major Field of Study | Date Degree Received (Month & Yr.) |
|---|---|---|---|---|---|---|
|  |  |  |  |  |  |  |
|  |  |  |  |  |  |  |
|  |  |  |  |  |  |  |

| C. MAJOR SUBJECTS | CHIEF UNDERGRADUATE SUBJECTS (Show Major on Line 1.) | Total Credit Hours Earned Semester — Quarter | CHIEF GRADUATE SUBJECTS (Show Major on Line 1.) | Total Credit Hours Earned Semester or Qtr. |
|---|---|---|---|---|
| 1 |  |  |  |  |
| 2 |  |  |  |  |
| 3 |  |  |  |  |

**22. LICENSES AND CERTIFICATION**

List any job-related licenses or certificates that you have (CPA, lawyer, registered nurse, etc.)

| | TYPE OF LICENSE OR CERTIFICATE (Specify Which One) | DATE ORIGINALLY LICENSED/ CERTIFIED | EXPIRATION DATE | NAME AND ADDRESS OF LICENSING OR CERTIFYING AGENCY |
|---|---|---|---|---|
| 1 |  |  |  |  |
| 2 |  |  |  |  |

**23. TYPING SPEED**

_____ WPM

**DICTATION SPEED**

_____ WPM

**24.** Explain a "YES" answer to Items 13 and/or 14 here. A "YES" ANSWER WILL NOT NECESSARILY BAR YOU FROM STATE EMPLOYMENT. WE WILL CONSIDER THE DATE, FACTS, AND CIRCUMSTANCES OF EACH INDIVIDUAL CASE. For Item 13, give the law enforcement authority (city police, sherrif, FBI, etc.), the offense, date of offense, place, and disposition of case.

_____

_____

Name _____

## STATE OF LOUISIANA APPLICATION—page 3

Name _____

| 25. | WORK EXPERIENCE — <u>IMPORTANT</u>: Read Item 11 of Instruction Page carefully before completing these items. List all jobs and activities including military service, part-time employment, self-employment, and volunteer work. BEGIN with your FIRST job in Block A; END with your MOST RECENT or PRESENT job. |
|---|---|

**A** EMPLOYER/COMPANY NAME | KIND OF BUSINESS

STREET ADDRESS | YOUR OFFICIAL JOB TITLE

CITY AND STATE | BEGINNING SALARY | ENDING SALARY

DATES OF EMPLOYMENT (MO/DA/YR) | AVERAGE HOURS WORKED PER WEEK | REASON FOR LEAVING | NO. OF EMPLOYEES YOU DIRECTLY SUPERVISED

FROM | TO

NAME/TITLE OF YOUR SUPERVISOR) | LIST JOB TITLES OF EMPLOYEES YOU DIRECTLY SUPERVISED

NAME/TITLE OF PERSON WHO CAN VERIFY THIS EMPLOYMENT (IF OTHER THAN SUPERVISOR)

DUTIES: List the major duties involved with job and give an approximate percentage of time spent on each duty.

| % OF TIME | MAJOR DUTIES |
|---|---|
| | |
| | |
| | |
| | |
| | |
| 100% | |

**B** EMPLOYER/COMPANY NAME | KIND OF BUSINESS

STREET ADDRESS | YOUR OFFICIAL JOB TITLE

CITY AND STATE | BEGINNING SALARY | ENDING SALARY

DATES OF EMPLOYMENT (MO/DA/YR) | AVERAGE HOURS WORKED PER WEEK | REASON FOR LEAVING | NO. OF EMPLOYEES YOU DIRECTLY SUPERVISED

FROM | TO

NAME/TITLE OF YOUR SUPERVISOR) | LIST JOB TITLES OF EMPLOYEES YOU DIRECTLY SUPERVISED

NAME/TITLE OF PERSON WHO CAN VERIFY THIS EMPLOYMENT (IF OTHER THAN SUPERVISOR)

DUTIES: List the major duties involved with job and give an approximate percentage of time spent on each duty.

| % OF TIME | MAJOR DUTIES |
|---|---|
| | |
| | |
| | |
| | |
| | |

## STATE OF LOUISIANA APPLICATION—page 4

100%

USE REVERSE SIDE OF THIS PAGE IF ADDITIONAL SPACE REQUIRED FOR WORK EXPERIENCE

Name _____

**25. WORK EXPERIENCE (Continued)**

**C** EMPLOYER/COMPANY NAME | KIND OF BUSINESS

STREET ADDRESS | YOUR OFFICIAL JOB TITLE

CITY AND STATE | BEGINNING SALARY | ENDING SALARY

DATES OF EMPLOYMENT (MO/DA/YR) | AVERAGE HOURS WORKED PER WEEK | REASON FOR LEAVING | NO. OF EMPLOYEES YOU DIRECTLY SUPERVISED

FROM | TO

NAME/TITLE OF YOUR SUPERVISOR | LIST JOB TITLES OF EMPLOYEES YOU DIRECTLY SUPERVISED

NAME/TITLE OF PERSON WHO CAN VERIFY THIS EMPLOYMENT (IF OTHER THAN SUPERVISOR)

DUTIES: List the major duties involved with job and give an approximate percentage of time spent on each duty.

| % OF TIME | MAJOR DUTIES |
| --- | --- |
| | |
| | |
| | |
| | |
| | |
| | |

100%

**D** EMPLOYER/COMPANY NAME | KIND OF BUSINESS

STREET ADDRESS | YOUR OFFICIAL JOB TITLE

CITY AND STATE | BEGINNING SALARY | ENDING SALARY

DATES OF EMPLOYMENT (MO/DA/YR) | AVERAGE HOURS WORKED PER WEEK | REASON FOR LEAVING | NO. OF EMPLOYEES YOU DIRECTLY SUPERVISED

FROM | TO

NAME/TITLE OF YOUR SUPERVISOR) | LIST JOB TITLES OF EMPLOYEES YOU DIRECTLY SUPERVISED

NAME/TITLE OF PERSON WHO CAN VERIFY THIS EMPLOYMENT (IF OTHER THAN SUPERVISOR)

DUTIES: List the major duties involved with job and give an approximate percentage of time spent on each duty.

| % OF TIME | MAJOR DUTIES |
| --- | --- |
| | |
| | |
| | |
| | |
| | |
| | |

# TEST-TAKING TECHNIQUES

Many factors enter into a test score. The most important factor should be ability to answer the questions, which in turn indicates the ability to learn and perform the duties of the job. Assuming that you have this ability, knowing what to expect on the exam and familiarity with techniques of effective test taking should give you the confidence you need to do your best on the exam.

There is no quick substitute for long-term study and development of your skills and abilities to prepare you for doing well on tests. However, there are some steps you can take to help you do the very best that you are prepared to do. Some of these steps are done before the test, and some are followed when you are taking the test. Knowing these steps is often called being "test-wise." Following these steps may help you feel more confident as you take the actual test.

"Test-wiseness" is a general term which simply means being familiar with some good procedures to follow when getting ready for and taking a test. The procedures fall into four major areas: (1) being prepared, (2) avoiding careless errors, (3) managing your time, and (4) guessing.

## BE PREPARED

Don't make the test harder than it has to be by not preparing yourself. You are taking a very important step in preparation by reading this book and taking the sample tests which are included. This will help you to become familiar with the tests and the kinds of questions you will have to answer.

As you use this book, read the sample questions and directions for taking the test carefully. Then, when you take the sample tests, time yourself as you will be timed in the real test.

As you are working on the sample questions, don't look at the correct answers before you try to answer them on your own. This can fool you into thinking you understand a question when you really don't. Try it on your own first, then compare your answer with the one given. Remember, in a sample test, you are your own grader; you don't gain anything by pretending to understand something you really don't.

On the examination day assigned to you, allow the test itself to be the main attraction of the day. Do not squeeze it in between other activities. Be sure to bring admission card, identification, and pencils, as instructed. Prepare these the night before so that you are not flustered by a last-minute search. Arrive rested, relaxed, and on time. In fact, plan to arrive a little bit early. Leave plenty of time for traffic tie-ups or other complications that might upset you and interfere with your test performance.

In the test room, the examiner will hand out forms for you to fill out. He or she will give you the instructions that you must follow in taking the examination. The examiner will tell you how to fill in the grids on the forms. Time limits and timing signals will be explained. If you do not understand any of the examiner's instructions, ASK QUESTIONS. It would be ridiculous to score less than your best because of poor communication.

At the examination, you must follow instructions exactly. Fill in the grids on the forms carefully and accurately. Misgridding may lead to loss of veteran's credits to which you may be entitled or misaddressing of your test results. Do not begin until you are told to begin. Stop as soon as the examiner tells you to stop. Do not turn pages until you are told to do so. Do not go back to parts you have already completed. Any infraction of the rules is considered cheating. If you cheat, your test paper will not be scored, and you will not be eligible for appointment.

The answer sheet for most multiple-choice exams is machine scored. You cannot give any explanations to the machine, so you must fill out the answer sheet clearly and correctly.

## HOW TO MARK YOUR ANSWER SHEET

1. Blacken your answer space firmly and completely. ● is the only correct way to mark the answer sheet. ◑, ✖, ⊘, and ⊘ are all unacceptable. The machine might not read them at all.

2. Mark only one answer for each question. If you mark more than one answer, you will be considered wrong, even if one of the answers is correct.

3. If you change your mind, you must erase your mark. Attempting to cross out an incorrect answer like this ✖ will not work. You must erase any incorrect answer completely. An incomplete erasure might be read as a second answer.

4. All of your answering should be in the form of blackened spaces. The machine cannot read English. Do not write any notes in the margins.

5. MOST IMPORTANT: Answer each question in the right place. Question 1 must be answered in space 1; question 52 in space 52. If you should skip an answer space and mark a series of answers in the wrong places, you must erase all those answers and do the questions over, marking your answers in the proper places. You cannot afford to use the limited time in this way. Therefore, as you answer each question, look at its number and check that you are marking your answer in the space with the same number.

6. For the typing tests, type steadily and carefully. Just don't rush, since that's when the errors occur. Keep in mind that each error subtracts 1 wpm from your final score.

## AVOID CARELESS ERRORS

Don't reduce your score by making careless mistakes. Always read the instructions for each test section carefully, even when you think you already know what the directions are. It's why we stress throughout this book that it's important to fully understand the directions for these different question-types before you go into the actual exam. It will not only reduce errors, but it will save you time—time you will need for the questions.

What if you don't understand the directions? You will have risked getting the answers wrong for a whole test section. As an example, vocabulary questions can sometimes test synonyms (words which have similar meanings), and sometimes test antonyms (words with opposite meanings). You can easily see how a mistake in understanding in this case could make a whole set of answers incorrect.

If you have time, reread any complicated instructions after you do the first few questions to check that you really do understand them. Of course, whenever you are allowed to, ask the examiner to clarify anything you don't understand.

Other careless mistakes affect only the response to particular questions. This often happens with arithmetic questions, but can happen with other questions as well. This type of error, called a "response error," usually stems from a momentary lapse of concentration.

### Example

The question reads: "The capital of Massachusetts is ...." The answer is (D) Boston, and you mark (B) because "B" is the first letter of the word "Boston."

### Example

The question reads: "8 - 5 = ...." The answer is (A) 3, but you mark (C) thinking "third letter."

A common error in reading comprehension questions is bringing your own information into the subject. For example, you may encounter a passage that discusses a subject you know something about. While this can make the passage easier to read, it can also tempt you to rely on your own knowledge about the subject. You must rely on information within the passage for your answers—in fact, sometimes the "wrong answer" for the questions are based on true information about the subject not given in the passage. Since the test-makers are testing your reading ability, rather than your general knowledge of the subject, an answer based on information not contained in the passage is considered incorrect.

## MANAGE YOUR TIME

Before you begin, take a moment to plan your progress through the test. Although you are usually not expected to finish all of the questions given on a test, you should at least get an idea of how much time you should spend on each question in order to answer them all. For example, if there are 60 questions to answer and you have 30 minutes, you will have about one-half minute to spend on each question.

Keep track of the time on your watch or the room clock, but do not fixate on the time remaining. Your task is to answer questions. Do not spend too much time on any one question. If you find yourself stuck, do not take the puzzler as a personal challenge. Either guess and mark the question in the question booklet or skip the question entirely, marking the question as a skip and taking care to skip the answer space on the answer sheet. If there is time at the end of the exam or exam part, you can return and give marked questions another try.

## MULTIPLE-CHOICE QUESTIONS

Almost all of the tests given on civil service exams are multiple-choice format. This means that you normally have four or five answer choices. But it's not something that should be overwhelming. There is a basic technique to answering these types of questions. Once you've understood this technique, it will make your test-taking far less stressful.

First, there should only be one correct answer. Since these tests have been given time and again, and the test-developers have a sense of which questions work and which questions don't work, it will be rare that your choices will be ambiguous. They may be complex, and somewhat confusing, but there will still be only one right answer.

The first step is to look at the question, without looking at the answer choices. Now select the correct answer. That may sound somewhat simplistic, but it's usually the case that your first choice is the correct one. If you go back and change it, redo it again and again, it's more likely that you'll end up with the wrong answer. Thus, follow your instinct. Once you have come up with the answer, look at the answer choices. If your answer is one of the choices, you're probably correct. It's not 100 percent infallible, but it's a strong possibility that you've selected the right answer.

With math questions you should first solve the problem. If your answer is among the choices, you're probably correct. Don't ignore things like the proper function signs (adding, subtracting, multiplying, and dividing), negative and positive numbers, and so on.

But suppose you don't know the correct answer. You then use the "process of elimination." It's a time-honored technique for test-takers. There is always one correct answer. There is usually one answer choice that is totally incorrect—a "distracter." If you look at that choice and it seems highly unlikely, then eliminate it. Depending on the number of choices (four or five), you've just cut down the number of choices to make. Now weigh the other choices. They may seem incorrect or they may be correct. If they seem incorrect, eliminate them. You've now increased your odds at getting the correct answer.

In the end, you may be left with only two choices. At that point, it's just a matter of guessing. But with only two choices left, you now have a 50 percent chance of getting it right. With four choices, you only have a 25 percent chance, and with five choices, only a 20 percent chance at guessing correctly. That's why the process of elimination is important.

## SHOULD YOU GUESS?

You may be wondering whether or not it is wise to guess when you are not sure of an answer (even if you've reduced the odds to 50 percent) or whether it is better to skip the question when you are not certain. The wisdom of guessing depends on the scoring method for the particular examination part. If the scoring is "rights only," that is, one point for each correct answer and no subtraction for wrong answers, then by all means you should guess. Read the question and all of the answer choices carefully. Eliminate those answer choices that you are certain are wrong. Then guess from among the remaining choices. You cannot gain a point if you leave the answer space blank; you may gain a point with an educated guess or even with a lucky guess. In fact, it is foolish to leave any spaces blank on a test that counts "rights only." If it appears that you are about to run out of time before completing such an exam, mark all the remaining blanks with the same letter. According to the law of averages, you should get some portion of those questions right.

If the scoring method is *rights minus wrongs*, such as the address checking test found on Postal Clerk Exam 470, DO NOT GUESS. A wrong answer counts heavily against you. On this type of test, do not rush to fill answer spaces randomly at the end. Work as quickly as possible while concentrating on accuracy. Keep working carefully until time is called. Then stop and leave the remaining answer spaces blank.

In guessing the answers to multiple-choice questions, take a second to eliminate those answers that are obviously wrong, then quickly consider and guess from the remaining choices. The fewer choices from which you guess, the better the odds of guessing correctly. Once you have decided to make a guess, be it an educated guess or a wild stab, do it right away and move on; don't keep thinking about it and wasting time. You should always mark the test questions at which you guess so that you can return later.

For those questions that are scored by subtracting a fraction of a point for each wrong answer, the decision as to whether or not to guess is really up to you.

A correct answer gives you one point; a skipped space gives you nothing at all, but costs you nothing except the chance of getting the answer right; a wrong answer costs you 1/4 point. If you are really uncomfortable with guessing, you may skip a question, BUT you must then remember to skip its answer space as well. The risk of losing your place if you skip questions is so great that we advise you to guess even if you are not sure of the answer. Our suggestion is that you answer every question in order, even if you have to guess. It is better to lose a few 1/4 points for wrong guesses than to lose valuable seconds figuring where you started marking answers in the wrong place, erasing, and re-marking answers. On the other hand, do not mark random answers at the end. Work steadily until time is up.

One of the questions you should ask in the testing room is what scoring method will be used on your particular exam. You can then guide your guessing procedure accordingly.

## SCORING

If your exam is a short-answer exam such as those often used by companies in the private sector, your answers will be graded by a personnel officer trained in grading test questions. If you blackened spaces on the separate answer sheet accompanying a multiple-choice exam, your answer sheet will be machine scanned or will be hand scored using a punched card stencil. Then a raw score will be calculated using the scoring formula that applies to that test or test portion— rights only, rights minus wrongs, or rights minus a fraction of wrongs. Raw scores on test parts are then added together for a total raw score.

A raw score is not a final score. The raw score is not the score that finds its way onto an eligibility list. The civil service testing authority, Postal Service, or other testing body converts raw scores to a scaled score according to an unpublicized formula of its own. The scaling formula allows for slight differences in difficulty of questions from one form of the exam to another and allows for equating the scores of all candidates. Regardless of the number of questions and possible different weights of different parts of the exam, most civil service clerical test scores are reported on a scale of 1 to 10. The entire process of conversion from raw to scaled score is confidential information. The score you receive is not your number right, is not your raw score, and, despite being on a scale of 1 to 100, is not a percentage. It is a scaled score. If you are entitled to veterans' service points, these are added to your passing scaled score to boost your rank on the eligibility list. Veterans' points are added only to passing scores. A failing score cannot be brought to passing level by adding veterans' points. The score earned plus veterans' service points, if any, is the score that finds its place on the rank order eligibility list. Highest scores go to the top of the list.

---

### Test-Taking Tips

1. Get to the test center early. Make sure you give yourself plenty of extra time to get there, park your car, if necessary, and even grab a cup of coffee before the test.

2. Listen to the test monitors and follow their instructions carefully.

3. Read every word of the instructions. Read every word of every question.

4. Mark your answers by completely darkening the answer space of your choice. Do not use the test paper to work out your answers.

5. Mark only ONE answer for each question, even if you think that more than one answer is correct. You must choose only one. If you mark more than one answer, the scoring machine will consider you wrong.

6. If you change your mind, erase completely. Leave no doubt as to which answer you mean.

7. If your exam permits you to use scratch paper or the margins of the test booklet for figuring, don't forget to mark the answer on the answer sheet. Only the answer sheet is scored.

8. Check often to be sure that the question number matches the answer space, that you have not skipped a space by mistake.

9. Guess according to the guessing suggestions we have made.

10. Stay alert. Be careful not to mark a wrong answer just because you were not concentrating.

11. Do not panic. If you cannot finish any part before time is up, do not worry. If you are accurate, you can do well even without finishing. It is even possible to earn a scaled score of 100 without entirely finishing an exam part if you are very accurate. At any rate, do not let your performance on any one part affect your performance on any other part.

12. Check and recheck, time permitting. If you finish any part before time is up, use the remaining time to check that each question is answered in the right space and that there is only one answer for each question. Return to the difficult questions and rethink them.

---

**PART TWO**

# What Kind of Work Will You Be Doing?

# THE STRUCTURE OF PROBATION AND PAROLE

How one goes about doing the job of a probation or parole officer is, believe it or not, fundamentally the same. The differences lie mostly in the organizational structure.

Where the probation and parole agencies lie in the overall structure of state government often dictates how the various duties are performed. In some states, probation and parole are a separate governmental unit with officers having responsibility for both probationers and parolees. Within individual offices, however, a distinction may be made (i.e., there may be a probation "staff" and a parole "staff").

In other states, probation and parole are separate divisions of a governmental unit, usually the Department of Corrections (or a similarly named division). In this structure, an officer is either a probation officer or a parole officer. In most cases, transfer between divisions is possible, as is transfer among other state agencies.

Probation generally functions at the county or local level. This means that although it operates as part of a state governmental unit, the job is done by and through the court systems. So in a sense, the probation officer has two masters: his or her "boss" within the state agency and the judge for whom he or she "works." There are times when these two masters come into conflict.

Probation and parole are often criticized for being uncoordinated and not communicating with each other or with other criminal justice agencies or departments. This lack of coordination and communication often leads to duplication of services and a general failure of "one hand knowing what the other is doing." This problem has improved as a number of both adult and juvenile probation agencies have partnered with law enforcement to investigate crimes and supervision of probationers.

Another arguable concern exists over the preparation a person interested in a career in probation/parole has to complete. Some say that there is no specialized body of knowledge a candidate must have to become a probation or parole officer. However, in some states (e.g., Alabama), probation/parole officers are sworn peace officers, and as such they are required to comply with the state's minimum standards for peace officers. Forty-six states require at least two years of education past high school, and most require a Bachelor of Science degree. While most states that require a degree do not specify what field the degree should be in, aspiring probation and parole personnel better prepare themselves for agency entry by enrolling in various criminal justice, sociology, social work, or psychology programs. Because most criminal justice programs are interdisciplinary, students who know they want to be a probation/parole officer should major in criminal justice and minor in social work or sociology.

## THE OFFICER'S ROLE

Historically, the role of the probation/parole officer has been considered a dichotomous one. The officer must enforce the law and provide social work assistance to the offender. Which role is more appropriate depends in large measure on the officer and the offender. With regard to the social work role, many officers have become resource brokers who match the offender with social workers and other assisting professionals in the community. In so doing, the officer is better able to focus more on the law enforcement role (which is more often the role society prefers).

What ultimate role, if any, the officer might take continues to develop as the responsibilities of the probation/parole officer change. For example, probation/parole officers' view of themselves has developed during the past thirty-five years. In the mid-1960s, a study found that probation officers identified more with corrections than social work. This same survey found that experienced officers believed that societal protection (i.e., surveillance) was their primary job. However, the officers of the new millennium see their job as more rehabilitative and hence more social work-related.

Whether this role conflict requires making a choice between one role or the other or whether it is simply inherent in the practice remains to be answered. Clearly, the mark of a professional is being whatever you need to be to get the job done. If an offender (particularly one on probation) is sufficiently integrated into the community, that offender probably needs to be watched more than anything else. Conversely, an offender who has a host of personal difficulties and problems will probably need some "assistance" in addition to or perhaps instead of surveillance. Of course, the orientation the officer brings to the job will also influence the role he or she undertakes. The organization's mission and vision and how its officers are trained and led also play a crucial role for obvious reasons.

## SAMPLE EXAMINATION AND JOB ANNOUNCEMENTS

The following examination and job announcements will give you a good idea of what will be required of you on the job, whether you are a probation officer, a parole officer, or a supervising probation officer.

---

### PROBATION OFFICER

#### Minimum Requirements

1. a baccalaureate degree from an accredited college, including or supplemented by 24 credits in psychology, social work, sociology, or criminal justice, and two years of full-time paid experience as stated in (2) or

2. education and/or experience in the social sciences.

All candidates must have at least a baccalaureate degree from an accredited college or university. Graduate courses in an accredited college or university in case work, group work, community organization, clinical or counseling psychology, or closely related fields may be substituted for experience on a year-for-year basis. Graduate courses in an accredited college or university in the field of criminal justice may be substituted for up to one year of experience.

Candidates who were educated in countries outside the United States must file an Application for Evaluation of Credentials (DP-398) with their Experience Paper Form A. Education received outside the U.S. is evaluated to determine its comparability to education received in domestic, accredited educational institutions to determine the extent to which it can be used toward meeting the requirements or for additional credit in this examination.

Experience in the determination of eligibility for income maintenance, unemployment insurance, social security, or related benefits; in routine police patrol work; or in care, custody, or control of inmates is not acceptable.

The minimum requirements must be met by the deadline date for the receipt of applications.

*continued*

---

All candidates must be able to write, understand, and be understood in English. Qualifying written and oral English tests are given by the Department of Personnel to all candidates who, in the opinion of the appointing officer, do not meet this requirement.

## Character

Proof of good character is a prerequisite to appointment. The following are among the factors that may be cause for disqualification.

- Conviction for an offense, the nature of which indicates lack of good moral character or disposition toward violence or disorder, or which is punishable by one or more years of imprisonment

- Repeated convictions for an offense, where such convictions indicate a disrespect for the law

- Discharge from employment, where such discharge indicates poor behavior or inability to adjust to discipline

- Addiction to narcotics or to a controlled substance or excessive use of alcoholic beverages

- Dishonorable discharge from the armed forces

## Age Requirements

In accordance with Section 257 of the Executive Law, eligible candidates must have reached their 21st birthday by the time of appointment. However, there is no minimum age in order for candidates to file for this position.

## Duties and Responsibilities

Under supervision, with some latitude for independent or unreviewed action or decision, performs difficult and responsible social work or special assignments in the field of probation, providing intake evaluation, investigation, and supervision services for persons within the jurisdiction of the courts; performs related work.

## Examples of Typical Tasks

The following are typical tasks that might be required of a probation officer.

- Testifies in court

- Makes preliminary investigations of crimes or offenses, covering such matters as the nature of the offense, the place and manner in which it was committed, the circumstances, and the statements of the complainant and defendant

- Obtains information on the offender's legal, economic, and psychosocial history and background

- Interprets conditions of sentence to persons placed under probation supervision; supervises probationers individually or in groups and provides services for their problems, such as alcohol and narcotic addiction, psychiatric disorders, unemployment, and marital difficulties

- Makes initial and supervising investigations of cases involving family problems, such as neglect, child abuse, adoption, and nonsupport

*continued*

■ Enforces payments of fines, restitutions, and reparations ordered by the court

■ Acts as a liaison between the department and the courts

■ Secures and clarifies information; answers questions; prepares and submits written reports and recommendations, including revocations of probation if necessary

■ Keeps track of court cases in which the department is involved

■ Refers probationers to social, government, or community agencies that may assist in probationers' rehabilitation

■ Performs fieldwork that includes home visits to individuals under investigation or supervision

■ Corresponds with and makes collateral visits to the probationer's friends, relatives, community agencies, employers, former employers, churches, schools, law enforcement agencies, and others

■ Prepares and maintains case records

■ Provides intake service to determine the necessity for court intervention or adjusts matters without referral to court

■ Provides specialized services in research and demonstration projects

■ Provides services related to placement of minors in foster homes, group homes, community-based programs, or institutions

■ Serves as department representative as required

■ May assist in the supervision of probation assistants and volunteers

## Tests

Education and experience, weight 100, 70 percent required; qualifying medical. There is no competitive test other than an evaluation of education and experience. After the minimum requirements are met, credit is given for a maximum of an additional six years of experience. Education and experience rating is based on candidate's statements on the Experience Paper Form A, which must be filled out completely and in detail, including dates and number of hours per week worked. In completing the Experience Paper Form A, candidates should list all graduate and undergraduate courses completed in psychology, sociology, social work, and related fields in the space provided. Candidates are to list all education and experience for which credit may be given as described below. Once they have filed their application, candidates are permitted to add additional education or experience for purposes of having such education and experience evaluated beyond the minimum requirements.

Education or experience will not be found acceptable unless it is verifiable. Education and experience listed on Experience Paper Form A will receive credit only to the extent that they are described clearly and in detail.

The maximum score on the Education and Experience Test is 100. Candidates who meet the minimum requirements receive a score of 70.

After the minimum requirements are met, credit may be given for up to six years of experience on the following basis.

■ An additional 3 points for each year of full-time, paid professional experience (after receipt of the baccalaureate degree) in case work and/or counseling in a recognized social services agency adhering to acceptable standards

*continued*

- An additional 5 points for each year of full-time, paid professional experience (after receipt of the baccalaureate degree) in case work and/or counseling in a recognized criminal justice agency adhering to acceptable standards
- An additional 1 point for a master's degree from an accredited college or university (if not used to meet the minimum requirements) in criminal justice
- An additional 3 points for a master's degree from an accredited college or university (if not used to meet the minimum requirements) in social work, clinical or counseling psychology, or a closely related field
- An additional 5 points for a doctoral degree from an accredited college or university in social work, clinical or counseling psychology, or a closely related field

Eligible candidates are required to pass a qualifying medical test prior to appointment. An eligible candidate will be rejected for any current medical and/or psychiatric impairment that inhibits his or her ability to perform the duties of the class of positions.

## Selective Certification

The eligible candidates list resulting from this examination may be selectively certified to fill vacancies that require a working knowledge of both English and another language. Those who are placed on the eligible candidate list may be permitted to take a qualifying oral test to determine ability to speak and understand another language. Candidates wishing to take this qualifying oral test must so indicate by filing the Language Proficiency Tests Form with their Experience Paper Form A. Candidates who do not so indicate at the time of filing are not permitted to take the qualifying oral test.

## Promotion Opportunities

Employees with the title of Probation Officer are accorded promotion opportunities, when eligible, to the title of Supervising Probation Officer.

## PAROLE OFFICER AND RELATED TITLES

Six exams leading to jobs with the State Parole Division are given by the State Civil Service Departments. The jobs pay up to $40,000 per year and require at least a baccalaureate degree. These exams are for Parole Officer Trainee and Parole Officer Trainee (Spanish Language), Parole Officer and Parole Officer (Spanish Language), and Parole Substance Abuse Counselor and Parole Substance Abuse Counselor (Spanish Language).

Eligible candidate lists, to be compiled based on exam scores, are created to fill current and future vacancies. Most hiring lists are active for four years. Health and safety positions such as these are exempt from the state's hiring freeze that is currently in effect.

### Job Description

Parole officers supervise offenders who have been released early from state and local correction facilities. Parole officers supervise, counsel, and assist with reintegration of the offenders into the community and with a variety of social problems as needed. Parole substance abuse counselors work with releases with alcohol or drug problems.

Parole officers are peace officers and must meet the minimum requirements for peace officers as required by state law.

### Minimum Requirements

The trainee positions require a bachelor's degree or higher in sociology, psychology, social work, counseling, criminal justice, rehabilitation counseling, or American studies, with a concentration in a minority culture.

To qualify to be a parole officer, applicants must have a bachelor's degree and three years of experience as a case worker or group worker with a social services or correctional or other criminal justice agency.

A bachelor's degree and three years of experience in an alcohol or substance abuse treatment program are required to take the exams for parole substance abuse counselors. A relevant master's degree may be substituted for some of the experience requirement. Counselors need not be state residents.

In addition to passing the written tests, parole officer and parole officer trainee applicants must meet physical and medical requirements. Candidates who seek Spanish language positions must show the ability to speak Spanish. Candidates with Spanish language capability are urged to apply for both exams for any title.

### Advancement

After completing a two-year training program, parole officer trainees advance to parole officer positions without further examination.

## THE INVESTIGATIVE REPORT

Regardless of whether one is a probation officer or a parole officer or does both, one of the primary responsibilities of the officer is investigation. This includes gathering information from a variety of sources about a variety of areas: past arrests/convictions, school performance, work performance, information about the charge(s), behavior considerations, etc. This information is gathered from law enforcement and corrections officials, neighbors, friends, family, and official records. Once this information has been obtained, perhaps the most important function (at least in relation to investigation) begins: the preparation of the report. The ability to communicate, both orally and in writing, is a paramount ability the probation/parole officer must possess. In many cases, the reputation of the officer hinges on his or her ability to communicate effectively.

For probation officers, this report is known as the Pre-sentence Investigation Report (PSI). For parole officers, it may be called the Parole Investigative Report or simply the Parole Report. While the PSI is better known, they are essentially the same. The PSI is important because sometimes this is the only information (or contact) the judge has on the offender (especially given that about 90 percent of all offenders plead guilty). Judges tend to lean heavily on the professional advice of probation officers, just as the parole board relies mostly on the parole report for their decision making. Judges concur with the recommendation in the PSI 85 percent of the time. The importance of this report (and its companion parole report) cannot be over-stated.

The primary purpose of these reports is to provide the decision maker with complete information regarding the offender. The purposes of these reports are to

- help the court determine the sentence.

- assist correctional authorities in classification and treatment in release planning.

- provide the parole board with useful information pertinent to parole consideration.

- help the probation officer during probation rehabilitation efforts.

- serve as a source of information for research.

This report must encompass any and all information available about the offender and the crime and other relevant information. In addition, all information should be verified, and, if opinions are included, they should be noted.

Many times, the evaluation and recommendations are the only part of the report the decision maker will read. It is in this section that the many purposes and functions of probation/parole are considered. It is the responsibility of the officer to make a recommendation that flows logically from the information contained in the report.

**IN SUM**

As you can see from the information provided in this section, the role of the probation/parole officer is a serious one, filled with responsibilities to both the offender and society. Now that you have a basic idea of the type of work you will be doing, you can use the next two sections to prepare for the exam you will most likely have to take as part of the application process.

# PART THREE

# Preparing for the Examination

# THE DEVELOPMENT AND EVOLUTION OF PROBATION AND PAROLE

## PROBATION

Probation is a sentence imposed on a criminal who must serve time in the community under supervision. Probation requires an offender to comply with certain terms and conditions. If an offender fails to comply with these terms and conditions, he or she will most likely be returned to prison to complete his or her sentence. Probation comes from the Latin *probatio*, meaning a period of proving or trial and forgiveness. As a result, while probation is a sentence (like fines, incarceration, or death), it is also a privilege that a judge grants during sentencing. That is, not all offenders are granted probation or are deemed worthy of it. The worthiness of an offender for probation is determined in part by the probation officer in his pre-sentence investigation report recommendation and the judge, who ultimately makes the decision after taking into account all the information.

Most criminal codes, in describing the sentence for a crime, will specify a monetary fine or a period of imprisonment not to exceed a certain amount of time. Judges, in using their discretion, may sentence someone to probation in lieu of imprisonment under "the following terms and conditions." If the offender fulfills those terms and conditions, he or she is released from supervision. Whether the offender is granted probation or has his or her probation revoked as recommended by the probation officer is ultimately the decision of the judge.

Like many of the other concepts in American criminal justice, probation has its roots in England. During the 1700s and 1800s, many judges in England used their discretion and granted convicted offenders a judicial reprieve. Judicial reprieves essentially suspended the incarceration of offenders and were granted in cases in which the offender did not have a prior record and had committed a minor offense and in which the judges had determined the punishment was excessive.

While its roots lie in the judicial reprieves of the English judges, probation itself is decidedly American. Boston shoemaker and philanthropist John Augustus is widely credited for conceiving probation in the mid-1840s. Influenced by the temperance movement of the time, Augustus underwent a concerted effort to rehabilitate alcoholics and those involved with alcohol-related charges. Appearing in a Boston municipal court, Augustus volunteered to supervise a "common drunkard" for three weeks and ensure the alcoholic's reappearance in court after that time. Given Augustus' reputation, the judge agreed and three weeks later, Augustus and the reformed alcoholic reappeared in court. The judge suspended the offender's sentence and fined him $.01 and $4.00 in court costs. From 1841 until his death in 1859, it is estimated that Augustus "saved" 2,000 people from incarceration by supervising them (on probation) for a fixed period of time. During that same time, Augustus enlisted other philanthropic volunteers to join him in serving as probation officers. Probation as a sentence took flight with the formation of juvenile courts in 1899 and now accounts for as many as 60 percent of all convicted offenders.

## MODERN PROBATION

While probation began as a rehabilitative effort, its emphasis has moved more toward the punitive vein. The "get tough" movement has shifted the focus of probation more on ensuring the offender follows the terms and conditions of the sentence and less on treatment by the probation officer. Regardless of whether the focus is on treatment and rehabilitation or simply following the rules, probation better allows for rehabilitation than does incarceration. The whole idea of the privilege of probation is to allow offenders to "prove" themselves capable of not doing crime. Those who can prove themselves capable don't do any "time," but those who cannot stay out of trouble will end up in prison at one point or another.

Offenders need to know that they will be punished for their crimes. Probation is a restriction of freedom and, depending on the conditions and the quality of the probation officer, can be as punitive as might be needed given the uniqueness of each offender. Within that context, the purposes of probation include crime control, reintegration, rehabilitation, and deterrence.

- **Crime control** is achieved through requiring offenders to comply with the terms and conditions set forth in the probation sentence. While clearly any offender who is not incarcerated has a greater opportunity to commit a crime against society than one who is imprisoned, the nature of the terms and conditions and the quality of the probation officer enforcing same can go a long way in achieving crime control. For example, the use of polygraphs with sex offenders on probation has helped keep them from committing additional sex crimes. In addition, most probationers know that failure to comply with the terms and conditions may very well send them back to prison, and this also helps control crime.

- **Reintegration and rehabilitation** are possible by the simple fact that the probationer remains in the community. As such, he or she is able to maintain (or find) a job, stay (or enroll) in school, maintain personal relationships, obtain counseling or drug/alcohol treatment, and otherwise avoid the "pains of imprisonment." In addition, any fines or restitution that might be required is much easier paid when the offender remains in the community. Paying the victim or the community back for their crimes goes a long way in achieving both reintegration and rehabilitation.

- **Deterrence** may or may not be achieved by probation. To measure deterrence is to attempt to measure something that does not occur: future crime. If a person leaves probation and never returns to the system, can it be said that probation deterred his or her future criminality, or was it some other variable (an education, marriage, stable employment, etc.)? Regardless, recidivism has been used to measure the effectiveness of probation (as well as incarceration, parole, and punishment in general), and while certainly not everyone "succeeds" on probation, the success rate is high. It should also be noted that some offenders view probation as "worse" than being incarcerated, as offenders actually have to work at bettering themselves for the greater good, instead of living off the state in a prison. This could also demonstrate the effectiveness of probation as a deterrent as well as serving its crime control purpose and its reintegration and rehabilitation purpose.

## TYPES OF PROBATION

Diversion, standard probation, intensive supervised probation, and shock probation are the four most common types of probation.

- **Diversion** is often used with first-time offenders who have committed a relatively minor crime and refers to the suspension of all legal proceedings contingent on the accused fulfilling certain terms and conditions. While technically not probation, as the accused has not been convicted of anything, it is similar in function and is often monitored by probation officers. Essentially, the accused is required to comply with a set of terms and conditions (e.g., stay out of trouble, get into treatment, pay restitution, etc.) for a fixed period of time and, upon successful completion, all charges are dropped. Such probation results in no formal official record for the accused.

■ **Standard probation** is at least part of what all offenders receive. It refers to the basic terms and conditions that all probationers are required to comply with. For some critics of probation, it is nothing more than the offender agreeing to do whatever tasks are required and never to be seen again. Part of this has to do with the large number of caseloads many probation officers have. The larger the caseload, the less likely the opportunity that the probation officer can adequately monitor each probationer. This leads to the increased likelihood that the offender will continue to commit crimes or at least not comply with the terms and conditions of probation.

■ **Intensive supervised probation** got a jumpstart in Georgia and New Jersey in the mid-1980s. It entails the probation officer and the probationer having much more frequent contact with each other than in standard probation. Such contact usually begins on a daily basis and is modified based on the compliance of the probationer. Probation officers usually handle about 15 – 25 cases each, which makes frequent contacts with probationers more easily attainable.

■ **Shock probation** involves a judge sentencing the offender to be incarcerated for a period of time. Upon completion of that time, the judge then resentences the offender to serve his or her remaining time on probation. It is hoped that the brief period of incarceration will "shock" the offender and make him or her see the importance of doing well on probation.

## PROBATION REQUIREMENTS

Home detention and electronic monitoring are common forms of keeping track of a probationer. These methods are usually used together, since requiring someone to remain at home is usually useless without some form of supervision, and electronic monitoring helps to provide this. Generally, the offender wears a monitoring device (ankle or wrist bracelet) and is required to remain at home. A computer will check in on the offender by phone, and the offender is required to respond. However, offenders have found ways to beat this system with the advent of call forwarding. The offender simply forwards her phone to wherever she is (or to her cell phone) so when the call comes in, the offender answers, the machine records her as "being home," and no alert is issued. Offenders have also gotten around electronic monitoring by having an answering machine pick up, which the computer assumes to be a live voice, so it does not issue an alert.

Some probationers are required to stay in a halfway house. Such houses are normally reserved for people on parole, but some people on probation are ordered into them as well. Here again, the judge believes the offender does not need to be in prison but also needs more structure than being "free" in the community. In addition to the terms and conditions of probation, the offender must also comply with the rules of the house.

In summary, probation is a sentence imposed at the discretion of the judge, as recommended by the probation officer. The primary benefit to probation is that the offender is allowed to remain in the community without being incarcerated. Parole, at least conceptually, is far different from probation.

## PAROLE

Unlike probation, parole is *not* a sentence handed down by a judge. Parole is a conditional release from prison before the offender completes his or her sentence. While the mechanics of parole is similar to probation, the fundamental (and important) difference is that the offender on parole has been in prison and subject to the "pains of imprisonment." These pains, which include loss of liberty, autonomy, and security, often make the parolee a more hardened individual than the probationer and thus more difficult to supervise. The parole officer must have a good sense of how the parolee has reacted to imprisonment to provide the best possible plan for reintegration and reduced criminalization.

Like probation, parole has its roots in the U.K. In the eighteenth century, Britain faced the same problem the United States currently faces: prison overcrowding. Having few prisons, Britain transported many of its prisoners to the American colonies. After the American Revolution, the United States no longer accepted Britain's prisoners, so Australia became Britain's new dumping ground. Because many of Australia's new "immigrants" needed to be housed, Australia began to build its own prisons. Two of the most notable were Norfolk Island and Van Diemen's Land.

A former Royal Navy officer, Alexander Maconochie, was appointed superintendent of Norfolk Island. Known as a reformer and humanitarian, Maconochie quickly became the bane of both his superiors and his colleagues. The prisoners, on the other hand, adored him. Believing that imprisonment should be rehabilitative instead of punitive, Maconochie established a number of policies designed to further this goal. One of his most important policies was his "marks of commendation." Maconochie believed that well-behaved prisoners should receive "marks of commendation" and be granted early release.

Maconochie's views and outspoken nature got him transferred from Norfolk Island and eventually dismissed from the British service. Despite his dismissal from the British penal service, Maconochie became instrumental in the passage of the English Penal Servitude Act in 1853. This act established many rehabilitative programs and abolished transportation to Australia. For these reasons and others, Maconochie is often referred to as the "Father of Parole."

Sir Walter Crofton, Director of Ireland's prison system (and also referred to as a "Father of Parole"), was so impressed with Maconochie's views that he introduced a three-tier system to Ireland's prisons. In this system, an inmate could earn an early release following a three-stage plan:

1. strict imprisonment for a period of time,

2. transfer to an "intermediate" prison where the inmate could participate in a variety of programs and work leading to the earning of good marks, and

3. a ticket of leave, which resulted in the inmate's release from prison into the community under the supervision of the police. Prisoners under a ticket of leave were required to submit to the police monthly reports noting their progress. The police assisted the inmates in finding work and had monthly contact with them.

In 1870, the National Prison Association met in Cincinnati, Ohio, with Crofton and several American prison reformers in attendance. Crofton's Irish system was the primary topic, and upon its adjournment, the association adopted a "Declaration of Principles" that promoted (in part) an indeterminate sentence and a classification system, both based on Crofton's Irish model.

Six years later, Z.R. Brockway, superintendent of Elmira Reformatory, led the fight for the establishment of the first indeterminate sentencing law. He is also credited with introducing the first "good time" system, whereby an inmate's release date was reduced by the number of good marks he or she received. With indeterminate sentencing, the legislature establishes a range of time to be served (e.g., one to ten years, ten years to life, etc.) and the parole board determines the actual amount of time served. Generally, an incarcerated offender is eligible for parole after serving one third of his or her sentence. A parole report (similar to a PSI) is put together, the parole officer attaches a recommendation, and the parole board determines whether the offender is a good candidate for parole.

While indeterminate sentencing and parole are certainly linked, a state that offered one did not automatically offer the other. However, by the mid-1940s, all states and the federal government provided some type of parole system, and by the mid-1960s all states offered a form of indeterminate sentencing.

## THE MODERN PAROLE SYSTEM

For a variety of reasons, beginning in the late 1970s the use of and support for indeterminate sentencing and parole gradually declined. This was replaced with an emphasis on a model more akin to fairness: the justice model. In this model, prison is more focused on executing the sentence rather than on rehabilitation of the offender. Critics of such an approach often point out that all (or most all) offenders return to society some day, and how they return should be the focus of corrections.

With this change in philosophical focus also came a shifting in sentencing models. Many states went from an indeterminate to a determinate sentencing model, i.e., the offender is sentenced to a specific time to be served. In many instances, a reduction in the discretion of parole boards and/or judges also occurred. By the 1990s, parole in many states had been completely abolished or severely restricted. Benefits to determinate sentencing include the idea that the inmate knows exactly when she will be getting out and that the public knows how much time she will serve (although this is far from the case). While rumors about the death of parole may be greatly exaggerated, where it exists, it serves remarkably similar purposes as probation. Following are five main purposes of probation.

1. Reintegrating rehabilitated offenders into society

2. Deterring previous offenders from committing more crimes

3. Alleviating prison overcrowding

4. Protecting the public

5. Remedying sentencing disparities

Parole decision making rests in the hands of a parole board. Parole boards are usually appointed by a state's governor or legislature, and often those who sit on parole boards are visible members of the community or political supporters of the governor. Rarely is it the case that one or more members of the board have any experience in criminal justice. Even then, experience does not necessarily translate into good parole decisions. The Alabama parole board (with a former police chief and victim's advocate) has come under fire for many of its decisions recently. In fact, the board has rewritten the rules for granting parole. One major rule change involves the requirement of certain classes of offenders (essentially Class A felons) to serve at least 85 percent of their sentences before they become eligible for parole. This is consistent with changes that are being made across the country.

Probation and parole are important tools in the implementation of corrections. While one is a sentence and one is not, they are both privileges granted at the discretion of a judge or parole board. They both involve release of the offender into the community to serve or finish out their sentences. While the future of probation seems "solid," parole has undergone a number of changes, particularly in the last seven years, and change should continue as the concern about crime continues.

# ESSENTIAL ELEMENTS OF AN EFFECTIVE PAROLE SYSTEM

"We know from experience that parole, when it is honestly and expertly managed, provides better protection for society than does any other method of release from prison."

—*Franklin Delano Roosevelt* at the National Parole Conference, Washington, April 1939.

The following are the essential elements of an adequate parole system.

1. Complete freedom from improper control or influence, political or otherwise

2. Sufficient flexibility in the laws governing sentences and parole to permit the parole of an offender at the time when release under supervision is in the best interest of society

3. A parole board composed of members qualified by intelligence, training, and experience to weigh the complex problems of human behavior involved in parole decisions and having the patience and integrity required to make wise and just decisions

4. A staff of supervisory and administrative personnel, parole officers, clerks, placement officers, and other personnel adequate in number to handle the caseload of the parole system

5. An administrative structure within the framework of the state government as a whole, which makes it possible for the parole system, without sacrifice of proper independence, to function in complete coordination with other departments and services, notably probation services, correctional institutions, and departments of health, mental hygiene, welfare, and public safety

6. A parole procedure that makes provision for orienting the prisoner toward parole, preparation of all data pertinent to the case for the parole board, a parole hearing based on careful study of such data, formulation of a satisfactory parole plan, and release under adequate supervision

7. Operation within the institution of a program that aims at using the period of confinement for preparing the inmate physically, vocationally, mentally, and spiritually for return to society and puts forth intensive effort at the close of the term toward effecting release under optimum conditions as far as the inmate, his or her dependents, and the community are concerned

8. A proper attitude toward the parolee so that he or she may be accorded fair and helpful treatment in the effort to make good, especially in matters of employment and social integration

## FREEDOM FROM POLITICS AND OTHER IMPROPER INFLUENCES

The parole system should be entirely free not only from political control, manipulation, or influence, but also from improper influences by pressure groups of any type. The weaknesses and failures of parole systems can be traced more often to political interference than to any other cause. The members of the parole board should be appointed on a nonpolitical basis, their actions should not be affected in any way by political consideration, and their tenure of office should not bear any relationship to any individual or political party in or out of power or to changes in administration. Government officials and political organizations should not be able to influence parole decisions in any way or to exert influence in the appointment of parole board members, parole officers, and other personnel.

While politics are the particular bane of parole as well as of all other correctional services, there is need also to establish safeguards against the undue influence of racial and religious groups and pressure groups in general. In short, all decisions with regard to parole should be made on the merits of the individual case, whether these concern the granting, denying, deferring, or revoking of parole; determining the conditions under which parole shall be granted; deciding when and to what extent the restrictions imposed shall be relaxed; and when final discharge shall be granted. Freedom from improper influences cannot be guaranteed by law, although the law can give the parole authorities the independence and security of tenure that they must have to be able to resist interference successfully. The best guarantee, however, lies in the appointment of able personnel who have the integrity and courage to carry on their work without fear or favor and who stand ready, if necessary, to inform the public whenever improper attempts are being made to influence their decisions.

## FLEXIBILITY IN THE LAW

Among the leading authorities in the correctional field there is general agreement in favor of indeterminate sentences—one to five years, five to ten years, twenty years to life, for example, or a maximum and no minimum—as opposed to definite sentences of a fixed term of years. The indeterminate sentence is firmly established in the practice of the leading states. Some states provide for sentences of one year to fifteen years, for example, or even one year to life, or no specified minimum. The Youth Correction Authority Plan, sponsored by the American Law Institute, goes further. It provides that the court shall determine guilt or innocence and commit the offender found guilty to the authority but shall not prescribe a term of imprisonment. The authority provided for under this plan would have power to utilize probation, institutional care, and parole with complete flexibility and to retain control over the convicted offender for as long or as short a time as it sees fit, with certain legal limitations that are flexible.

The usual parole provision in jurisdictions where there is an indeterminate sentence law is that the prisoner can be paroled at any time after the completion of the minimum sentence—minus whatever good conduct time (five days, a month, etc.) has been earned, as provided by law—or after the completion of a specified fraction of the minimum sentence. It has long been recognized that "good conduct time" credits are a holdover from old laws passed prior to the adoption of an adequate indeterminate sentence law whereby the severity of a fixed sentence was mitigated and that a fixed credit system is incompatible with the indeterminate sentence theory. Giving time off for good conduct becomes a complication whenever a paroling authority has the legal power to fix and change terms and grant paroles when it sees fit.

Provisions governing eligibility for parole should allow a measure of flexibility, but there is a sound basis for requiring service of a minimum period of reasonable proportions before parole eligibility. Where there are definite sentences only, the law customarily provides that the prisoner is eligible for parole after serving a certain fraction of the sentence, usually one third to one half. The laws of some states provide that prisoners serving a life sentence are eligible for parole consideration after they have served a fixed number of years, usually ten, twelve, or fifteen.

The general opinion of correctional authorities is against rigid provisions prohibiting the parole of persons convicted of certain offenses, such as murder in the first degree, kidnapping, and armed robbery. Similarly, provisions that certain categories of offenders cannot be paroled until they have served a fraction of their sentences in excess of the usual fraction destroy the essential flexibility of parole and should not be imposed by the parole law.

To summarize, correctional authorities generally endorse the principle of the indeterminate sentence and believe in provisions that allow a prisoner to become eligible for parole at the end of the minimum sentence, minus earned good conduct time, or at the end of a fraction of a minimum sentence. However, the prisoner is not necessarily paroled as soon as he or she becomes eligible. When there is no legal provision for indeterminate sentences, correctional authorities generally endorse the idea of eligibility for parole at the end of a minimum period set by the board or at some fixed fraction, such as one third of the sentence. They believe that the law should make flexibility of action possible and impose only restrictions that seem absolutely essential to protect the rights of the parolee and society. The proper aim of parole authorities is to release each prisoner when he or she is most nearly ready for release and chances of succeeding on parole are greatest. Determining when that time has come is not an easy task, and the mechanics of parole make it impossible to release every person at the moment when he or she is ready for it. Nevertheless, it should not be made more difficult or completely impossible by rigid legal restrictions.

## THE PAROLE BOARD

### FUNCTION

The paroling authority, by whatever title it is known, may be given by law two functions: one of granting and revoking paroles and the other of directing the parole staff, including those engaged in the work of parole supervision. These functions are sometimes assigned to different bodies, an official or board exercising the first, while the task of parole supervision is given to the state department of corrections, the welfare department, or another agency. Sometimes the parole officers who supervise parolees are a part of the institution staff and have no direct responsibility to the authority that grants parole.

### SIZE AND COMPOSITION

There should be a full-time parole board of at least three members in jurisdictions having a large enough parole load to warrant it. If a larger board consisting of five or more members is provided in a state having a heavy parole load, a policy under which the board may split up into panels in order to handle the work more expeditiously can be adopted under careful administrative safeguards. Such panels should function under policies set up by the entire board. There should be enough flexibility to permit panels to refer special cases to the board as a whole for decision.

In states having so few prisoners and parolees that a full-time board is not justified, various practices are followed for the granting of paroles. A method sometimes encountered is to have a board of *ex officio* members: the lieutenant governor, attorney general, and secretary of state, for example. Correctional authorities do not consider this a desirable method on the ground that *ex officio* members are bound to be chiefly concerned with their primary duties, and they often view parole duties as having secondary importance. Moreover, these individuals are likely to be sensitive to political influences. The same arguments hold against another common method: vesting parole authority in the governor. The objections to this method are increased by the fact that the governor often turns over parole decisions to another individual on staff who usually has no experience in the parole field. The practice of having a single parole commissioner in lieu of a parole board has not met with general approval.

A recommended practice for states with small caseloads is to have a single full-time parole commissioner who staffs a parole board with two qualified citizens serving on a part-time basis. The commissioner or one of his or her staff may chair the board. The commissioner supervises the staff and is responsible for records, statistics, and reports; preparation of cases for hearing; and the administration of parole supervision. Some states include parole commissionership as part of the responsibilities of a commissioner of corrections, a director of institutions, or a similar official. In states where there is no corrections department but the correctional institutions are under the department of welfare, the welfare commissioner, a deputy, or the head of the division of correction institutions may be authorized to act as parole commissioner. In any event, two carefully chosen and well-qualified laypersons should be appointed to act with this person as a parole board.

## APPOINTMENT AND TENURE

Members of the parole board are appointed by the Board of Corrections in instances where there is a coordinated correctional system. Where no such system exists, the governor will generally appoint parole board members. Appointments are usually made from a list of eligible candidates that is established by competitive merit examinations and for permanent tenure. If appointments are made for a term of years, the terms are generally staggered to ensure continuity. Members may be eligible for as long as their mental vigor, judgment, capacity for sustained concentration, and physical stamina do not become impaired by age or other factors.

## QUALIFICATIONS

Parole board members should be selected on the basis of general ability, intelligence, character, personality, education, training, and experience. Political or other extraneous considerations should not enter in any way into their appointment or retention in office. In an ideal world, a parole board should contain a lawyer, a businessperson, a social worker, an educator, a psychiatrist, and a penologist. At least one member of the board should be professionally trained in correctional work or in another closely related field such as social work, education, or psychology. The professional standing of such person should include graduate work and practical experience or a satisfactory combination of education and experience. It is not unreasonable to require that all members of the board be college graduates.

There are certain qualifications of education and experience that should not be compromised when making appointments to a parole board. In general, however, it is not wise to limit the choice narrowly and specifically on grounds of occupation, sex, race, or religion. The need is for intelligent, understanding, conscientious individuals with a good background of education and experience but above all with genuine interest in human problems, sound judgment, capacity for hard work, and unquestionable integrity.

## SALARIES

Part-time parole board members should be paid at a liberal *per diem* rate, plus actual expenses, for all time spent on the business of the board. The salaries of full-time board members should be high enough to attract and hold persons of the desired type. In general, the salaries of full-time members should compare favorably with those of judges of the higher courts of the state. The guiding principle should be that the qualifications for this work and the grave responsibilities the board members must assume call for substantial compensation.

## PAROLE STAFF

A parole staff should include, as a minimum, a chief parole officer or chief supervisor of parolees, sufficient parole officers to carry on the work of investigation and supervision of parolees without excessive caseloads (generally no more than 50 – 75 cases, unless the officer is assigned exclusively to investigation, in which case no more than 15), enough senior supervisory officers to maintain supervision over the parole officers, an adequate clerical force, and at least one placement officer. There should also be a statistician and a personnel director charged with the procurement and training of personnel if the size of the parole system warrants it.

## APPOINTMENT AND TENURE

All parole staff members should be employed under civil service, appointed from lists of eligible candidates established by competitive examinations (qualifying examinations should be held for personnel already in service when civil service provisions go into effect), and provided security of tenure as long as their performance of duty and their conduct are satisfactory. Members of the staff are appointed from civil service lists by the paroling authority on recommendation of the chief parole officer or whoever administers the supervision of parolees.

## QUALIFICATIONS

The parole staff members are selected on the basis of having the highest professional and technical standards possible. Applicants for clerk and statistician positions are required to meet accepted standards for hire. In the case of parole officers, placement officers, and others dealing directly with parolees, the qualifications specified not only cover education, special training, and experience but also age, physical requirements, personality, and character. If candidates lack previous training and experience in the parole field, they are given an intensive course of training when they enter the service. All personnel receive in-service training, including periodic refresher courses.

Some states, because of lack of funds to pay higher salaries, cannot recruit a parole staff with a high level of education and professional training. These states, however, can still maintain high standards of general intelligence, conscientiousness, sincerity of interest in parole work, capacity for hard work, personality, and integrity. As public understanding and acceptance of the value of good parole work increases, these states can gradually raise the educational and training requirements of its applicants.

- **Education:** A bachelor's degree or its equivalent is generally required, with preference given to those who have done major work in education, psychology, economics, political science, and history or who have had specific training in a school of social work.

- **Experience:** Since maturity and experience in living are necessary in the guidance of others, it is felt that 25 years should be the minimum age for appointment, except in exceptional cases.

  There should be a minimum of two years of practical experience, preferably in social case work, correctional or penal work, law enforcement, teaching, recreation, vocational guidance, personnel work, or other types of occupation directly related to the guidance of human behavior.

- **Equivalents to the above:** In place of a college degree, additional practical experience may be substituted.

  In place of one year only of practical experience, graduate study in a school of social work or graduate study with a master's degree may be substituted.

- **Personality:** In addition to the other qualifications necessary to be hired, candidates are also evaluated on their appearance, manner, voice, and emotional stability.

## SALARIES

Salaries of the parole staff members in most states will ordinarily have to conform to the scale of salaries for government workers on a professional, semiprofessional, and technical level in those particular states rather than to the salary scale in states where parole is securely established and well financed.

No state should be content to place parole workers' salaries on a low level and expect to maintain a satisfactory parole system on that basis. Salaries should be high enough to attract and hold workers with the required qualifications, usually in competition with the fields of education, social work, personnel work, and law enforcement. There should be regular promotions and salary increases on merit.

## PAROLE IN THE STATE'S ADMINISTRATIVE STRUCTURE

Of the two major functions of a parole system—the granting of paroles and the supervision of parolees—the former calls for a high degree of independence while the latter requires effective coordination with other state and local agencies and services.

Whatever administrative plan is established with reference to the parole board, it is vital that the board maintains an independent status to the extent that it can retain complete independence in its parole decisions. In the exercise of the function of supervision, however, complete independence is neither necessary nor desirable. In fact, the parole staff must often utilize the services of a variety of agencies to help solve problems presented by parolees and their families; consequently, complete coordination with such other agencies is necessary.

There are at least four administrative plans in the various states with reference to parole. The *first* is to set up an independent parole board on the general administrative level of state departments and the most important state commissions. This plan, through a chief parole officer or other executive, makes the board responsible for the work of the parole staff, which coordinates its efforts with but is administratively independent of institutional and probation services staffs. The *second* is to establish a state board of probation and parole that acts as a parole board and supervises probationers as well as parolees but is not a part of the department that administers institutions. The *third is* to make the parole system an integral part of a state department of corrections or public welfare that administers institutions but has no responsibility for probation supervision. The *fourth* is to make the parole system (board and staff) an integral part of a fully coordinated state department of corrections or public welfare that also administers institutions and probation supervision.

If one accepts the principle of continuity of the correctional process and the desirability of establishing a fully coordinated state correctional system embracing probation supervision, institutions, and parole, as discussed earlier, the fourth plan is the appropriate one. If, on the other hand, it does not prove feasible to include probation supervision, the third plan is appropriate and a department of corrections the preferred form of organization. None of the plans involves sacrificing the independence of the parole board in making decisions. Nor do the plans involve subordination of parole to other divisions and functions of the state correctional department.

## PROPER PAROLE PROCEDURE

The following are the successive steps in proper parole procedure.

### 1. ORIENTING THE INMATE WITH RESPECT TO PAROLE

This process should be initiated at the time of the prisoner's arrival. Confinement should be considered preparation for parole, except in long sentences where prisoners have been recidivists and have been on parole several times and there is little likelihood that parole can be considered in the foreseeable future. In general, the new inmate should be taught the meaning of parole, how it is earned, and how he or she must conduct himself or herself while on parole. This important matter cannot be left entirely to the last few weeks of the prisoner's stay at the institution. For orientation to be successful, the entire staff of the institution must also become familiar with the meaning of parole, the rules and practices of parole supervision, and the conditions under which parole is granted.

The inmate must understand that earning parole requires positive effort. This fact emphasizes the necessity of having the institution make an analysis of the inmate's problems soon after arrival, especially in the case of the improvable offender, and charting what needs to be accomplished before the parole hearing.

### 2. PREPARING THE CASE FOR THE PAROLE HEARING

This step involves compiling a basic history; a summary of available social, medical, psychiatric, and psychological findings; institution progress reports; and personality evaluations. In institutions where there is a classification program, preparation of this material is a function of the classification staff. Some parole systems require parole officers to reside in the institution; as a rule, such officers either cooperate with the institution staff in preparing cases or take major responsibility for preparing them with the aid of data supplied by other institutional departments or outside sources. In some systems, those who prepare the case indicate, by reference to parole prediction tables, the factors in a given case that point to probable success or failure on parole.

## 3. ATTENDING THE PAROLE HEARING

The inmate should be present at the parole hearing. The hearing is not a retrial of the case. Consequently, legal counsel, prosecutors, witnesses, and relatives are not permitted to attend. At this hearing parole is approved, deferred, or denied, or no affirmative action is taken, and the inmate is advised of the decision. If the action is adverse, the inmate is told the reason for which parole was denied, unless the board determines it a wise decision to withhold that information from the inmate.

It is not possible here to discuss all the criteria used in making a parole decision. However, it is useful to point out that the weight of opinion is against placing undue emphasis upon such factors as length of time served, nature of the offense, and similar items; a far more important basic factor is the personality makeup of the offender.

The parole board must clarify to the inmate that his or her sentence is limited by the maximum; that he or she has no right to demand parole; that parole is a matter of leniency; that the parole board decides whether the part of the sentence imposed by the court in deference to the law is to be served outside rather than inside; and that the extent of time that he or she can serve outside depends, under restrictions, upon himself or herself. Such a statement will avoid the misconceptions that most prisoners believe that their minimum is their maximum and that any action of the parole board in holding them beyond their minimum sentence is an invasion of their rights.

## 4. PREPARING A PAROLE PLAN

This step, if the inmate is granted parole, involves assurance of a satisfactory home and job and sometimes the securing of an acceptable "first friend" or parole adviser. However, it should be noted that the supervisory services of a volunteer are not an adequate substitute for supervision by a qualified parole officer. The board may require that the parole plan be completed by the institution or parole staff (or both of them working together) before the hearing, or it may vote approval on condition that a satisfactory parole plan is developed later.

## 5. RELEASING THE PAROLEE

The parolee is released under supervision of a parole staff and under such special conditions as the parole board may see fit to impose in addition to the general conditions imposed in all cases. General conditions are usually that the parolee report to the parole officer at prescribed intervals and that the parolee may not leave the state, change residence or employment, get married or divorced, or secure a license to operate a motor vehicle without permission of the parole officer or the parole officer's supervisor and, in some cases, the parole board. The parolee is not only required to lead a law-abiding life but also to avoid places and persons of questionable character.

Samples of special conditions include requirements that the parolee stay away from specified communities, neighborhoods, and people; refrain from accepting certain types of employment; make restitution; keep up alimony payments and support dependents; and abstain entirely from liquor and gambling. It is customary for parole officers to cooperate closely with law enforcement agencies but not to notify them routinely of the whereabouts of parolees.

The Interstate Compact for the Supervision of Parolees and Probationers has not been accepted by all fifty states. The Compact is being used more and more as an effective measure of rehabilitation and crime control under which all states assume certain responsibilities for the supervision of parolees and probationers from other states and in return secure supervision of their own parolees and probationers located in other states. A great deal of material has been accumulated on the administration of the Compact. A parole system serves its own as well as the public interest by engaging in active cooperation, under terms of this Compact, with the parole authorities in other states.

## 6. STRICT BUT HELPFUL SUPERVISION

The parole staff requires the parolee to make periodic reports in writing or in person, makes regular visits to the parolee at home and work, and checks up on the parolee through his or her employer and relatives. In many states parole officers have been trained in case work techniques. The parole officer should be able to detect the danger signals of forthcoming criminal activity so that he or she may take prompt and appropriate action. The parole officer must make every effort to understand a parolee's personal and family problems, help with wise counsel toward solving these problems, or bring the parolee in touch with other state and local agencies that can help him or her. Parole supervision is designed to afford protection to the community and to help the parolee without being vengeful or punitive in the enforcement of its conditions.

### 7. RELAXING SUPERVISION GRADUALLY

Supervision is relaxed gradually as it proves practicable by requiring less frequent reports and visits and relaxing restrictions originally imposed on such things as types of employment, travel, and operation of motor vehicles. The varying degrees of supervision may be designated by such terms as "maximum," when the parolee is perhaps required to report as often as once a week; "normal," with reports required less frequently; and "minimum," when he or she is required to report only occasionally or not at all.

### 8. FINAL DISCHARGE FROM PAROLE

This step takes place either at expiration of the sentence or by legally authorized action of the parole board before the expiration date.

### 9. CERTIFICATE OF REHABILITATION

In the final step, a certificate of rehabilitation is issued by the parole board, the governor, or a special commission authorized to do so when the parolee has maintained a satisfactory record for a required term of years after release. In some states, conviction does not result in loss of the rights of citizenship. Where such loss does result, the certificate of rehabilitation should carry with it restoration of all rights of citizenship as well as impounding of the person's criminal record so that it is available to law enforcement agencies only.

## PRERELEASE PREPARATION

As stated before, the period of confinement must serve as preparation for parole. While good institutions may not be, strictly speaking, essential elements of a good parole system, they are vital to its success. How high the percentage of success will be depends in large part on whether or not the institutions have the philosophy, policies, programs, and personnel required to prepare prisoners for successful return to free life. The individual treatment program of the institution should train the inmate vocationally to resume a place in the free world, put her in good physical condition, give her insight into personal problems, teach her to make proper use of leisure time, and help her assume responsibilities as a useful, law-abiding citizen. However, the prisoner needs help in bridging the gap between prison and the free world. To turn this person loose without proper preparation, or to fail to give guidance after she leaves, is manifestly unfair.

Assuming that the institution has done its part during the period of confinement toward preparation for release, there is need of special activity in this respect after the board has approved parole. There should be adequate group counseling and guidance on such topics as parole rules, relationship to parole and law enforcement officers, the common causes of parole failure, attitude toward employers, budgeting financial resources, helpful community resources and agencies, adjustment to family life, and leisure time activities.

Effort is made to discover whether the prospective parolee faces any special problems, either personal or family-related, and preparations should be made to help the parolee deal with them. When advisable, advance contact is made with the appropriate community agency. Arrangements are made for sufficient clothing and money to tide the parolee over until the first payday. In some systems, the inmate is helped to make the transition by removing some of the restraints to which she has grown accustomed and placing her in honor blocks or camps, minimum custodial facilities, special cell blocks, and the like.

## A PROPER PUBLIC ATTITUDE TOWARD THE PAROLEE

The parole board and the institution have a large part to play in returning the parolee to society. However, the manner in which the public receives the parolee—the attitude it assumes—is vital to the parolee's success. The public must give the parolee a chance. That means an opportunity to earn a living and to support dependents; it means fair and helpful treatment in efforts to make good.

Institution and parole personnel must actively seek to foster the proper attitude on the part of the public. To do so, they may secure the cooperation of such organizations as the Prisoners' Aid Association, the Salvation Army, Volunteers of America, and others who have an interest in seeing the parolee readjust to society properly. A program of public information must be carried on constantly. Prison and parole officials must seize every opportunity to address luncheon clubs, chambers of commerce, church groups, and other interested bodies. Industrial personnel officers and other responsible citizens must be invited to the institutions so that they may see the treatment program at work, thus furthering the parolee's chances of securing employment. Law enforcement officers and industrial executives must be enlisted to take part in the prerelease preparation program. Through such activity, much can be done toward creating the proper attitude on the part of the public, thereby making the path of the parolee easier and increasing chances of successful readjustment to life in the free world.

Whenever possible, the parole board should invite representative law enforcement officials, judges, adult students, and interested citizens to attend parole hearings. These visitors should be limited to a small number at any one hearing. Such visits will afford opportunity for creating a positive interest in the administration of criminal justice and foster a wider understanding of parole and institutional problems and procedures as well as of the underlying philosophy of parole.

# PRINCIPLES OF PAROLE SUPERVISION

There are two irreconcilable points of view regarding the criminal. There is the point of view of the average citizen who has neither studied the problem of crime nor had any contact with individual offenders and who, therefore, forms an opinion from the press, the screen, and the detective story. No small part of the population builds up a sort of hero worship for the criminal. But for the most part, the average citizen thinks of the criminal as a menace to life and property. His ideas as to the treatment of crime, if he has any at all, are restricted to protecting society by keeping the criminal within the walls of a prison and to punishing the offender by making prison life as uncomfortable as possible.

The average citizen does not think of the criminal as an individual human being with family ties, personal interests, and emotional problems similar to those of other human beings. Criminal habits are not conceived of as the result of heritage, environment, and personality factors. Because criminals are thought of as a class, rather than as individual offenders, the only treatment thought of is mass treatment in the form of punishment.

The second point of view is held largely by penologists, social workers, psychologists, psychiatrists, and psychoanalysts who have studied both the general problem of crime and the problems of individual offenders. These individuals, for the most part, go to the other extreme and stress as the only cure for crime a therapeutic treatment of the individual offender.

In the first point of view, the protection of society is the paramount idea, and the treatment of the individual as such is overlooked, whereas in the second point of view, the treatment of the individual offender is the paramount idea, and the protection of society is incidental.

The laws of the State of New York put upon the Division of Parole in the Executive Department responsibility for performing both these apparently irreconcilable functions.

"Parole officers shall be selected because of definite qualifications as to character, ability, and training and primarily with regard for their capacity and ability for influencing human behavior; they shall be persons likely to exercise a strong and helpful influence upon persons placed under their supervision. The executive director, under the direction and authority of the board of parole, shall direct and supervise the work of the board of parole and, with its approval, shall formulate methods of investigation and supervision in its work and develop various processes in the technique of the case work of the official staff of the board, including interviewing, consultation of records, analysis of information, diagnosis, plan of treatment, correlation of effort by individuals and agencies, and methods of influencing human behavior....

"... If the parole officer having charge of a paroled prisoner shall have reasonable cause to believe that such prisoner has lapsed, or is probably about to lapse into criminal ways or company, or has violated the conditions of his parole in an important respect, such parole officer shall report such fact to a member of the board of parole, who thereupon shall issue a warrant for the retaking of such prisoner and his return to the designated prison or the Elmira reformatory."

The first paragraph in the quotation, from the law creating the Division of Parole, clearly implies that the parole officer is intended to be primarily a social worker whose chief business is to influence human behavior. The second paragraph in the quotation, from the general laws pertaining to paroled prisoners from state prisons or the Elmira reformatory, clearly implies that the parole officer is also charged with duties as an officer of the law.

Superficial thinking regarding parole often leads to the conclusion that there exists an inherent conflict between the social case work approach—which requires that the parole officer, in the capacity of a social worker, shall treat the parolee as a client to whom he or she owes a professional service—and the legal approach—which requires that the parole officer, in the capacity of an officer of the law, shall treat the parolee as a criminal offender against whom he or she must, when occasion demands, take disciplinary action. This concept leads to the further conclusion that a parole officer who is a successful social worker will be unsuccessful in the disciplinary phase of work as an officer of the law and vice versa. While it is true that the parole officer is called upon at times to act in the capacity of defense counsel and at other times as a prosecutor, it is likewise true that the social worker, even in a private agency, is frequently called upon to fill these two opposing roles, at least in a figurative sense.

As a matter of fact, actual social case work practice, both in public and private agencies, consists in large part of professionally guided discipline. The relief-giving agency must discipline its clients against asking for or accepting unnecessary aid and in living within a budgetary allowance and assuming self-support as promptly as possible. In child-care and medical social work, much discipline is required in order to bring about on the part of the clients an acceptance of the services or the plan proposed by the social agency. In private agencies, social workers themselves have as tools of discipline only their professional skill and the control of the agency's service, such as granting or withholding relief. When the private agency social worker cannot meet the problem through these means, either the case is closed or the matter is taken to court. Resorting to court action is an important factor in the handling of desertion and nonsupport cases by private family agencies and also in the handling of neglect or improper guardianship by private child-caring agencies.

The addition of legal force to persuasion in case work practice, which occurred with the development of probation and later of parole, seems, however, to introduce an element of conflict. Fundamentally, legal force is no different from the private agency's exercise of force through threatened or actual withdrawal of service or through the resort to court action.

Like any social worker, the parole officer is primarily interested in the rehabilitation of the individual offender. The parole officer, as a social worker, can afford to be patient with a parolee's weaknesses so long as these weaknesses neither jeopardize life or property nor indicate the resumption of an antisocial attitude. When a parolee engages in illegal activities, the parole officer's greater responsibility turns to the general good.

In fact, when a parole officer suspects that a parolee is engaged in illegal activities, the officer as a social worker is responsible for checking on all possible clues to determine the true facts. If the parolee is found to be engaged in illegal activities, the parole officer's responsibility is clearly to take such steps as common sense may dictate—for example, arrest the parolee and place her in custody pending further investigation and a final decision by the board.

There arises here the objection that these situations transform the parole officer into a police officer, nullifying the status of social worker. There is further objection that, with investigation as part of the work, the parole officer may become a detective rather than a social worker. Because the parole officer frequently is called upon to meet a dual responsibility, some conflict of ideas is bound to arise.

As a good social worker, a parole officer will make every effort to assist the parolee in adjusting to the community. When such efforts fail, the parole officer will take disciplinary action against the parolee for the good of the community just as a parent who deprives a child of a pleasure, or a teacher who deprives a pupil of a privilege. The only difference is that the parole officer deals with the state; the behavior condemned by the group is usually of a grave nature, often involving serious loss of property or even loss of life; and the penalty involved restricts the individual offender's liberty and pursuit of happiness.

However, since apprehending criminals is ordinarily the business of the police, this disciplinary phase of the parole officer's work connotes police methods and police motives. This natural connotation of ideas probably accounts for the frequent assumption that this phase of parole work is not in keeping with social case work. Insofar as police methods and police psychology involve making arrests for the purpose of establishing a record, these types of police methods may not be adopted by a social worker. But insofar as police methods involve keen observation, alertness to situations, and ability to sense clues and to follow them up, these are among the essentials of the social worker's craft.

Famous detectives, when asked the secret of their success, frequently state that there is no secret except dogged perseverance in relentlessly following clues. Social case work is based primarily on the discovery of clues, a search for their significance, and a planned effort to meet the problems involved. In other phases of social work, the clues or symptoms sought and followed have to do with sickness, mental defect, mental disease, personality problems, family conflicts, desertion, nonsupport, and neglect of children. In parole, clues have to do not only with all these social problems but also with actual or suspected crime.

The discovery and use of evidence is the basis of social diagnosis quite as much as it is the basis of the detective business. That the parole officer, as a social worker, is expected to be on the alert for any problems presented by the parolee, particularly any manifestation of antisocial behavior, is a truism. The parole officer's task, however, neither begins nor ends with this. It should begin with a careful analysis of the causes of the parolee's behavior, and it should end in removing these causes. Failure to help parolees overcome antisocial habits requires the parole officer, as a social worker, to take whatever action against the parolee that may be necessary to protect society.

The greater success the parole officer has as a social worker, the more society will benefit. In every case in which the parole officer succeeds in rehabilitating the parolee and thus removing him from the criminal group, the parole officer saves society from possible loss of property or life, and from the further cost of apprehending and detaining the offender. In cases in which the parole officer fails in this ultimate purpose, yet uses skill in securing evidence to bring about the return of a parole violator to prison, he is rendering society a similar service.

In fact, the removal from parole supervision of those who are not amenable to case work treatment is an obligation that the parole officer, as a social worker, owes not only to the state but also to his profession. Under existing laws, many people who have had previous opportunities to benefit from case work treatment must be released on parole. Because of a fundamental personality defect or other deep-rooted cause, the individual does not respond to the social worker's best skill. As long as such a parolee does not violate the law or violate any condition of parole, the parole officer must assume responsibility for supervision. When such a parolee violates the law or parole conditions, it is clearly the business of the parole officer, as a social worker, to remove the parolee from the community.

If one recognizes that it is the business of the social worker to be conversant with all the important facts of the client's present situation, not merely as represented by the client but as verified through outside sources of information, it becomes clear that by fulfilling this elementary requirement of social case work, the parole officer lays the best possible foundation for a stringent check upon the activities of the parolee.

As part of a special project, the parole officers in a certain district office were asked to submit a list of cases in which valuable aid had been given the police in detecting or preventing crimes. A study of the cases submitted indicated that in every case it was the social worker's careful check on the parolee's statements and the skillful pursuit of clues obtained that made the detection of actual or potential criminal acts possible. The practical experience revealed in the case histories thus bears out the theory that proficiency as a case worker is the parole officer's most valuable asset from the point of view not only of rehabilitating the individual but also of protecting society.

This discussion of the apparent conflict between the duties of the parole officer as a social worker and as an officer of the law has been set down for the purpose of clarifying the question that frequently arises in the minds of parole officers and the general public.

## SOCIAL INVESTIGATION

Social case work is a combined art and science in which the case worker, by means of a professional relationship established to meet a special problem, works toward effecting in the client an adjustment to her social situation that will permit the fullest possible development of her own personality.

Social case work is a science inasmuch as it has developed certain general principles and built up a body of systematized knowledge regarding its methods and objects. It is an art inasmuch as the successful practice of social case work involves not only knowledge but skill in performing certain actions that must be acquired through observation, study, and experience. The relationship between the social worker and the client is the dynamic force that serves as the medium of operation. The goal is an adjustment between the individual client and the social environment. This at once implies that there must be a dual approach to the problem—a psychological approach to the personality problem involved and a sociological approach to the environmental problem. There is also a clear implication that each of these two approaches to the case must be integrated with the other.

Treatment implies a process in which skilled technique, based on a thorough knowledge and understanding of the facts, aims toward a planned objective. Whether the treatment involves a sick person, a mentally deranged patient, a quarreling husband and wife, or the antisocial conduct of a paroled prisoner, it is first of all necessary to know the facts. Securing the facts is the inevitable first step in the treatment of any problem.

In social case work this process of getting the facts is called social investigation. In common with other types of fact finding, it predicates solicitous effort to obtain complete, accurate, and impartial information. In addition, it involves a particular emphasis on social evidence and a particular skill in obtaining and interpreting this evidence.

To understand the present problem of any prisoner, it is necessary to take a long look back into the life history of that individual. To plan treatment wisely, it is necessary to take a long look ahead into the possibilities of the future.

The social worker, while conducting an investigation, is not merely collecting facts but weighing and measuring the significance of these facts regarding their contribution to an explanation of the present problem as well as their value in revealing resources that may be used in future treatment. A thoroughly satisfactory social investigation uses the past to interpret the present and lays the foundation for future planning.

Not only is this broad perspective of time necessary in social investigation but also a broad perspective of human behavior that recognizes both the sociological or environmental factors and the psychological or personality factors that enter into any given situation.

It is not sufficient to know, for example, that at age 8 a certain prisoner fell from a fire escape and injured his right knee so seriously that he has since walked with a slight limp. It is more important to find out the psychological effect this physical injury has had on the individual; to know how it affected him as a boy and later as a man. Did it make him self-conscious and keep him from indulging in athletic games? Did his family or his schoolmates taunt him in any way? Did it give him any sense of inferiority?

Nor is it sufficient to know that at age 18 another prisoner transformed from a cheerful and agreeable boy into a morose and disagreeable youth. It is necessary to attempt to find out what environmental factors may have contributed to this change in disposition and mental outlook. Was it, for example, the death of a parent? Loss of economic security in the home? Disappointment in failing some test, such as for admission to the Army? A clandestine love affair? A new group of associates? Drugs?

In other words, the social worker must always think about the interrelation between personality and environment so that when a concrete external experience is reported, questions regarding the psychological reaction of the individual will immediately arise. When a specific mental trait or psychological reaction is reported, questions regarding the external factors that may have produced this effect will immediately arise.

## ANALYSIS AND PLAN OF TREATMENT

Ideally, a plan of treatment is based on an exhaustive investigation covering the psychological and sociological factors that have, in turn, been carefully analyzed. The plan of treatment should utilize constructive factors already presented in the situation, aim to counteract the destructive factors therein, and include treasures intended to foster and develop new resources within the individual, the environment, or both. To be successful, the plan must be accepted by the parolee and supported by the family group and often by interested individuals and other social agencies.

Thorough investigation, careful analysis, intelligent planning, and skillful presentation of the plan to the parolee and others involved are all steps that presuppose adequate personnel to give to the individual case ample time for planned treatment. Under existing conditions, when parole officers supervise as many as 100 cases, it is obviously impossible to give such treatment in every case.

In these instances, there is grave danger that haphazard treatment may be substituted for planned treatment. Although ideal planning cannot be done in all cases, it is still possible and highly necessary for the parole officer to recognize that a planned approach to a case will make it easier to accomplish her goals.

In the hurry and confusion that result from pressure of work, there is also danger that the term "case work plan" may be interpreted in a highly technical sense and assumed to involve an elaborate and comprehensive program that an overworked parole officer cannot be expected to carry out. This could result in the whole concept of planned treatment being discarded as impractical.

Another problem that impacts the formation and execution of a formal postparole treatment plan is that parole cases involve many unique situations. The parolee's attitude may be so antagonistic that it prevents the acceptance of any proposed plan. On the other hand, the parolee may be a white-collar offender who is entirely capable of making plans and effecting adjustment with little or no aid from the parole officer. The parolee may be so secretive and outside sources of information so meager that it is exceedingly difficult to arrive at any real understanding of the underlying problems. Or the parolee's thinking may be so dominated by an immediate acute problem such as homelessness or unemployment that a home and a job are the total focus of his attention.

Common sense dictates that under conditions such as any of these, preparing, recording, and attempting to follow an elaborate plan of treatment should be discarded as folly. Common sense also dictates that, in any of the above or similar situations, the parole officer is under obligation to plan an intelligent approach to the immediate situation. In the case of the antagonistic parolee, some method of approach must be planned that will first break down this antagonism and allow the parole officer to reach the parolee. In the case of the self-sufficient white-collar offender, the parole officer must recognize that there may be undiscovered underlying problems and develop the confidence in the parolee so that the parolee will be encouraged to discuss personal problems with the parole officer. The secretive parolee, with no family sources of information, requires a planned effort on the part of the parole officer to break down barriers and uncover possible sources of information.

While none of the four approaches suggested above may be called a well-rounded social case work plan, common sense indicates that under any of the given situations, the only feasible plan is an approach to the immediate problem. However thoroughly the parole officer studies and analyzes the parolee's situation, the approach to the problem should be modified by the degree of insight into the problem that the parolee possesses. Because this so largely determines the parole officer's approach, it is important to record the parolee's own interpretation of his problem insofar as the parole officer is able to learn this.

Since the parolee's attitude toward parole and toward his parole officer also determines in large part the type of treatment undertaken by the parole officer, this likewise merits recording. Within the limits set by the parolee's insight into his problems and his attitudes toward his parole officer, the latter will plan the best approach to the situation. This approach may be on one or more of the various levels of case work treatment.

# PAROLE PROBLEMS

## PREPARATION FOR PAROLE

Prison life at its best is a hard and bitter experience. If the years spent in prison are spent in overcrowded conditions that are unsanitary, corrupting, and dangerous and tremendously increase the risk of criminal "cross infection," the chances of rehabilitation are considerably reduced. If, in addition to such overcrowding, the years spent in prison are years of idleness, the degrading effect of mental stagnation—which is an inevitable byproduct of idleness—can easily be imagined.

The part of educational and vocational training in any prison program that attempts to prepare the inmate for release is of prime importance. Yet thousands of prisoners are untouched by any educational program. Moreover, comprehensive educational programs exist in only a few institutions. Indiscriminate educational or vocational training of the prisoner is not sufficient. In fact, from the standpoint of removing the causes of delinquency, it may be wholly irrelevant. What is needed, then, is a service of diagnosis and classification based on medical, psychological, and psychiatric examinations of the offender.

Since the institution and parole are parts of one continuous process for the rehabilitation of the offender, the work of the receiving station, the social worker in connection with the institution, the psychiatric clinic, the prison officials, and the parole board and parole officers should be closely coordinated. Such coordination of the work of the prison and parole authorities is the best guarantee for successful prison and parole program operation.

The preparation of a prisoner for release on parole should begin the day he or she enters the prison. It cannot be postponed until the last few weeks or days of incarceration. Both the prison authorities and the prisoner should look upon parole as the logical, natural means of terminating a prison sentence, and the offender should receive instruction in regard to the behavior that will be expected of him or her on parole. An important element of pre-parole preparation is the contact of the prisoner with the parole officer. A friendly relationship with the officer will do much to prepare the prisoner for future release and to ensure the right attitude to parole supervision. Furthermore, it will help the parole officer become familiar with the home, environment, and problems of the inmate before he or she leaves the institution.

A partial answer to the problem of parole preparation may be found in a transitional stage between imprisonment and release that the inmate would spend in a supervised halfway house. The few recent experiments in this direction indicate that such a stage may greatly facilitate the difficult transition from the living conditions in prison to life in a free community. These experiments should be watched closely for they may provide a distinct contribution to a more effective parole system.

## TREATMENT OF PAROLE VIOLATORS

The reasons for declaring a parolee to be a violator are related to, among other factors, the type and extent of parole supervision in any one jurisdiction. In those states in which there is no personal supervision by parole agents, a parolee is seldom declared a violator unless he or she is apprehended on suspicion of having committed, or in the commission of, another criminal offense. On the other hand, in jurisdictions where supervision is strict, violators are frequently returned for breaches of the conditions of parole since the parole authorities believe it to be their duty to prevent new crime before its occurrence.

Between the extremes of reincarceration for the commission of a new offense only and reincarceration for the violation of any parole condition, most states exercise varying degrees of control in determining when parolees should be declared violators, retaken, and remanded to penal custody.

In general, the authority to revoke parole and the power to arrest a parolee for an alleged violation rests with the agency of the state vested with the authority to grant parole. In some states, parole may be revoked by more than one agency, each acting independently of the other.

Hearings on the violation of parole are, as a general rule, discretionary with the parole authorities. The purpose of these hearings is to give the alleged violator the opportunity to present his or her side of the case. As a matter of administrative practice in many of the states, the parole authorities conduct hearings to avoid any possible faulty judgment or bias on the part of the parole agents.

In most states certain penalties other than the mere fact of reincarceration are incurred by a parole violator. In those states where an indeterminate sentence law is in existence, the parole authorities generally prolong the period of incarceration until the ex-parolee appears again to be a fit subject for parole or until the full maximum term of his or her sentence has expired.

The procedures involved in the disciplinary treatment of parole violators subsequent to their arrest and reimprisonment are varied and generally involve the following questions.

- Should the violator forfeit prison good time prior to his or her release upon parole?

- Should the violator be allowed to receive good time credits for subsequent good behavior?

- Should the violator receive credit on his or her sentence for the time he or she was at large on parole?

If the correctional process is completely integrated from the time the offender first enters prison until he or she is finally discharged from parole, a parole violation might warrant the rescinding of prison good time previously granted and perhaps even the forfeiting of good time deductions for subsequent good behavior. The answer to these questions should lie within the discretion of the parole authorities in accordance with the individual circumstances of each case.

Certain states have placed definite restrictions upon the parole authorities in the matter of making parole violators ineligible for further parole consideration or of delaying the time of further parole consideration. It appears that the greater the flexibility of parole and indeterminate sentence laws, the greater the possibility for an individualized approach to re-parole in the interest of social protection and rehabilitation. If society may be best served by extending supervision over repeaters as well as over first offenders, there is justification for extending the practice of re-parole far beyond its present bounds.

Parole violation rates are used (1) as a measure of efficiency of parole systems; (2) as a basis for comparing the effectiveness of different parole systems; and (3) as a measure of the adequacy or inadequacy of the parole administrative personnel. In the methods currently used in computing violation rates, there is a lack of uniformity in defining the number of cases placed on parole, the number of violators, and the time period under consideration. These three terms must be defined uniformly before violation rates can be used for comparative purposes.

The use of violation rates for comparative purposes must also take into consideration the following.

- The selective process

- The general environmental conditions to which parolees are subject

▓ The policies used in determining what constitutes a parole violator

▓ The supervision of parolees

▓ The length of the parole period

The selective process, as it makes greater use of rehabilitative methods other than incarceration, is likely to parole more "poor risks," thus leading to a high violation rate. Again, a selective policy for parole that entails the supervision of poor risks, along with the good risks, may lead to a high violation rate. For example, the greater the degree of revocation for technical violations of parole conditions, the greater the violation rate will be. The stricter the supervision leading to the detection of crimes committed on parole, the greater the violation rate could be. The longer the time under supervision, that is, the longer the period of "exposure to crime," the greater the violation rate may be. Again, parole violation rates may be merely a reflection of the influence of the incentives for crime in metropolitan centers or the greater facilities for police detection in these areas.

## FINAL DISCHARGE FROM PAROLE

The most important question surrounding final discharge from parole is the length of the parole period. In this connection three groups of jurisdictions may be distinguished.

1. The time of discharge is specified by statute

2. The maximum parole period is provided for but the parole authorities have discretion to grant final discharge before the period elapses

3. The parole authorities have full discretion regarding length of the parole period

The length of the parole period is of considerable importance in regard to the social effectiveness of parole as a rehabilitative process. Obviously, if a parolee has to be discharged from parole because of legal provisions at a time when actual rehabilitation has not been fully tested, society is not as adequately protected as it should be. The most ideal plan in this respect is that of giving the parole authorities full discretion in determining the length of the parole period.

Inasmuch as environmental conditions should be made as nearly normal as possible for the discharged parolee if rehabilitation is to be brought about, civil rights should be restored to the parolee at least at the time of final discharge from parole.

# REPORTS

In probation and parole work, reports are normally required. In some instances, a report might be an informal, oral reply to a request for information. In other instances a report might be a full written statement based upon careful study.

## PURPOSE OF REPORTS

Before delving into the methods of creating reports, let's discuss the purpose behind them.

### WHAT IS THE PRIMARY REASON FOR MAKING REPORTS?

- They supply the information needed by officials.

- They are necessary in order to maintain control of operations.

- Top management must have full knowledge of what goes on in order to plan properly.

### WHY ARE PROBATION AND PAROLE OFFICERS RESPONSIBLE FOR WRITING THE REPORTS?

- Probation and parole officers are the best source of information about the work.

- Probation and parole officers are closest to operations and know the most about the working conditions.

- The points of view of probation and parole officers are more practical and realistic than those of people further removed from operations.

- It is the responsibility of the probation or parole officer as part of the management team to contribute to the smooth running of the organization.

## WHO RECEIVES PROBATION AND PAROLE REPORTS?

In general, as a probation or parole officer, you will be required to submit reports to the following groups.

**Line**

- Direct supervisor
- Division chief
- Commanding officer
- Headquarters offices
- Departmental offices

**Staff**

- Management office
- Safety office
- Personnel office
- Medical office

**Committees**

- Promotion
- Deferment
- Career development
- Board of examiners

## PREPARING THE REPORT

Now let's discuss how to create a report, whether it is oral or written, special or periodic.

### 1. KNOW EXACTLY WHAT IS WANTED

- Check the instructions.
- Understand what is needed.
- Ask for explanation of unclear points.
- Set limits; provide only what is wanted.
- Find out who will use the report.
- Plan to meet the needs of those who will use it.

### 2. GET THE FACTS TOGETHER

- Decide on the kind of information needed.
- Use data already available in records.

- Find new facts that are pertinent.

- Ask questions of colleagues and staff members.

- Probe to find out why people have certain opinions.

- Record information on paper so it will not be lost.

## 3. ORGANIZE THE FACTS

- Bring together facts that are related regarding time, place, persons, cause, and effect.

- Discard irrelevant facts.

- Arrange facts in a smooth order.

- Check for breaks in continuity and rough spots.

- Be sure the facts make sense.

- Build up to an effective culmination of facts.

- When desired, state conclusions and recommendations based upon the facts.

## PREPARING AN ORAL REPORT

Probably the most common method of reporting is by word of mouth. Many times we are asked questions such as:

- How did Mr. Jones's parole hearing go today?

- Will you find out whether your staff is using too much sick leave?

In these cases, somebody wants a report quickly and it is not necessary to write it out.

## ANSWERING WITHOUT OPPORTUNITY TO STUDY THE SITUATION

What do you do when your chief wants an answer to a question right now? In these instances:

- There is little time to prepare a reply.

- You have a chance to pause for a moment to get your thoughts in order.

- You recall what you know about the situation: the facts.

- You quickly organize your information so that it makes sense as you tell it.

- You protect yourself with an expression such as:

    - "This is the condition as I understand it now."
    - "Without a complete check, it would appear that …."
    - "As I see it at this time …."

## ORAL REPORTING AFTER PREPARATION

If you have an opportunity to get ready to tell your story, how can you make your presentation effective?

- Know what you are going to say.

- Have a brief outline or notes.

■ If visual aids will help, have the material ready (charts, graphs, photos).

■ Be alert.

■ Speak clearly.

■ Stop talking as soon as you have presented the information.

An effective public speaker once said that when he appeared before an audience he tried to remember the following three things.

1. Stand up so they would see him.

2. Speak up so they could hear him.

3. Shut up so they would like him.

This is sound advice, even when your audience is limited to one person.

## PREPARING A WRITTEN REPORT

For many people, it is a difficult task to prepare a written report. Writing reports involves a great deal of organization, clear presentation of the facts, and a logical conclusion. Following are some guidelines to use in writing a formal report.

### USE OUTLINES

Using an outline to prepare your written report will

■ help organize the material you have collected for inclusion in the report.

■ allow you to think through the report as a whole.

■ enable you to ensure that all important points are included, and that unimportant details are left out.

■ allow you to make changes to the order and contents of the report before the report is written.

### STICK TO THE POINT

It is important to include only the pertinent facts in your report. By avoiding the inclusion of extraneous information, you will

■ enable the reader to understand the report easily.

■ save your reader valuable time.

■ communicate to the reader that you are able to think and present information clearly.

### BE CONCISE

Presenting information in your report in a brief succinct manner will

■ save the time of the writer, typist, or reader.

■ make the report much more powerful.

■ make information in the report easy to find.

### GET A CRITICAL REVIEW
Asking a colleague to review you report will help you

- find parts that are not clear.

- recognize "rough spots," where flow of thought is not smooth.

- reduce wordiness.

### USE TABS AND ATTACHMENTS
If your written report becomes lengthy, it may be helpful to organize the report using tabs to divide sections and attachments to present information that may be too lengthy or involved to include in the body of the report. By using tabs and attachments you will

- permit the report to be shorter and more readable.

- enable the reader to refer to supporting data or illustrative materials if desired.

- permit the reader to find quickly the exact items he or she wants to see.

- support the body of the report with factual data.

- add to the strength of the report without adding to the length.

## EFFECTIVE REPORTING
The quality of the reports you make to officials in the organization has a great deal to do with your reputation as a good manager. Ask yourself the following questions when putting together a report.

### IS THIS REPORT NECESSARY?

- In some instances, a report that was useful in the past is no longer needed.

- The same data you are presenting in your report may be available from another source.

- A tactful question regarding how your report is used will show your supervisor that you are alert and interested.

### IS THIS REPORT ADEQUATE?

- Put yourself in the position of the recipient of the report. Are you providing enough information to satisfy him or her?

- Read your report again. Are there corrections or changes that could be made to increase its effectiveness?

- Review the report in terms of its purpose. Does it achieve its goals?

### IS THIS REPORT TIMELY?

- Decisions at a higher level may depend on the contents of your report. Make sure you meet your deadlines.

- Your supervisor may be under pressure to provide information to his or her superiors.

- Remember: a report that is delivered too late most likely has lost its usefulness.

## MECHANICAL MAKEUP OF A REPORT

Reports can be divided into two categories: long and short. The long report is one that usually consists of six or more pages and is usually bound. It contains a letter of transmittal, a formal introduction, a discussion of the facts, conclusions, and recommendations. The short report may be set up in one of two ways: as a letter or a memorandum. Short reports should also include an introduction, discussion of the facts, conclusions, and recommendations.

## STYLE AND TONE

In the long report, it is not customary to refer to yourself as I or we. In general, a report is written in the third person and passive voice may be used. For example, "Upon investigation it was learned that …," instead of "During my investigation I learned…." The reason you do not refer to yourself personally in the long report is so that the report sounds objective and scientific rather than subjective or personal. The report should give the impression that the material in the report consists of actual, unbiased facts that were discovered through investigation, and that you are not injecting your personal views or prejudices. In short reports, however, you may use those personal references, as these types of reports are less formal.

## OPINION VERSUS FACT

You must be able to distinguish between a fact and an opinion if you are going to write a good report. A fact is a verifiable truth. In other words, it is something that can be proved. An opinion, on the other hand, has no weight as evidence. It cannot be proved.

In a report you should state the facts upon which your conclusions are based. If your report contains facts rather than opinions, the person for whom the report is intended need not agree with your conclusions or recommendations. The facts will allow him or her to form his or her own conclusions and recommendations.

Suppose your supervisor has called on you to write a report about a person under your supervision. You have had a great deal of trouble with this individual. She comes in too late and has proved herself to be very inefficient. You would like to recommend that her services be dispensed with. These are all general statements that should be based on facts. If you were to study your employee's time sheet, you could report, for example, that she is required to begin work at 8:45 a.m. every day. However, on January 2, your employee came in at 9:25 a.m.; January 3, at 9:17 a.m.; January 4, at 9:22 a.m., etc. Regarding inefficiencies, you would report the same types of activities. For example, on January 4, you asked your employee to make 10 copies of a recommendation for parole in time for the parole hearing at 2:00 that afternoon. At 1:45 p.m. that day, she was still at lunch and had not completed the task. To make the hearing on time, you had to make the copies yourself. On the basis of those facts, you can conclude that this particular person has been negligent.

## EFFECTIVE EXPRESSION

A useful report that is not well written is generally not well received. Take a look at the following grammar guidelines and keep them in mind as you write your reports.

### SELECTED RULES OF GRAMMAR

1.  The subject of a verb is in the nominative case even if the verb is understood and not expressed.

    *Example:*   They are as old as *we.* (as we are)

2.  The word *who* is in the nominative case. *Whom* is in the objective case.

    *Examples:*   The trapeze artist who ran away with the clown broke the lion tamer's heart. *(Who is the subject of the verb ran.)*

    The trapeze artist whom he loved ran away with the circus clown. *(Whom is the object of the verb loved.)*

3. The word *whoever* is in the nominative case. *Whomever* is in the objective case.

   *Examples:* Whoever comes to the door is welcome to join the party. *(Whoever* is the subject of the verb *comes.)*

   Invite whomever you wish to accompany you. *(Whomever* is the object of the verb *invite.)*

4. Nouns or pronouns connected by a form of the verb *to be* should always be in the nominative case.

   *Example:* It is *I.* (Not *me)*

5. The object of a preposition or of a transitive verb should use a pronoun in the objective case.

   *Examples:* It would be impossible for *me* to do that job alone. *(Me is* the object of the preposition *for.)*

   The attendant gave *me* the keys to the locker. *(Me is* the indirect object of the verb *gave.)*

6. *Each, either, neither, anyone, anybody, somebody, someone, every, everyone, one, no one,* and *nobody* are singular pronouns. Each of these words takes a singular verb and a singular pronoun.

   *Examples: Neither likes* the pets of the other.

   *Everyone* must wait *his* turn.

   *Each* of the patients *carries* insurance.

   *Neither* of the women *has* completed *her* assignment.

7. When the correlative conjunctions *either/or* and *neither/nor* are used, the number of the verb agrees with the number of the last subject.

   *Examples:* Neither John nor *Greg eats* meat.

   Either the cat or the *mice take* charge in the barn.

8. A subject consisting of two or more nouns joined by a coordinating conjunction takes a plural verb.

   *Example:* Paul *and* Sue *were* the last to arrive.

9. The number of the verb is not affected by the addition to the subject of words introduced by *with, together with, no less than,* and *as well as.*

   *Example:* The *captain,* together with the rest of the team, *was* delighted by the victory celebration.

10. A verb agrees in number with its subject. A verb should not be made to agree with a noun that is part of a phrase following the subject.

    *Examples: Mount Snow,* one of my favorite ski areas, *is* in Vermont.

    The *mountains* of Colorado, like those of Switzerland, *offer* excellent skiing.

11. A verb should agree in number with the subject, not with the predicate noun or pronoun.

    *Examples:* Poor study *habits are* the leading cause of unsatisfactory achievement in school.

    The leading *cause* of unsatisfactory achievement in school *is* poor study habits.

12. A pronoun agrees with its antecedent in person, number, gender, and case.

    *Example:* Since you were absent on Tuesday, you will have to ask Mary or Beth for her notes on the lecture. (Use *her,* not *their,* because two singular antecedents joined by *or* take a singular pronoun.)

13. *Hardly, scarcely, barely, only,* and *but* (when it means *only*) are negative words. Do NOT use another negative in conjunction with any of these words.

    *Examples:* He had *but* one hat; or, he had *only* one hat. (NOT: He *didn't* have *but* one hat.)

    I can *hardly* read the small print; or, I *can't* read the small print. (NOT: I *can't hardly* read the small print.)

14. *As* is a conjunction introducing a subordinate clause, while *like* is a preposition. The object of a preposition is a noun or phrase.

    *Examples:* Winston tastes good *as* a cigarette should. *(Cigarette* is the subject of the clause; *should* is its verb.)

    He behaves *like* a fool.

    The gambler accepts only hard currency *like* gold coins.

15. When modifying the words *kind* and *sort,* the words *this* and *that* always remain in the singular.

    *Examples:* *This kind of* apple makes the best pie.

    *That sort of* behavior will result in severe punishment.

16. In sentences beginning with *there is* and *there are,* the verb should agree in number with the noun that follows it.

    *Examples:* There isn't an unbroken bone in her body. (The singular subject *bone* takes the singular verb *is.*)

    There are many choices to be made. (The plural subject *choices* takes the plural verb *are.*)

17. A noun or pronoun modifying a gerund should be in the possessive case.

    *Example:* *Is* there any criticism of Arthur's writing? *(Writing* is a gerund. It must be modified by Arthur's, not by Arthur.)

18. Do not use the possessive case when referring to an inanimate object.

    *Example:* He had difficulty with the management *of* the store. (NOT: He had difficulty with the *store's* management.)

19. When expressing a condition contrary to fact or a wish, use the subjunctive tense.

    *Example:* I wish I *were* a movie star.

20. Statements equally true in the past and in the present are usually expressed in the present tense. The contents of a book are also expressed in the present tense.

    *Examples:*  He said that Venus is a planet. (Even though he made the statement in the past, the fact remains that Venus is a planet.)

            In the book *Peter Pan*, Wendy says, "I can fly." (Every time one reads the book, Wendy *says* it again.)

## ANTECEDENTS AND MODIFIERS

1. *It,* when used as a relative pronoun, refers to the nearest noun. In your writing, you must be certain that the grammatical antecedent is indeed the intended antecedent.

    *Example:*  Since the mouth of the cave was masked by underbrush, *it* provided an excellent hiding place. (Do you really mean that the underbrush is an excellent hiding place, or do you mean the cave?)

2. *Which* is another pronoun with which reference errors are often made. In fact, whenever using pronouns, you must ask yourself whether or not the reference of the pronoun is clear.

    *Examples:*  The first chapter awakens your interest in cloning, which continues to the end of the book. (What continues, cloning or your interest?)

            Jim told Bill that he was about to be fired. (Who is about to be fired? This sentence can be interpreted to mean that Jim was informing Bill about Bill's impending termination or about his, Jim's, own troubles.)

            In your writing, you may find that the most effective way to clear up an ambiguity is to recast the sentence.

    *Examples:*  The first chapter awakens your interest in cloning. The following chapters build upon this interest and maintain it throughout the book.

            Jim told Bill, "I am about to be fired." Or, Jim told Bill, "You are about to be fired."

3. Adjectives modify only nouns and pronouns. Adverbs modify verbs, adjectives, and other adverbs.

    *Examples:*  One can swim in a lake as *easily* as in a pool. (NOT: One can swim in a lake as *easy* as in a pool.)

            I was *really* happy. (NOT: I was *real* happy.)

Sometimes context determines the use of adjective or adverb.

    *Examples:*  The old man looked *angry. (Angry* is an adjective describing the old man. [angry old man])

            The old man looked *angrily* out the window. *(Angrily* is an adverb describing the man's manner of looking out the window.)

4. Phrases should be placed near the words they modify.

    *Examples:*  *In the first chapter,* the author says that he intends to influence your life. (NOT: The author says that he intends to influence your life *in the first chapter.*)

            He played the part of Jud *in "Oklahoma."* (NOT: He played the part *in "Oklahoma"* of Jud.)

5. Adverbs should be placed near the words they modify.

   *Example:* The man was willing to sell *only* one horse. (NOT: The man was *only* willing to sell one horse.)

6. Clauses should be placed near the words they modify.

   *Example:* *He who sows early will* reap a good harvest. (NOT: *He will* reap a good harvest *who sows early.*)

## SENTENCE STRUCTURE

1. Every sentence must contain a verb. A group of words, no matter how long, without a verb is a sentence fragment, not a sentence. A verb may consist of one, two, three, or four words.

   *Examples:* The boy *studies* hard. The boy *will study* hard. The boy *has been studying* hard. The boy *should have been studying* hard.

   The words that make up a single verb may be separated.

   *Examples:* It is not *snowing.* It will almost certainly *snow* tomorrow.

2. Every sentence must have a subject. The subject may be a noun, a pronoun, or a word or group of words functioning as a noun.

   *Examples:* *Fish* swim. (noun)

   *She* is young. (pronoun)

   *Running* is good exercise. (gerund)

   *To argue* is pointless. (infinitive)

   That *he* was *tired* was evident. (noun clause)

   In commands, the subject is usually not expressed but is understood to be you.

   *Example:* Mind your own business.

3. A phrase cannot stand by itself as a sentence. A phrase is any group of related words that has no subject or predicate and that is used as a single part of speech. Phrases may be built around prepositions, articles, gerunds, or infinitives.

   *Examples:* *The* boy *with* curly hair is my brother. (prepositional phrase used as an adjective modifying *boy*)

   *My* favorite cousin lives *on* a farm. (prepositional phrase used as an adverb modifying *lives*)

   *Beyond the double white line* is out of bounds. (prepositional phrase used as a noun, the subject of the sentence)

   *A* thunderstorm preceding a cold *front* is often welcome. (participial phrase used as an adjective modifying *thunderstorm*)

   We eagerly awaited the pay envelopes *brought by the messenger.* (participial phrase used as an adjective modifying *envelopes*)

   *Running a day camp* is an exhausting job. (gerund phrase used as a noun, subject of the sentence)

   The director is paid well for *running the day camp.* (gerund phrase used as a noun, the object of the preposition *for*)

*To breathe unpolluted air* should be every person's birthright. (infinitive phrase used as a noun, the subject of the sentence)

The child began *to unwrap his gift.* (infinitive phrase used as a noun, the object of the verb *began*)

The boy ran away from home to *become a marine.* (infinitive phrase used as an adverb modifying *ran away*)

4. A *main, independent,* or *principal* clause can stand alone as a complete sentence. A main clause has a subject and a verb. It may stand by itself or be introduced by a coordinating conjunction.

    *Example:* The sky darkened ominously and rain began to fall. (two independent clauses joined by a coordinating conjunction)

    A *subordinate* or *dependent* clause must never stand alone. It is not a complete sentence, only a sentence fragment, despite the fact that is has a subject and a verb. A subordinate clause usually is introduced by a subordinating conjunction. Subordinate clauses may act as adverbs, adjectives, or nouns. Subordinate adverbial clauses are generally introduced by the subordinating conjunctions *when, while, because, as soon as, if, after, although, as before, since, than, though, until,* and *unless.*

    *Examples:* *While we were waiting for the local,* the express roared past.

    The woman applied for a new job *because she wanted to earn more money.*

    Although a subordinate clause contains both subject and verb, it cannot stand alone because it is introduced by a subordinating word.

    Subordinate adjective clauses may be introduced by the pronouns *who, which,* and *that.*

    *Examples:* The play *that he liked best* was a mystery.

    I have a neighbor *who served in the Peace Corps.*

    Subordinate noun clauses may be introduced by *who, what,* or *that.*

    *Examples:* The stationmaster says *that the train will be late.*

    I asked the waiter *what the stew contained.*

    I wish I knew *who backed into my car.*

5. Just as a subordinate clause cannot stand alone but must be incorporated into a sentence that features an independent clause, so two independent clauses cannot share one sentence without some form of connective. If they do, they form a run-on sentence. Two principal clauses may be joined by a coordinating conjunction, by a comma followed by a coordinating conjunction, or by a semicolon. They may form two distinct sentences. Two main clauses may never be joined by a comma without a coordinating conjunction. This error is called a comma splice.

*Examples:*

| **Correct** | **Incorrect** |
|---|---|
| A college education has never been more important than it is today, and it has never cost more. | A college education has never been more important than it is today it has never cost more. (run-on sentence) |
| A college education has never been more important than it is today; it has never cost more. | A college education has never been more important than it is today, it has never cost more. (comma splice) |
| A college education has never been more important than it is today. It has never cost more. | A college education has never been more important than it is today and it has never cost more. (The two independent clauses are not equally short, so a comma is required before the coordinating conjunction.) |
| | A college education has never been more important than it is today; and it has never cost more. (A semicolon is never used before a coordinating conjunction.) |

6.  Comparisons must be logical and complete. Train yourself to concentrate on each sentence so that you can recognize errors.

    *Examples:*  Wilmington is larger than any *other* city in Delaware. (NOT: Wilmington is larger than any city in Delaware.)

    He is as fat *as,* if not fatter than, his uncle. (NOT: He is as fat, if not fatter, than his uncle.)

    I hope to find a summer job other than *that* of lifeguard. (NOT: I hope to find a summer job other than a lifeguard.)

    *Law* is a better profession than *accounting*. (NOT: *Law* is a better profession than *an accountant*.)

7.  Avoid the "is when" and "is where" construction.

    *Examples:*  A limerick is a short poem with a catchy rhyme. (NOT: A limerick *is when* a short poem has a catchy rhyme.)

    To exile a person is to force him to live in another place. (NOT: To exile is where a person must live in another place.)

8.  Errors in parallelism are often quite subtle, but you should learn to recognize and avoid them.

    *Examples:*  *Skiing* and *skating* are both winter sports. (NOT: Skiing and to skate are both winter sports.)

    She spends all her time *eating, sleeping,* and *studying*. (NOT: She spends all her time eating, asleep, and on her studies.)

    The work is neither difficult nor interesting. (NOT: The work is neither difficult nor do I find it interesting.)

    His heavy *drinking* and *gambling* make him a poor role model. (NOT: His heavy drinking and the fact that he gambles makes him a poor role model.)

# KNOW YOUR COURTS

To the layperson who has had minimal contact with the courts, the judicial system may appear to be complex and involved. Actually, court organization is quite systematic and logical. Each state is unique; each has its own court system. The structure of the court system in some states differs greatly from that in others. Information about the New York court system is NOT interchangeable with information about the court system of any other state. But the logic behind the organization of a court system is instructive and universally applicable. This section focuses on court organization in the State of New York and serves as a good example of the levels and jurisdictions of courts in a complex arena.

Prior to the comprehensive New York court reform of 1962, the administration of the various courts was completely decentralized. Each court more or less ran itself. The result was, on one hand, inefficiency and duplication of processes and, on the other hand, inflexibility. One court could be overloaded and heavily backlogged while another sat idle. But a case could not be transferred from one court to another because jurisdictions were conflicting and incompatible. The mission of court reform was to eliminate this untenable state of affairs. With the court reform, courts were combined to allow for greater flexibility and heavy savings in administrative and supervisory work.

Courts may be classified according to three criteria. The *first* of these criteria is the power that created the court: the state constitution or legislative action. Constitutional courts are provided for in the Constitution of the State of New York. Statutory courts have been created out of necessity. Statutory courts may arise from legislation originating with the legislature of the State of New York or from local legislation.

A *second* criterion by which courts may be classified relates to the type of case tried therein. Civil courts try cases dealing with civil matters—that is, suits for the recovery of damages, property matters, etc. Criminal courts try people accused of violations of laws the conviction for which would make them criminals. Both criminal and civil courts may be either constitutional or statutory.

The *third* criterion relates to whether or not a court's verdict sets precedent for future cases and trials. A court of record is one in which the decisions are recorded and may be referred to as a basis for future decisions involving similar circumstances. Civil court is a court of record. Its decisions set precedents for the trying of future cases.

## TYPES OF COURTS

### COURT OF APPEALS

**Organization:** The court of appeals is the highest court in the state. The court of appeals is composed of a chief judge and six associate judges elected for fourteen-year terms. The governor, at the request of the court, may assign no more than four justices of the Supreme Court to act as associate judges of the court of appeals when warranted by the court's calendar. No more than seven judges sit on any one case. Five constitutes a quorum and four must concur to arrive at a decision.

**Jurisdiction:** This court is restricted to reviewing questions of law, except where the judgment is death or where the appellate division makes new findings of fact and enters judgment or orders based on these findings. Appeals are heard as of right direct from the trial court where the question involved tests the validity of a statutory provision of the state or the United States and in criminal cases where the sentence is death. Appeals are heard by the appellate division of the Supreme Court as a matter of right from a judgment or order handed down by the appellate division granting a new trial. Appeals are also heard when a construction of the Constitution of the State or of the United States is involved, or in a case where a justice of the appellate division dissents. Finally, appeals are heard when order of reversal is given or when questions of law certified by the appellate division, in its opinion, ought to be reviewed.

*Note:* Only one appeal is allowed in a criminal case as a matter of right. No appeal from a final order of the appellate division in civil cases originally commenced in a court other than the Supreme Court. Surrogates, county court, court of claims, or board of audit shall be reviewed except by permission of the appellate division. Death penalty appeals go directly to this court.

## THE COURT ON THE JUDICIARY

**Organization:** This court is made up of the chief judge of the court of appeals who presides over its hearing, the senior associate judge of the court of appeals who presides in the absence of the chief judge, and one justice from each department of the appellate division.

**Jurisdiction:** This court has power to remove or retire a judge among the following: court of appeals, justice of the Supreme Court, judge of the court of claims, surrogate, special surrogate, county court judge, justice of any city court of record.

## COURT OF CLAIMS

**Organization:** The law provides that this court is composed of twelve judges appointed by the governor with the approval of the state senate. Appointees must be attorneys with at least ten years of experience.

**Jurisdiction:** The state is sovereign and cannot be sued in the usual manner. However, under the Court of Claims Act, the state waives its right to immunity for the acts of its employees and officers and consents to have its liability for acts of officers or employees determined in accordance with the same rules of law as apply to actions in the Supreme Court against an individual or corporation. Jurisdiction is conferred on the court of claims to hear and determine all claims against the state to recover damages, injuries to property, or personal injury because of misfeasance or negligence of the officers or employees of the state while acting in their official capacity. It also has the power to hear and determine such private claims against the state as may be authorized by the state legislature. It may also hear and determine any claim on the part of the state against a claimant. Appeals from this court may be taken to the appellate division in the state capital.

## COURT FOR THE TRIAL OF IMPEACHMENTS

**Organization:** This court is composed of the state senators, the associate judges of the court of appeals, and the chief justice who presides.

**Jurisdiction:** To try impeachments presented by the state assembly against the governor or lieutenant governor. The court may remove the accused from office, disqualify him or her from holding office under the state, or both. There is no provision for an appeal from this court.

## SURROGATE'S COURT

**Organization:** Surrogates are chosen by voters of their respective counties. Their term of office is six years except in the New York City counties of New York, Kings, Bronx, and Queens, where the term is fourteen years. New York County has two surrogates.

**Jurisdiction:** Tries will and inheritance cases; conducts probate proceedings, with or without a jury; appoints guardians and public administrators; issues letters of administration; and grants adoptions. Appeals from actions of the surrogate court are taken to the appellate division of the appropriate department.

*Note:* The distinctive office of surrogate does not exist in many of the counties outside of the City of New York. In counties where there is no separate office of surrogate, the county judge acts in that capacity.

## THE SUPREME COURT—ALL COUNTIES

**Organization:** The State of New York is divided into eleven judicial districts and four judicial departments. A number of Supreme Court Justices are elected by the voters of each judicial district. Each department includes one or more districts. In the New York metropolitan area, the First District includes the counties of New York and the Bronx. The Second District takes in Kings and Richmond (Brooklyn and Staten Island) and seven nearby counties. The Tenth District includes Nassau and Suffolk. Queens is the Eleventh District. The appellate division of each department, in the fall of each year, assigns the various Supreme Court Justices within the department to hold the different special and trial terms of the Supreme Court. If the criminal calendar within a county warrants it, a Justice of the Supreme Court is assigned to sit in the criminal branch when felony cases are tried.

**Jurisdiction:** The court has unlimited civil jurisdiction in both civil and criminal cases, even where the death penalty is involved. In criminal cases, the Justice passes upon questions of law, and a petit jury of 12 determines the facts. However, in civil cases, the justice may try the case with or without a jury. Appeals from this court are taken to the appellate division within the same department, except that in cases where the penalty is death the appeal goes directly to the court of appeals.

## APPELLATE TERM OF THE SUPREME COURT

**Organization:** This branch of the court exists only in the First and Second Departments. It consists of not fewer than three and not more than five Supreme Court Justices designated from among the Supreme Court Justices by the appellate division of the department for a month at a time. Three sit to hear an appeal; two must concur for a decision.

**Jurisdiction:** Reviews cases on appeal from the civil court and criminal court.

## APPELLATE DIVISION OF THE SUPREME COURT

**Organization:** This is the second-highest state court, ranking just below the court of appeals. Justices are appointed by the governor to five-year terms from among the Supreme Court Justices. In the larger districts, there are seven justices, in other districts there are five.

**Jurisdiction:** Normally, all cases on appeal must be heard by the appellate division, except where the judgment has been the death penalty, before going to the court of appeals. This division hears appeals from the appellate term and trial and special terms of the Supreme Court, surrogate's courts, and the family court. This court admits attorneys to practice and may, after a hearing, disbar them. It may also, after a hearing, remove from office magistrates, civil court justices, and justices of the criminal court. It has the power to issue writs of habeas corpus and judgments pursuant to the Civil Practice Law and Rules in the nature of mandamus, prohibition, and certiorari.

## JUSTICE OF THE PEACE COURTS

**Organization:** In a number of counties outside of New York City, elected justices of the peace serve in civil capacity and hear cases involving lesser claims.

**Jurisdiction:** Roughly equivalent to that of small claims courts. Cases are tried either with or without a jury.

## GRAND JURY—ANY COUNTY

**Organization:** The grand jury is an essential part of the judiciary system of the county. It consists of 23 citizens, usually selected for a term of one month by the clerk of the Division of

Jurors. One member is designated by the court as foreman, another as assistant foreman. A secretary is selected by the body itself. Sixteen jurors constitute a quorum. In order to secure an indictment, also known as a "true bill," 12 must vote for it.

**Jurisdiction:** To inquire into the crimes of the grade of felony, criminal libel, or other misdemeanors as are presented by the district attorney. The jury may also inquire into the condition and arrangement of public prisons and into willful and corrupt conduct of public officers in the county. The proceedings of the grand jury are called ex parte as the only witnesses heard are those for the state although occasionally, upon request, the defendant is heard.

## CIVIL COURT

**Organization:** The judges of the New York City civil court have citywide jurisdiction and are elected for ten-year terms.

**Jurisdiction:** Civil court has jurisdiction over civil cases up to $25,000. The civil part of the Supreme Court sits in judgment over cases involving more than that sum. Appeals from this court are directed to the appellate term of the Supreme Court.

## CRIMINAL COURT OF NEW YORK CITY

**Organization:** The judges who preside over this court are appointed by the mayor for a ten-year term.

**Jurisdiction:** The criminal court of New York City tries violations, misdemeanors, and, in general, lesser crimes. The criminal part of the Supreme Court is empowered to try felonies in New York City as it previously had been empowered to handle crimes of this nature in other parts of the state. This court has jurisdiction over

1. arraignment of persons arrested for all crimes.

2. narcotics proceedings.

3. trials of persons charged with an offense or misdemeanor.

4. arraignments, pleadings, examinations, trials, and sentences of persons at least 16 years of age but who have not yet reached their 19th birthday.

5. weekend and holiday arraignments and pleadings of persons arrested and charged with certain misdemeanors and offenses.

6. arraignments, pleadings, examinations, trials, and sentences of persons charged with violations of the

    a. administrative code of the City of New York.
    b. local laws of the City of New York.
    c. rules and regulations of a department of the City of New York.
    d. statutes of the State of New York.

7. issuing warrants of arrest and court summonses.

8. arraignments, pleadings, examinations, trials, and sentences of persons charged with a violation of the gambling laws.

9. arraignments, pleadings, trials, and sentences of persons charged with prostitution.

10. arraignments, pleadings, trials, and sentences of persons charged with being drunk and disorderly.

11. arraignments and pleadings of persons who are arrested after the day's courts are closed. They may try and sentence people who are charged with offenses and misdemeanors.

Appeals from this court are directed to the appellate term of the Supreme Court.

## THE FAMILY COURT

**Organization:** "The Family Court of the State of New York" is followed by the name of the county in which it is located. The court is presided over by judges who are appointed by the mayor for a ten-year term.

**Jurisdiction:** This court has jurisdiction over

1. neglect of children proceedings.

2. support of children proceedings.

3. paternity proceedings.

4. custody proceedings of children by reason of neglect.

5. adoption proceedings.

6. proceedings concerning juvenile delinquency and the determination of whether or not delinquents are in need of supervision.

7. proceedings involving acts which would constitute disorderly conduct or an assault between spouses or between parent and child or between members of the same family or household.

Appeals from this court are directed to the appellate division of the Supreme Court.

## A NEW YORK CITY CIVIL COURT IN OPERATION

The purpose of this section is to present the forms and procedures employed in prosecuting a case in the civil court of the City of New York. This is a court of civil jurisdiction handling actions to $25,000.

### VENUE

In order to bring suit against a person in the civil court, the plaintiff may first determine the appropriate county in which to institute the action. A suit may be started in any county where either of the parties resides or has a place of business or where cause of action arose. In accordance with this rule, attorneys usually bring their actions in the county most convenient to them. "Venue" is the term applied to the county in which an action is brought.

### THE SUMMONS AND COMPLAINT

Any number of plaintiffs may sue any number of defendants in the same action, but all the names must appear on the summons. The caption of the summons includes the name of the court and the parties to the action. The same caption must be used on all papers subsequently used in court in the same action. Captions are extremely important since they specify by whom and against whom a case is brought.

One side of a summons orders the defendant to appear before the clerk of the court 10 or 30 days after the service of the summons in order to answer the complaint. In civil actions, every attorney is an officer of the court and possesses the power to issue a summons asking the defendant to appear in court and answer the complaint. The party summoned does not have to appear to defend himself or herself, but, by not appearing, truth of the complaint is thereby admitted and judgment is obtained by default.

### THE COMPLAINT

On the reverse side of the summons, usually in the lower part, are the words "the nature and substance of the plaintiff's cause of action is as follows." Under this, the attorney for the plaintiff writes the complaint, which might take the following form: "Action to replevy personal property rightfully belonging to the plaintiff." Though written, this is called an oral complaint because it is not sworn to.

---

**Form: Affidavit of Service:**

STATE OF NEW YORK ) 
COUNTY OF KINGS ) ss:

<u>John Doe</u> being duly sworn, deposes and says: that on the <u>10th</u> day of <u>May, 20xx</u>, at No. <u>480 Marcy Avenue</u>, in the Borough of <u>Brooklyn</u>, City of New York, he served the within summons and complaint on <u>Richard Roe</u>, the defendant therein named, by delivering to and leaving a true copy thereof with said defendant personally; deponent knew the said person so served as aforesaid to be the same person mentioned and described in said summons and complaint as the defendant therein. Deponent is over the age of 18 years and is not a party to the action.

JOHN DOE

Sworn to before me this <u>11th</u> day of <u>May, 20xx</u>

ALTON BING

Notary Public, Kings County

---

## SERVICE OF THE SUMMONS

Any person over 18 who is not a party to the action may serve the summons at any time, except on Sunday. The defendant must be found and the summons personally handed to him or her. It may be left on a table, or anywhere in the person's presence, should he or she refuse to accept it. However, the defendant must first be informed by the person leaving it that he or she is being served with a summons. The server should never take a summons back. After a copy of the summons has been served to the defendant, the server must make an affidavit of service, which must be in writing and sworn to. The printed form of summons usually has a form of affidavit on the outside with blank space to be filled in.

## SUBSTITUTED SERVICE

When there is good reason to believe that the defendant is expecting to be served and is deliberately evading service by any number of ruses, the process server may make an affidavit in which he or she details the attempts to serve the summons or subpoena and the attempts at evasion on the part of the defendant. If the facts are in good form, and it appears that diligent efforts have been made to serve the evading defendant, then an order is issued in which the judge permits the summons to be mailed to the defendant's last known address and a copy of the summons to be affixed to the door of that address. Proof of such service shall be filed with the clerk of the court within 20 days. Service is complete 10 days after such filing.

## SERVICE BY PUBLICATION

When a defendant leaves the state in order to evade service, and under certain other conditions, service may be consummated by publication after a diligent effort to locate the defendant has been made and it appears certain that the defendant has left. An affidavit must be submitted before the judge issues an order permitting service by publication. Usually the judge specifies the newspapers in which the service is to be publicized and the number of times the statement must appear. This procedure does not apply in the civil court except where a warrant of attachment has been granted.

## TRAVERSE

When a defendant has not been properly served, the defendant's attorney may claim that a traverse has occurred and may make a motion to vacate the service of the summons and dismiss the complaint on those grounds. Although cases are not usually closed on the grounds of traverse, the process server should avoid falling into such an error because it may be costly in that the defendant can utilize it to delay the trial.

## FILING THE SUMMONS

Seven days after the copy of the summons is served, the original with the affidavit of service must be filed with the clerk of the court named in the summons. At this time, the case receives an index number that must be used on all subsequent papers filed in the case.

## THE ANSWER

The answer to the summons and complaint must be given within 10 or 30 days. The answer may be made orally to the clerk or on a regular printed form of answer. It usually contains a general denial, to which defenses may be added and even "counterclaims."

## COUNTERCLAIMS

Counterclaims are included in the answer when the defendant, instead of admitting that he or she has done any wrong, claims that he or she has been wronged and recites the details in very much the same manner as the complaint.

## BILL OF PARTICULARS

The plaintiff and the defendant have the right to ask for a "bill of particulars," and in such a case a detailed statement of charges must be furnished by the party making the charges.

## NOTICE OF TRIAL

After receiving an answer, any party, or that party's attorney, may serve a notice of trial on the other party. The notice, of course, indicates when and where the trial is to be held.

## THE TRIAL CALENDAR

Except in a court of arraignment, a calendar of cases to be tried during the day is posted by the clerk of every court. This calendar is called at the opening of court to determine which cases are to be adjourned and which are to be tried. Both sides must be represented at the calendar call, and when their case is reached, both must indicate what disposition of the case they desire for the day. If both sides are ready, the case will be called for the day. If there is a request for adjournment, it must be accompanied by an affidavit giving the reasons for such a request.

## INQUESTS

Should the plaintiff be ready and the defendant fail to answer, an inquest may be held before the judge or clerk depending upon the nature of the case. A judgment may be rendered in an inquest with only the plaintiff reciting the details, but judgments by inquest are subject to rehearing on motion by the defendant.

## STIPULATIONS AND ADJOURNMENTS

If one side is not ready for trial on a certain date, the attorneys may arrange, with court approval, to postpone the trial to a more convenient time. When such an arrangement is made a few days before the date set, then both attorneys sign a "stipulation" or agreement. A copy of this agreement is mailed to the clerk of the court who takes note of the postponement, altering the court calendar in accordance.

## SUBPOENAS

If there is doubt that a witness will appear in court, he or she must be served with a subpoena, which is a command to come to court and testify. The courts have given all attorneys the power to issue subpoenas. Like a summons, a subpoena must be served personally upon the witness. In fact, exactly the same procedure applies in the service of subpoenas with this addition: the person serving a subpoena must pay the witness a fee for appearance in the civil court and a mileage allowance if his or her home is outside the confines of the court. An affidavit of service must be obtained because if the witness does not appear, the affidavit is essential to the institution of proceedings for contempt of court. A subpoena *duces tecum* is a special form of subpoena that not only orders the witness to appear but also commands the witness to produce books, papers, or other evidence in court.

## MOTIONS

Motions are formal requests made by an attorney to a judge asking that the judge order an adversary to do something he or she is required to do so as to facilitate justice. Sometimes a motion requests a favor or even to be relieved of the consequence of one's own mistake. There is an almost unlimited number of different motions that may be made. Thus, a defendant to whose store a marshal comes to collect a judgment may make a motion to "vacate" the judgment that was entered by "default" on the grounds that through an error he was not notified that he had to appear to defend himself on the preceding day.

On the proper day, the attorneys for both sides appear before the judge who listens to the arguments and decides whether or not to grant the motion.

## ORDER TO SHOW CAUSE

This is practically the same as notice of motion except that it must be signed by the judge and may prevent the other party from taking any action until the motion is decided. Thus with an "Order to Show Cause," the marshal may be restrained from levying until the motion to reopen the case has been heard.

## MOTION FOR SUMMARY JUDGMENT

This type of motion is made frequently and is consequently worthy of note. The plaintiff has the right to make a motion for a summary judgment in any action. In this motion it is claimed that there is no merit in the defense, and a request is made that the answer be stricken out.

The effect of a motion for a summary judgment is to force the defendant to submit an affidavit in which the grounds for his or her answer must be specified. The judge then examines the affidavits of both parties and from this decides whether or not there is a real issue involved in the case. If the judge concludes that the arguments of the defense are not pertinent to the case, then that judge may hand down judgment without a regular trial—in other words, a summary judgment.

## JUDGMENT BY DEFAULT

If no answer to the summons has been made in 10 or 30 days after its receipt, the plaintiff makes out a "deposition of judgment" in which he or she attests to exactly what the damages and claims are. This affidavit enables the clerk to enter the judgment.

## COSTS

After a trial has been held, the defeated shall bear the court costs. These costs are determined from a schedule based on the amount of money being sued for. In the event the defendant is successful and the case is dismissed, the plaintiff must not only assume the court costs but also the cost of the disbursements, which include the fees paid for filing and service of process.

If a defendant is neither in business nor working but is suspected of having property of some kind that he or she is concealing, then supplementary proceedings are started following execution. At these proceedings the plaintiff or some other person who is familiar with the facts swears that an execution after judgment has been returned unsatisfied by the marshal and that the judgment debtor must be examined under oath to discover whether or not he or she has property from which the judgment can be collected. If the judge desires to grant the request, he or she signs an order requiring the defendant to appear for examination. The judgment debtor is examined under oath by the attorney for the plaintiff. No judge is present in the room, but if the debtor refuses to answer a question he or she may be brought before a judge, who, if the question is reasonable, will order the debtor to answer or be held in contempt of court.

# INTRODUCTION TO THE QUIZZERS

The following sections include five brief quizzers.

1. Narcotics and Drugs Quizzer

2. Reading Comprehension Quizzer One

3. Reading Comprehension Quizzer Two

4. Reading Comprehension Quizzer Three

5. Courts Quizzer

Although these exact questions may not appear on any of the examinations you may take, they will help you with understanding some of the material you may encounter, as well as practicing your reading comprehension, a most valuable skill for any written examination.

# NARCOTICS AND DRUGS QUIZZER

> **Directions:** Read each question and circle the letter of the answer you select.

1. Most narcotic drugs are derived from which of the following drugs?

   (A) Morphine
   (B) Codeine
   (C) Heroin
   (D) Opium

2. Drug addicts, when under the influence of a drug, are a menace to the community because they

   (A) are flagrantly immoral.
   (B) become violently insane.
   (C) ruin their health.
   (D) feel no restraint in committing crimes.

3. Which narcotic is used by a majority of addicts?

   (A) Phenobarbital
   (B) Opium
   (C) Cocaine
   (D) Morphine

4. A suspect was arrested for possession of narcotics. He agrees to help the authorities as an operator for the purpose of getting evidence against other violators. The best procedure is to

   (A) cross-examine him to learn the names of other violators.
   (B) promise him that he will not be prosecuted for his illegal possession of narcotics because he is aiding the authorities.
   (C) release him but keep him shadowed in the hope that he will lead authorities to other violators.
   (D) give him marked money with which to make a specified purchase of narcotics.
   (E) send him to frequent his habitual places in the company of a plain-clothes officer.

*Questions 5 – 8 are based on the following situation.*

Information received from a reliable informant reveals that a "tea" party is taking place almost every night at a private residence in the suburbs. From this information there is an indication that the "tea" parties are directly tied in with what is believed to be a new source of supply of narcotics.

5. From this information, the best procedure is to

   (A) assemble the best available narcotics officers and raid the house immediately.

   (B) arrange to have two men just out of the academy stake out the residence for a few days to obtain additional information.

   (C) have two well-known, experienced officers stake out the residence to obtain the identity of all the visitors.

   (D) have two officers force an entry to the building and hide out until a party is in progress, then make the arrests.

   (E) send a reliable "stool" or "user" in to participate in a party to obtain additional information before raiding.

6. A visitor arrives. The "hostess" admits him and he turns out to be a dealer making a delivery of heroin. You, the officer, apprehend him in the act of handing the narcotics to the "hostess." He admits the narcotics belong to him and that he is a heavy user himself but will not reveal his source of supply. Which of the following is the best procedure to use under these circumstances to obtain additional information?

   (A) Make a deal to let him go if he'll provide you with the desired information.

   (B) Take the narcotics but release the dealer and put a tail on him to determine where he makes his contacts and who they are.

   (C) Arrest him and wait to see who posts bail for him.

   (D) Put him in jail for a while and talk to him when his fix wears off.

7. Authorities can confiscate certain property directly connected with a narcotics violation. Of the following combinations, which is most nearly correct in this particular situation?

   (A) All apparatus used in connection with narcotics addiction, the furnishings of the house, and all narcotics

   (B) All apparatus used in connection with narcotic addiction, the dealer's automobile, and all narcotics

   (C) All apparatus used in connection with narcotic addiction, the cars of all suspects booked as a result of the raid, and all narcotics

   (D) All apparatus used in connection with narcotic addiction, the cars of all suspects booked as a result of the raid, the furnishings of the house, and all narcotics

   (E) All apparatus used in connection with narcotic addiction and all narcotics

8. From information obtained from one of the suspects picked up in the raid, you are able to locate several small-time dealers. One of these dealers is a newspaper boy who sells occasionally. In order to get to his source of supply, the best procedure is to

   (A) make several small buys, and then ask for a large party supply hoping he will take you to his source to make a buy.

   (B) check all of his newspaper customers.

   (C) put a tail on the boy to see where he contacts his source.

   (D) make a general sweep of the area for known dealers.

9. Police operators are most likely to be successful in undercover narcotic investigations aimed at revealing major sources of supply if they pose as

(A) users.
(B) pushers.
(C) runners.
(D) jobbers.
(E) importers.

10. One of the most frightening aspects of narcotics addiction is the tendency to increase the dose. This is due to the development of body tolerance, which proceeds most rapidly in the use of

(A) cocaine.
(B) heroin.
(C) marijuana.
(D) morphine.
(E) opium.

11. From the standpoint of physiological effect, narcotic drugs are commonly and roughly classed as

(A) spinals and cerebrals.
(B) cumulative and noncumulative.
(C) depressants and stimulants.
(D) ingestants and injectants.
(E) intoxicants and soporifics.

12. The physiological effect of marijuana is in general most comparable to that of

(A) barbiturates.
(B) benzedrine.
(C) morphine.
(D) antihistamine.

13. In a person fully addicted to morphine or heroin, the first withdrawal symptoms (runny nose, watering eyes, perspiration, etc.) ordinarily appear within what period after the last dose is taken?

(A) 1 to 4 hours
(B) 4 to 24 hours
(C) 24 to 48 hours
(D) 48 to 60 hours
(E) 72 to 96 hours

14. While there is considerable controversy about the direct effects of marijuana on the user's behavior, the main argument for suppressing the use of marijuana is that

(A) its use frequently leads to more serious types of addiction.
(B) failure to suppress would encourage violation and disrespect of other laws.
(C) the public expects vigorous enforcement regardless of the threat to public welfare.
(D) users have come to expect certain effects and react accordingly even in the absence of physiological stimulation.

15. A confirmed marijuana user, when not under the direct influence of the drug, is generally characterized by

(A) a waxy, florid complexion.
(B) a persistently runny nose.
(C) a somewhat jerky and discoordinated gait.
(D) general lassitude and torpor.
(E) none of the above; there is no characteristic symptomology.

16. Considering the current high rate of addiction to drugs among youths throughout the country, which of the following statements is the least correct?

    (A) A relatively large number of children and youths who experiment with drugs become addicts.
    (B) Youths who use narcotics do so because of some emotional and personality disturbance.
    (C) Youthful addicts are found largely among those who suffer deprivations in their personal development and growth to an abnormal extent.
    (D) The great majority of youthful addicts have had unfortunate home experiences and practically no contact with established community agencies.

17. The biggest roadblock to the effective enforcement of narcotics laws is the

    (A) availability of the drugs and the ease with which they can be transported and sold.
    (B) lack of effective cooperation between local and federal police to suppress drug traffic.
    (C) lack of effective laws to regulate the distribution of newer drugs.
    (D) phenomenally high rate of addiction among teenagers.
    (E) unfortunately high degree of recidivism among drug addicts.

18. Barbiturates, as a class of drugs, are of concern to police officers. Which of the following statements is true of barbiturates as a class?

    (A) Postmortem appearances of barbiturate poisoning have pronounced characteristics.
    (B) There are approximately three related drugs that are classified as the only barbiturates.
    (C) They are essentially a variety of stimulant much favored by persons under age 21.
    (D) They are incapable of being synthesized in any appreciable commercial amount.
    (E) They are much favored by attempters of suicide and less commonly by murderers.

19. "Snow" in criminal parlance is

    (A) opium.
    (B) morphine.
    (C) cocaine.
    (D) heroin.

20. To the narcotic addict, "yellow jacket" commonly means

    (A) Nembutal.
    (B) heroin that has been cut for the ultimate consumer.
    (C) bromides, caffeine compounds, and other nonprescription pharmaceuticals.
    (D) narcotic capsules that can be swallowed and recovered intact.
    (E) a plainclothes officer.

21. One of the more common methods by which attempts are made to supply prisoners with narcotics is

    (A) stamps with narcotic-impregnated glue.
    (B) visitors blowing smoke in the face of the prisoner.
    (C) letters written with a narcotic base ink that can be scraped off and consumed.
    (D) importation with food supplies.

22. From a criminological standpoint, the relationship between marijuana and crime is most commonly thought to spring essentially from

(A) the efforts of addicts to obtain adequate supplies.

(B) physiological deterioration and organic brain damage resulting from continued use.

(C) intense but short-lived aphrodisiac effects.

(D) personality disintegration and unwholesome escape from reality.

23. Drugs that cause the pupils of the user's eyes to become dilated include

(A) cocaine, codeine, and morphine.

(B) heroin, cocaine, and marijuana.

(C) morphine and codeine.

(D) cocaine and marijuana.

(E) codeine and marijuana.

24. Conflicting statements have been published regarding the British system of narcotics control, both regarding the nature of the methods used by the British and the success of their methods as compared with those used in the United States. Most of those who advocate adoption of the British system believe that it is characterized mainly by

(A) making narcotics available to addicts at a low cost through any doctor, removing the opportunity for large profits in illicit narcotics traffic.

(B) extreme emphasis on control of imports.

(C) heavy penalties for anyone selling or transferring any narcotic to another.

(D) special laws governing narcotics arrests and evidence, thus simplifying enforcement.

(E) a government monopoly on the possession and prescription of narcotics.

25. In attempting to classify the various narcotics on the basis of their effect on the user, considerable confusion can be avoided by carefully distinguishing between

(A) occasional and continuous use.

(B) users in the early stages of addiction and those in later stages.

(C) use by ingestion and use by injection.

(D) physiological effects and behavioral effects.

(E) age of first use and age upon arrest.

26. As commonly adulterated for use by addicts, heroin is taken in doses of most nearly

(A) .1 to .2 grain.

(B) 1 to 2 grains.

(C) 10 to 20 grains.

(D) 50 to 90 grains.

(E) 100 to 200 grains.

27. "Marijuana smoking creates homicidal tendencies." This statement is best described as

(A) valid, in the light of generally accepted evidence.

(B) controversial; there is evidence both pro and con.

(C) invalid, in the light of generally accepted evidence.

28. It has been frequently suggested that the sale of narcotics to addicts be made legal under strict governmental control. In this way, the narcotics black market and attendant crimes will end. The major objection to this suggestion is that

(A) the evils that are involved in licensing users and controlling selling places will defeat the purpose of the plan.

(B) crime resulting from addiction will not be reduced since the cause is not eliminated.

(C) legalized sale will increase rather than decrease control costs.

(D) the problems of addiction are not ended, but are merely legalized.

(E) there is no evidence to indicate that such control will affect bootlegging and associated crime.

## ANSWERS

| | | | |
|---|---|---|---|
| 1. B | 8. A | 15. E | 22. D |
| 2. D | 9. B | 16. B | 23. E |
| 3. C | 10. B | 17. A | 24. A |
| 4. D | 11. C | 18. E | 25. D |
| 5. E | 12. A | 19. C | 26. B |
| 6. D | 13. B | 20. A | 27. B |
| 7. E | 14. A | 21. A | 28. D |

## EXPLANATIONS

1. **The correct answer is (B).** Codeine is a major part of all drugs.
2. **The correct answer is (D).** When high, individuals have fewer inhibitions.
3. **The correct answer is (C).** Cocaine is the drug of choice for most addicts. Also, heroin has seen resurgence in use lately.
4. **The correct answer is (D).** The marked money would provide independent corroboration of the narcotics dealing.
5. **The correct answer is (E).** Use of undercover operatives is a staple in narcotics investigations. They, too, provide independent corroboration of the activity under investigation.
6. **The correct answer is (D).** Jail often softens up the offender and makes him more amenable to talking.
7. **The correct answer is (E).** This is known as asset forfeiture; however, it has come under fire recently.
8. **The correct answer is (A).** This would be the most effective way to get to his source. Your knowledge of the offender and the circumstances will help you make the best choice.
9. **The correct answer is (B).** People who deal need a constant supply source.
10. **The correct answer is (B).** More heroin is needed to achieve the same kind of high a user had during his or her initial use.
11. **The correct answer is (C).** Narcotics either slow down the body or speed it up.
12. **The correct answer is (A).** Barbiturates can give one a "high" similar to marijuana.
13. **The correct answer is (B).** It may take as few as 4 or as many as 24 hours.
14. **The correct answer is (A).** Marijuana has been referred to as a gateway drug, i.e., its use leads people to try other drugs. Whether true or not, marijuana use puts the individual in contact with other drugs and the people who use them.
15. **The correct answer is (E).** This is one reason that many advocate the legalization of marijuana.
16. **The correct answer is (B).** It is extremely likely that most youths who use narcotics probably do so out of peer pressure, not necessarily emotional or personality disturbances.
17. **The correct answer is (A).** These factors increase the number of consumers, making drug enforcement difficult.
18. **The correct answer is (E).** Suicide by overdose is most often accomplished through the use of this class of drugs. Murders are almost never committed with barbiturates.
19. **The correct answer is (C).** "Snow" is a street term for cocaine.
20. **The correct answer is (A).** "Yellow jacket" is a street term for Nembutal.
21. **The correct answer is (A).** There is no end to the attempts to smuggle narcotics into prisons (many of which work well).

22. **The correct answer is (D).** People who are not in touch with reality are more likely to involve themselves in criminality.
23. **The correct answer is (E).** Codeine and marijuana use causes a person's pupils to dilate.
24. **The correct answer is (A).** Many European countries have used this method relatively successfully.
25. **The correct answer is (D).** Each narcotic has physiological and/or behavioral effects.
26. **The correct answer is (B).** Heroin is usually administered in this amount to avoid overdosing.
27. **The correct answer is (B).** This statement is more emotion driven than scientifically derived.
28. **The correct answer is (D).** The root causes of addiction and the cost to society are not addressed.

# READING COMPREHENSION QUIZZER ONE

**Directions:** This test consists of several reading passages, each followed by a number of statements. Analyze each statement solely on the basis of the material given. Then circle the letter

(A) if the statement is entirely true.

(B) if the statement is entirely false.

(C) if the statement is partially false and partially true.

(D) if the statement cannot be judged on the basis of the facts given in the excerpt.

## Reading Passage A

The objective of prison education, in its broadest sense, should be the socialization of inmates through varied impressionistic and expressional activities, with emphasis on individual inmate needs. The objective of this program shall be the return of these inmates to society with a more wholesome attitude toward living, a desire to conduct themselves as good citizens, and the skill and knowledge that will give them a reasonable chance to maintain themselves and their dependents through honest labor. To this end, each prisoner shall be given a program of education, which, on the basis of available data, seems most likely to further the process of socialization and rehabilitation.

1.  Machine shop work is a good example of an expressional activity.

2.  The educational program advocated for prisoners is designed for their rehabilitation, but not their socialization.

3.  Group needs, as distinguished from individual needs, should be given the greater consideration in the socialization of prison inmates.

4.  A confirmed criminal can rarely be induced to become a good citizen.

5.  The socialization process includes the acquisition of skills and knowledge on the part of prison inmates.

## Reading Passage B

No officer or employee in any prison shall inflict any blows whatsoever upon any prisoner, except in self-defense or to suppress a revolt or insurrection. When several prisoners or any single prisoner offers violence to any officer of a state prison or to any other prisoner, attempts to harm or vandalize the building or any workshop or any property therein, attempts to escape, or resists or disobeys any lawful command, the officers of the prison shall use all suitable means to defend themselves, enforce observation of discipline, secure the offenders, and prevent any such attempt or escape.

6. A prison officer may go to any suitable extreme in preventing prison breaks.

7. If a prisoner is escaping, the prisoner should be ordered to a halt before being fired upon.

8. A prison guard may strike a prisoner only if the latter provokes him or her verbally.

9. The duties of prison officers include the enforcement of discipline on the part of inmates, but under no circumstances may a prison officer strike a prisoner in the enforcement of such discipline.

10. Self-defense is the only legitimate excuse for physically inflicting injury upon a prison inmate.

## Reading Passage C

Whenever any prisoner confined in a state prison, and not released on parole, shall escape therefrom, it shall be the duty of the warden to take all proper measures for the apprehension of the escaped prisoner; and in his or her discretion he or she may offer a reward not to exceed $50 for the apprehension and delivery of every such escaped prisoner. Any such prisoner escaped from any state prison in this state and afterwards arrested shall serve out the full balance of the sentence remaining unexpired at the time of such escape. All rewards and other sums of money paid for advertising and apprehending any such escaped prisoner shall be paid by the warden out of the funds of the prison.

11. An escaped prisoner, upon being apprehended, must serve a year in prison if this is the amount of the full balance of the sentence remaining unexpired at the time of the escape.

12. An apprehended prisoner, returned to a state prison after having escaped, must serve the entire sentence again.

13. State prisoners are generally released on parole.

14. Reward money for an escaped prisoner's apprehension is generally paid out of the warden's funds.

15. The warden is most concerned with the apprehension of an escaped prisoner and may offer an unlimited reward for delivery.

## Reading Passage D

The Commissioner of Corrections may make rules and regulations for the promotion or reduction of the prisoners from one classification to another and shall transfer from time to time the prisoners in the state prisons from one prison to another with reference to the respective capacities of the several state prisons, with reference to the health or reformation of the prisoners, or with reference to including all prisoners of one classification as nearly as may be practical in one prison, or may direct the separation from each other of the prisoners of different classifications so far as practicable within each state prison.

16. Health conditions sometimes necessitate the transfer of prisoners from one state prison to another.

17. Prisoners are classified regarding the nature of their crime and are kept in those prisons that correspond exactly to their particular classification.

18. A state prisoner may be promoted or demoted from one classification to another in accordance with the rules and regulations set forth by the Commissioner of Corrections.

19. Prisoners are sometimes transferred from one prison to another by the Commissioner of Corrections, the chief purpose of the transfer being the bringing together of prisoners of dissimilar classification.

20. It is the duty of the prison guard to effect the transfer of prisoners from one prison to another.

## Reading Passage E

Whenever there shall be a sufficient number of cells in the prison, it shall be the duty of the warden to keep each prisoner single in a cell during both day and night when the prisoner is not employed, in a hospital, or engaged in other duties or recreation in accordance with the rules of the Department of Correction. The clothing and bedding of the prisoners shall be manufactured as far as practicable in the prison. The prisoners shall be supplied with a sufficient quantity of wholesome food.

21. Prison rules require that prisoners' food be adequate as well as healthful.

22. All prisoner clothing is manufactured by the prisoners themselves.

23. Under no circumstances are more than two prisoners kept in a prison cell.

24. No prison bedding is ever manufactured outside of the prison.

25. No more than one unemployed prisoner is generally kept in a cell during the daytime.

## Reading Passage F

If, in the opinion of the warden of a state prison, it shall be deemed necessary to inflict unusual punishment in order to produce the entire submission or obedience of any prisoner, it shall be the duty of such warden to confine such prisoner immediately in a cell, upon a short allowance, and retain the prisoner therein until reduced to submission and obedience. The short allowance of each prisoner shall be prescribed by the physician, whose duty it shall be to visit such prisoner and examine daily into the state of his or her health until the prisoner is released from solitary confinement and returned to labor.

26. Solitary confinement is prescribed only when a prisoner is disobedient or will not submit to orders.

27. A prisoner ordered to solitary confinement may not be released until reduced to submission and obedience.

28. It falls within the duties of the warden to put a prisoner upon a short allowance and it is the warden who prescribes its nature.

29. A prisoner on short allowance does not necessarily need a physician's attention.

30. Solitary confinement and a short allowance is not considered an unusual punishment.

## ANSWERS

| | | | | | | | | | |
|---|---|---|---|---|---|---|---|---|---|
| 1. D | | 7. D | | 13. D | | 19. C | | 25. A |
| 2. C | | 8. B | | 14. B | | 20. B | | 26. D |
| 3. B | | 9. C | | 15. C | | 21. A | | 27. A |
| 4. D | | 10. B | | 16. A | | 22. D | | 28. C |
| 5. A | | 11. A | | 17. D | | 23. D | | 29. B |
| 6. A | | 12. B | | 18. A | | 24. B | | 30. B |

## EXPLANATIONS

1. **The correct answer is (D).** There is nothing in the passage to support this statement.
2. **The correct answer is (C).** The objective of the program is to achieve both rehabilitation and socialization.
3. **The correct answer is (B).** The first sentence states "… with emphasis on individual inmate needs."
4. **The correct answer is (D).** There is nothing in the passage to support this statement.
5. **The correct answer is (A).** This is the essence of the passage.
6. **The correct answer is (A).** "The officers … shall use all suitable means …."
7. **The correct answer is (D).** There is nothing in the passage to support this statement.
8. **The correct answer is (B).** Refer to the first sentence.
9. **The correct answer is (C).** Refer to the first sentence.
10. **The correct answer is (B).** The passage talks about defending one's self, not inflicting injury.
11. **The correct answer is (A).** This is stated in the second sentence.
12. **The correct answer is (B).** They serve the remaining unexpired time at the time of escape.
13. **The correct answer is (D).** There is nothing in the passage to support this statement.
14. **The correct answer is (B).** Reward is paid *by* the warden but out of *prison* funds.
15. **The correct answer is (C).** The reward cannot exceed $50.
16. **The correct answer is (A).** This is stated clearly in the passage.
17. **The correct answer is (D).** There is nothing in the passage to support this statement.
18. **The correct answer is (A).** This is stated at the beginning of the passage.
19. **The correct answer is (C).** The purpose is to include prisoners of the same classification.
20. **The correct answer is (B).** The Commissioner of Corrections "shall transfer … the prisoner …."
21. **The correct answer is (A).** This is stated in the last sentence.
22. **The correct answer is (D).** There is nothing in the passage to support this statement.
23. **The correct answer is (D).** There is nothing in the passage to support this statement.
24. **The correct answer is (B).** The passage states that the bedding must be "manufactured as far as practicable in the prison."
25. **The correct answer is (A).** This is stated in the first sentence.
26. **The correct answer is (D).** There is nothing in the passage to support this statement.
27. **The correct answer is (A).** This is stated in the first sentence.
28. **The correct answer is (C).** The short allowance is prescribed by a physician.
29. **The correct answer is (B).** The last sentence says that each prisoner will be examined daily.
30. **The correct answer is (B).** The first sentence refers to "unusual punishment."

# READING COMPREHENSION QUIZZER TWO

**Directions:** This test consists of several reading passages, each followed by a number of statements. Analyze each statement solely on the basis of the material given. Then circle the letter

(A) if the statement is entirely true.

(B) if the statement is entirely false.

(C) if the statement is partially false and partially true.

(D) if the statement cannot be judged on the basis of the facts given in the excerpt.

## Reading Passage A

In case any pestilence or contagious disease shall break out among the prisoners of any of the state prisons or in the vicinity of such prisons, the Commissioner of Corrections may cause the prisoners confined to such prison, or any of them to be removed to some suitable place of security where they shall receive all necessary care and medical assistance. Such prisoners shall be returned as soon as possible to the state prison from which they were taken and will be confined therein according to their respective sentences.

1. Medical assistance must be provided to a sick patient removed from a prison to a place of security.

2. An epidemic raging in a nearby town may necessitate the removal of all inmates of a state prison to a place of security, but their return is imperative upon the cessation of the epidemic.

3. When a contagious disease breaks out among the prisoners of a state prison, only the sick may be ordered removed.

4. If the illness of a patient necessitates removal to a hospital for a period of six months, this period constitutes part of the sentence served and need not be served again.

5. A prisoner recovered from a contagious disease, having been removed to a hospital during the course of illness, has the option of remaining there to complete the sentence.

## Reading Passage B

The Commissioner of Corrections and the superintendents of all penitentiaries in the state shall, so far as practicable, cause all the prisoners in the state correctional institutions and such penitentiaries who are physically capable thereof to be employed at hard labor for no longer than eight hours of each day other than Sundays and public holidays. Such hard labor shall be either for the purpose of production of supplies for said institutions or for the state or any political division thereof, or for any public institution owned or managed and controlled by the state; or for the purpose of industrial training; or partly for one and partly for the other of such purposes.

6. State convict labor may be used to supply products for any institution controlled by the state.

7. Supplies manufactured by prisoners in a state prison must be utilized within the said institution.

8. A prisoner in good physical condition may generally be employed beyond eight hours at hard labor in a state prison.

9. The chief aim in forcing prison inmates to work is to provide them with industrial training.

10. Although state prisoners do not work on Sundays, they generally must put in a half day on public holidays.

## Reading Passage C

The Commissioner of Corrections may employ or cause to be employed the prisoners confined in the state prisons in the repair, maintenance, construction, or improvement of the public highways at any place within the state, outside of an incorporated village or city, upon request or with the consent of the superintendent of public works in the case of state or county highways. When engaged in the maintenance and repair of a highway under the jurisdiction of county or town authorities, the county or town receiving the benefit of such labor shall pay such reasonable compensation as may be agreed upon, not exceeding $1 per day for each prisoner.

11. A public highway within a city may not be constructed by state prison labor.

12. When a highway under the jurisdiction of a town is being repaired by state prison labor, such labor must be compensated for at the rate of more than $1 per day for each prisoner.

13. State prisoners may be assigned to work on the public highways of the state; however, they may not be employed on public highways under the jurisdiction of a town or county.

14. State highways are generally maintained by prison labor.

15. Prison labor may be used on state highways only with the consent or upon the request of the superintendent of public works.

## Reading Passage D

Any person interfering with or in any way interrupting the work of any prisoner employed upon the public highways or any person giving or attempting to give any intoxicating liquors, beer, ale, or other spirituous beverage to any prisoner so employed shall be guilty of a misdemeanor. Any officer or employee of any state correctional institution having in charge the convicts employed upon such highways may arrest without a warrant any person violating any above-mentioned provision.

16. Only non-intoxicating liquors may be offered by a civilian to a prisoner working on a state highway.

17. Under no circumstances may a state prisoner be allowed intoxicating liquors or beer.

18. It is unlawful for a civilian to interfere with a prisoner working on a public highway.

19. A person offering any spirituous beverage to a state prisoner working on a highway may be arrested by the correction officer in charge in the event the latter can provide a warrant.

20. A misdemeanor is not generally considered a serious offense.

## Reading Passage E

The warden of a state prison shall take charge of all money and other articles that may be brought to the prison by the convicts and shall cause the same, immediately upon the receipt thereof, to be entered by the warden or the chief clerk among the receipts of the prison. Whenever the convict from whom such money or articles was received shall be discharged from prison, or if such money or articles are otherwise legally demanded, such money and other articles shall be returned by the said warden to such convict or other person legally entitled to the same, and vouchers shall be taken therefor.

21. A convict, upon entering a state prison, must relinquish all but personal articles.

22. A prisoner's money and other articles, taken upon entrance to a state prison, may be withheld from the prisoner and returned to some other person when legally demanded.

23. It is the duty of the chief clerk in a state prison to take charge of all money brought into a prison by a convict as well as to enter it among the receipts of the prison.

24. It is not necessary to make out a voucher for money returned from the prison receipts to a discharged prisoner.

25. As a rule, money taken from a convict is not returned upon discharge unless legally demanded.

## Reading Passage F

Whenever the transfer of prisoners from one state prison to another shall be ordered by the Commissioner of Corrections, the warden of the prison from which such transfer is to be made shall cause the prisoners to be sufficiently chained in pairs so far as practicable and transferred to the prison to which they are so ordered. The persons so employed to transport such prisoners shall prohibit all intercourse between them and may inflict any reasonable and necessary correction upon such prisoners for disobedience or misconduct in any respect. In making such transfers, the Commissioner of Corrections shall take into consideration the adaptability of the prisoners to the industries in the prisons to which they are transferred.

26. Motor vehicles are generally used to convey prisoners in groups from one prison to another.

27. A factor in the transfer of state prisoners from one institution to another is the nature of the type of industry in the prison.

28. Prisoners need not necessarily be chained in being transferred from one state prison to another.

29. A prison guard employed in the transfer of prisoners from one state prison to another may inflict any necessary punishment upon a prisoner for disobedience.

30. Prisoners being transferred from one state prison to another are not generally permitted to hold conversations among themselves.

## ANSWERS

| | | | | |
|---|---|---|---|---|
| 1. A | 7. B | 13. C | 19. C | 25. B |
| 2. A | 8. B | 14. D | 20. D | 26. D |
| 3. B | 9. D | 15. A | 21. B | 27. A |
| 4. D | 10. C | 16. B | 22. A | 28. B |
| 5. B | 11. A | 17. D | 23. C | 29. A |
| 6. A | 12. B | 18. A | 24. B | 30. A |

## EXPLANATIONS

1. **The correct answer is (A).** This is stated clearly in the passage: "... where they shall receive all necessary care and medical assistance."
2. **The correct answer is (A).** This is stated in the first sentence.
3. **The correct answer is (B).** All prisoners should be moved if there is any contagious disease.
4. **The correct answer is (D).** There is nothing in the passage to support this statement.
5. **The correct answer is (B).** The last sentence says that they will "be returned as soon as possible to the state prison from which they were taken ...."
6. **The correct answer is (A).** The second sentence states that prisoners may be employed "... for any public institution ... controlled by the state."
7. **The correct answer is (B).** See the second sentence.
8. **The correct answer is (B).** The first sentence states "... for no longer than eight hours of each day ...."
9. **The correct answer is (D).** There is nothing in the passage to support this statement.
10. **The correct answer is (C).** They do not work on Sundays, but there is no mention of half days.
11. **The correct answer is (A).** Prisoners can only work on construction "outside of an incorporated village or city ...."
12. **The correct answer is (B).** The second sentence states that compensation may not exceed $1 per day.
13. **The correct answer is (C).** They can work on both public state highways as well as those under town or county jurisdiction.
14. **The correct answer is (D).** There is nothing in the passage to support this statement.
15. **The correct answer is (A).** This is stated clearly in the passage.
16. **The correct answer is (B).** Prisoners cannot be interrupted in the work in any way.
17. **The correct answer is (D).** There is nothing in the passage to support this statement.
18. **The correct answer is (A).** This is stated in the beginning of the passage.
19. **The correct answer is (C).** A warrant is unnecessary in order to make the arrest.
20. **The correct answer is (D).** There is nothing in the passage to support this statement.
21. **The correct answer is (B).** All personal articles must be relinquished at the time of imprisonment.
22. **The correct answer is (A).** See the second sentence.
23. **The correct answer is (C).** It is the warden, not the chief clerk, who takes charge of the money.
24. **The correct answer is (B).** A voucher is required.
25. **The correct answer is (B).** The money is returned upon release. See the second sentence.
26. **The correct answer is (D).** There is nothing in the passage to support this statement.
27. **The correct answer is (A).** See the third sentence.
28. **The correct answer is (B).** The first sentence states that they must be "sufficiently chained in pairs."
29. **The correct answer is (A).** The second sentence states that "any reasonable and necessary correction" may be inflicted for disobedience.
30. **The correct answer is (A).** The second sentence states that "all intercourse between them" shall be prohibited.

# READING COMPREHENSION QUIZZER THREE

**Directions:** This test consists of several reading passages, each followed by a number of statements. Analyze each statement solely on the basis of the material given. Then circle the letter

(A) if the statement is entirely true.

(B) if the statement is entirely false.

(C) if the statement is partially false and partially true.

(D) if the statement cannot be judged on the basis of the facts given in the excerpt.

## Reading Passage A

The Commissioner of Corrections may permit any prisoner confined in a state prison, except one awaiting the sentence of death, to attend the funeral of a father, mother, child, brother, sister, husband, or wife within the state or to visit such relative during his or her illness if death is imminent. Any expenses incurred under these provisions with respect to any prisoner shall be deemed an expense of maintenance of the prison and paid from monies available therefor; but the warden, if the rules and regulations of the Commissioner of Corrections shall so provide, may allow the prisoner or anyone in his or her behalf, to reimburse the state for such expense.

1. If a near relative is on the point of death, a state prisoner is generally permitted to leave the prison for a visit.

2. The traveling expenses of a state prisoner who attends the funeral of a relative are paid for either by the prisoner or the warden.

3. The only circumstances under which a state prisoner is granted permission to leave the prison is in the event of a funeral for a near relative.

4. Under no circumstances is a state prisoner forbidden to attend the funeral of his wife, provided it takes place within the state.

5. Under no circumstances is a state prisoner ever permitted out of the state to attend the funeral of a close relative.

## Reading Passage B

The Board of Parole is charged with the duty of determining which prisoners serving an indeterminate sentence in either the state prisons or the Elmira Reformatory are subject to release on parole, when, and under what conditions. The Board also has the responsibility for supervising all prisoners released on parole from state prisons, for making such investigations as may be necessary in connection therewith, and for determining whether violation of parole conditions exists in specific cases. The Board must make a personal study of the prisoners confined in the prisons under indeterminate sentence in order to determine their fitness for parole.

6. Only prisoners in state prisons are subject to parole.

7. An indeterminate sentence can be likened to an indefinite sentence.

8. Only prisoners serving indeterminate sentences may be considered for parole.

9. The Board of Parole has jurisdiction over prospective parolees.

10. Although the Board of Parole has the responsibility for supervising paroled prisoners, their fitness for parole is determined by an impersonal study of the prisoners.

## Reading Passage C

Every person sentenced to an indeterminate sentence and confined to a state prison, when he or she has served a period of time equal to the minimum sentence imposed by the court for the crime for which he or she was convicted, is subject to the jurisdiction of the Board of Parole. The time of release is within the discretion of the Board, but no such person may be released until he or she has served such minimum sentence or until he or she has served one year. The action of the Board in releasing prisoners is deemed a judicial function and is not reviewable if done according to law. No person may be released on parole merely as a reward for good conduct or efficient performance of duties assigned in prison but only if the Board of Parole is of the opinion that there is reasonable probability that, if such prisoner is released, he or she will live and remain at liberty without violating the law and that release is not incompatible with the welfare of society.

11. A paroled prisoner generally remains in the legal custody of the prison from which he or she was paroled.

12. When the Board of Parole releases a prisoner on parole, the Board's power is like that of a judge and may not be reviewed if lawful.

13. Prisoners under an indeterminate sentence are subject to the jurisdiction of the Board of Parole, but only when they have served their maximum sentence.

14. Prisoners are generally paroled on the basis of good conduct entirely.

15. No prisoner may be paroled without having served a minimum of a year in any case.

## Reading Passage D

A sentence of imprisonment in a state prison for a definite fixed period of time is a definite sentence. A sentence to imprisonment in a state prison having minimum and maximum limits fixed by the court or the governor is an indeterminate sentence. Every prisoner confined to a state prison or penitentiary may, in the discretion of the governor, receive, for good conduct and efficient and willing performance of duties assigned, a reduction of his or her sentence not to exceed ten days for each month of the minimum term in the case of an indeterminate sentence or of the term as imposed by the court in the case of a definite sentence. The maximum reduction allowable under this provision shall be four months per year, but nothing herein contained shall be construed to confer any right whatsoever upon any prisoner to demand or require the whole or any part of such reduction.

16. Only prisoners under indeterminate sentence are subject to parole.

17. Prisoners given indeterminate sentences are allowed time off for good behavior and conduct which is not the case with prisoners under definite sentence.

18. A definite sentence generally has prescribed minimum and maximum limits.

19. Under the law, all prisoners must receive time off their sentence for good conduct and efficient and willing performance of duties assigned.

20. The maximum limit of an indeterminate sentence may be set by the governor or the judge of the court in which sentence is imposed.

## ANSWERS

| | | | |
|---|---|---|---|
| 1. A | 6. B | 11. D | 16. D |
| 2. C | 7. D | 12. A | 17. C |
| 3. B | 8. D | 13. C | 18. B |
| 4. B | 9. A | 14. B | 19. B |
| 5. D | 10. C | 15. A | 20. A |

## EXPLANATIONS

1. **The correct answer is (A).** This is stated clearly in the first sentence.
2. **The correct answer is (C).** The money is paid from available monies, not from the warden, although the prisoner may reimburse the state.
3. **The correct answer is (B).** They may also leave if death of a family member is imminent.
4. **The correct answer is (B).** Prisoners awaiting the death sentence are not permitted to leave the prison.
5. **The correct answer is (D).** There is nothing in the passage to support this statement.
6. **The correct answer is (B).** According to the passage, prisoners in state prisons as well as Elmira Reformatory may be paroled.
7. **The correct answer is (D).** There is nothing in the passage to support this statement.
8. **The correct answer is (D).** There is nothing in the passage to support this statement.
9. **The correct answer is (A).** This is stated in the first sentence.
10. **The correct answer is (C).** The last sentence states that the "board must make a *personal* study."
11. **The correct answer is (D).** There is nothing in the passage to support this statement.
12. **The correct answer is (A).** The third sentence states that the decision of the Board of Parole "is not reviewable if done according to law."
13. **The correct answer is (C).** Every prisoner is subject to the board's jurisdiction regardless of time served.
14. **The correct answer is (B).** The prisoners are released if the board believes they will be able to live without violating the law.

15. **The correct answer is (A).** The second sentence says that they must serve the minimum sentence.

16. **The correct answer is (D).** There is nothing in the passage to support this statement.

17. **The correct answer is (C).** Prisoners under defined sentences may also be given time off at the discretion of the governor.

18. **The correct answer is (B).** There is no minimum or maximum limit—only a definite prescribed time.

19. **The correct answer is (B).** Time off is only granted at the discretion of the governor, but it is not required.

20. **The correct answer is (A).** See the second sentence.

# COURTS QUIZZER

> **Directions:** Read each question and circle the letter that precedes the answer you choose.

1. The first paper served in a civil action in the Supreme Court is the

   (A) complaint.
   (B) summons.
   (C) injunction.
   (D) subpoena.

2. Which of the following includes the plaintiff's statement of claims?

   (A) Reports
   (B) Writ of attachment
   (C) Notice to produce
   (D) The complaint

3. The paper containing the defendant's statement of defense is

   (A) the answer.
   (B) reports.
   (C) bill of particulars.
   (D) opening proclamation.

4. Should the defendant allege a claim against the plaintiff, it would be known as the

   (A) execution.
   (B) charge.
   (C) counterclaim.
   (D) challenge.

5. When the defendant's claim is denied by the plaintiff, the paper is known as

   (A) the deposition.
   (B) the motion.
   (C) the reply.
   (D) the lien.

6. To bring a witness into court with books and papers, he or she must be served with a(n)

   (A) injunction.
   (B) subpoena *duces tecum.*
   (C) affidavit.
   (D) summons.

7. A paper having the written testimony of a witness taken outside of the state is the

    (A) framed issues.
    (B) partition proceedings.
    (C) discontinuance.
    (D) deposition.

8. A list of cases ready to be tried is the

    (A) calendar.
    (B) panel.
    (C) board.
    (D) proceedings.

9. When referring to the "venue" in an action one means

    (A) the place of trial.
    (B) opening proclamation.
    (C) the scene of the crime.
    (D) residence of the witness.

10. A paper that has been properly entered and calls for the collection of a judgment for money is

    (A) special term, *ex parte*.
    (B) presumptive evidence.
    (C) bill of particulars.
    (D) the execution.

11. The provisions regulating practice in the Supreme Court of New York are known as the

    (A) Charter of New York State.
    (B) Civil Practice Laws and Rules, Code of Criminal Procedure Law.
    (C) New York Law Journal.
    (D) Long's Civil Cases.

12. The paper containing the official notice and memoranda of the courts and published daily in New York is the

    (A) Lawyer's Reports.
    (B) Criminal Procedure Law.
    (C) New York Law Journal.
    (D) Court of Record.

13. The books containing the decisions of the New York courts are known as the

    (A) Framed Issues.
    (B) References.
    (C) Citations.
    (D) Reports.

14. The rules governing the practice in the Supreme Court of New York are formulated by the

    (A) appellate division of the Supreme Court.
    (B) governor of New York State.
    (C) Bar Association of New York State.
    (D) senate of New York State.

15. To prove the service of a paper, one signs what is known as an

    (A) answer.
    (B) acknowledgment.
    (C) affidavit.
    (D) affirmation.

16. To obtain more complete details of the plaintiff's claim, the defendant must obtain a
    - (A) bill of exceptions.
    - (B) bill of particulars.
    - (C) secondary evidence.
    - (D) writ of inquiry.

17. For the cessation of harmful acts, one applies in **Supreme Court** for a(n)
    - (A) discontinuance.
    - (B) duress.
    - (C) injunction.
    - (D) bill of exceptions.

18. In order for a creditor to seize certain property belonging to a nonresident, he or she must apply in the Supreme Court for a
    - (A) writ of attachment.
    - (B) deposition.
    - (C) mandatory injunction.
    - (D) prohibition.

19. The proceedings that are taken in order to punish a person who causes a disturbance in court are known as
    - (A) condemnation proceeding.
    - (B) exhibit.
    - (C) measure of damages.
    - (D) contempt proceedings.

20. Papers filed in the Supreme Court are in the custody of the
    - (A) presiding judge.
    - (B) county clerk.
    - (C) board of county judges.
    - (D) attorney general.

21. The term applied to a person appointed to represent an infant in an action in the Supreme Court is the
    - (A) administrator.
    - (B) referee.
    - (C) guardian-*ad-litem*.
    - (D) talesman.

22. The announcement made at the opening of court is the
    - (A) summons.
    - (B) opening proclamation.
    - (C) cause of action.
    - (D) judgment roll.

23. Justices in the Supreme Court obtain their positions for full terms through
    - (A) election by voters of the various judicial districts in states.
    - (B) appointment by governor.
    - (C) appointment by the Bar Association of New York State.
    - (D) civil service appointment.

24. A Supreme Court justice's full term is
    - (A) 10 years.
    - (B) 7 years.
    - (C) lifetime appointment with good behavior.
    - (D) 14 years.

25. The provisions of a will left by a deceased person may be challenged in the

    (A) U.S. Supreme Court.
    (B) civil court.
    (C) court of claims.
    (D) surrogate court.

26. A witness of sufficient age and intellect has been called to the stand. What does the court now do before the witness can testify?

    (A) Swears in the court attendant first
    (B) Asks the witness to state political affiliation
    (C) Swears in or affirms the witness
    (D) Immediately begins to question the witness

27. A group of jurors selected to serve during a term of court is known as a

    (A) panel.
    (B) board.
    (C) jury.
    (D) judicial group.

28. The papers containing the trial jurors' names are known as the

    (A) document.
    (B) ballots or slips.
    (C) reference.
    (D) calendar.

29. Should a juror be objectionable to an attorney, the attorney

    (A) challenges the juror for "cause"; if sustained, the juror is excused.
    (B) asks clerk to dismiss the juror.
    (C) refuses to continue the case.
    (D) asks the judge to drop the charge.

30. The result of a jury's agreement is known as the

    (A) verdict.
    (B) judgment.
    (C) plea.
    (D) opinion.

31. The statement made by the judge to the jury is known is the

    (A) accusation.
    (B) warrant.
    (C) order.
    (D) charge.

32. One knows the agreement signed by attorneys during a trial as a(n)

    (A) agreement.
    (B) bargain.
    (C) stipulation.
    (D) notion.

33. In a trial by jury, questions of fact are decided by the

    (A) clerk.
    (B) jury.
    (C) judge.
    (D) two opposing attorneys.

34. In a trial by jury, questions of law are decided by the

    (A) judge.
    (B) clerk.
    (C) court attendant.
    (D) jury.

35. In order to prevent a witness from answering a question, the attorney may

    (A) write disapproval on paper.
    (B) do nothing about it.
    (C) protest to the clerk.
    (D) object.

36. Should an attorney be dissatisfied with a ruling of a judge, he or she may

    (A) rule the judge in contempt of court.
    (B) protest to the clerk.
    (C) take an exception to a judge's charge.
    (D) ask for a new trial.

37. The clerk's records kept during a trial of action are known as the

    (A) proceedings.
    (B) minutes.
    (C) information.
    (D) details.

38. In a contested action, what would an attorney do to obtain an order of the court?

    (A) Object
    (B) Ask for a recess
    (C) Resort to a compromise
    (D) Bring on a motion

39. The title of the person to whom a case is sent if the judge decides to try the case out of court is

    (A) clerk.
    (B) court attendant.
    (C) referee.
    (D) district attorney.

40. By whom are the parts in which the Supreme Court justices sit determined?

    (A) Appellate division
    (B) Governor
    (C) Lieutenant governor
    (D) Attorney general

41. The number of justices in the appellate term is

    (A) 7 to 9.
    (B) 5 to 7.
    (C) 6 to 8.
    (D) 3 to 5.

42. The justices are given their seats in the appellate term by the

    (A) governor.
    (B) appellate division.
    (C) senate.
    (D) people.

**43.** The appellate term receives appeals from which of the following courts?

(A) Court of appeals
(B) Criminal court
(C) Court of the judiciary
(D) Court of claims

**44.** Of the following, the one who designates justices to sit in the appellate division is

(A) the governor.
(B) the people.
(C) the Supreme Court.
(D) the attorney general.

**45.** What is the maximum number of justices sitting in any case in the Appellate Division First Department?

(A) 4
(B) 7
(C) 3
(D) 5

**46.** What is the number of justices in the Appellate Division First Department, if the governor has appointed extra judges?

(A) 8
(B) 7
(C) 4
(D) 3

**47.** Of the following groups, which one contains courts from which appeals are taken to the appellate division?

(A) Court of appeals
(B) Court of impeachment
(C) Court of impeachment and court of appeals
(D) Family court and criminal court

**48.** What is the number of appellate divisions in New York State?

(A) 5
(B) 4
(C) 7
(D) 8

**49.** From the appellate division, appeals are taken to the

(A) court of appeals.
(B) Supreme Court of U.S.
(C) city court.
(D) county court.

**50.** Suits for the recovery of small sums in an informal manner may be instituted in the small claims court. This court is part of the

(A) Supreme Court.
(B) court of claims.
(C) court of the judiciary.
(D) civil court.

51. A court whose jurisdiction includes the hearing of divorce actions and marriage separations is the

    (A) family court.
    (B) Supreme Court.
    (C) civil court.
    (D) justice of the peace court.

52. A part of a state court that is in existence to promote the welfare of children is connected to the

    (A) civil court.
    (B) family court.
    (C) Supreme Court.
    (D) surrogate court.

53. A court whose judges are appointed rather than elected to office is the

    (A) family court.
    (B) surrogate court.
    (C) civil court.
    (D) Supreme Court.

54. The conduct of attorneys who practice in New York State is governed by rules and procedures formulated by the

    (A) court of appeals.
    (B) court of the judiciary.
    (C) appellate division of the Supreme Court.
    (D) court of claims.

## ANSWERS

| | | | | |
|---|---|---|---|---|
| 1. B | 12. C | 23. A | 34. A | 45. D |
| 2. D | 13. D | 24. D | 35. D | 46. B |
| 3. A | 14. A | 25. D | 36. C | 47. D |
| 4. C | 15. C | 26. C | 37. B | 48. B |
| 5. C | 16. B | 27. A | 38. D | 49. A |
| 6. B | 17. C | 28. B | 39. C | 50. D |
| 7. D | 18. A | 29. A | 40. A | 51. B |
| 8. A | 19. D | 30. A | 41. D | 52. B |
| 9. A | 20. B | 31. D | 42. B | 53. A |
| 10. D | 21. C | 32. C | 43. B | 54. C |
| 11. B | 22. B | 33. B | 44. A | |

## EXPLANATIONS

1. **The correct answer is (B).** The summons requires one to appear in court.
2. **The correct answer is (D).** The complaint tells the court what the plaintiff's concerns and/or problems are.
3. **The correct answer is (A).** The defendant replies to the plaintiff in the answer.
4. **The correct answer is (C).** This is the counter to the defendant's answers.
5. **The correct answer is (C).** The reply is the response by the plaintiff.
6. **The correct answer is (B).** A subpoena *duces tecum* is a legal document requiring one to bring documents.
7. **The correct answer is (D).** Depositions are taken in a number of cases, whether the claimants are in state or out of state.
8. **The correct answer is (A).** The calendar lists where and when the cases are to be heard.
9. **The correct answer is (A).** Venue is important in relation to where the problem occurred.
10. **The correct answer is (D).** The execution requires the court's judgment to be exercised or complied with.
11. **The correct answer is (B).** Every state has rules that are to be followed.
12. **The correct answer is (C).** This kind of publication is unique to each state.
13. **The correct answer is (D).** Again, each state calls it something different.
14. **The correct answer is (A).** This is the rule-making body.
15. **The correct answer is (C).** Signing an affidavit confirms that you have received the paper.
16. **The correct answer is (B).** A bill of particulars is a more specific listing of the claims.
17. **The correct answer is (C).** An injunction, if granted, stops whatever is going on.
18. **The correct answer is (A).** A writ of attachment attaches the property so the user cannot continue to use it or dispose of it.
19. **The correct answer is (D).** When a person violates the rules of the court, he or she can be held in contempt.
20. **The correct answer is (B).** The county clerk is the keeper of the records.

21. **The correct answer is (C).** A guardian-*ad-litem* is appointed not only to an infant, but to almost all juveniles in certain types of proceedings.
22. **The correct answer is (B).** The opening proclamation introduces the judge and sets the ground rules.
23. **The correct answer is (A).** Most states elect their Supreme Court justices.
24. **The correct answer is (D).** This varies with each state.
25. **The correct answer is (D).** This is a New York court established to deal with these kinds of matters.
26. **The correct answer is (C).** Swearing in or affirming the witness is a ritual that requires the individual to testify truthfully.
27. **The correct answer is (A).** The legal term is impaneling of the jury.
28. **The correct answer is (B).** Each state has its own name for the list of jurors' names.
29. **The correct answer is (A).** Each attorney has a specified number of challenges.
30. **The correct answer is (A).** This is the legal term referring to the decision of the jury.
31. **The correct answer is (D).** In the charge, the judge gives the jury their rules and the law as to the case at hand.
32. **The correct answer is (C).** The stipulation saves people from testifying as to facts that both attorneys agree on.
33. **The correct answer is (B).** The jury decides on questions of fact in a trial by jury.
34. **The correct answer is (A).** The judge decides on questions of law in his role as referee.
35. **The correct answer is (D).** An objection requires the judge to decide generally a rule of law or whether the question was improper or inappropriate.
36. **The correct answer is (C).** Although some attorneys might like to rule a judge in contempt, all they can do is offer an exception (which may provide a point for appeal later).
37. **The correct answer is (B).** The clerk's records kept during a trial of action are known as the minutes.
38. **The correct answer is (D).** Motions are filed to achieve or question certain actions.
39. **The correct answer is (C).** The referee is someone who acts as a judge.
40. **The correct answer is (A).** The appellate division is the rule-making body.
41. **The correct answer is (D).** This number is established by law or constitution.
42. **The correct answer is (B).** Again, the appellate division is the rule-making body.
43. **The correct answer is (B).** Criminal cases go to appellate term; civil cases are appealed elsewhere.
44. **The correct answer is (A).** The governor is usually given this responsibility by the constitution.
45. **The correct answer is (D).** The number of justices is established by law, constitution, or tradition.
46. **The correct answer is (B).** Appointing extra judges is an option given the governor.
47. **The correct answer is (D).** Family court hears cases involving juvenile delinquents (i.e., criminal cases in which juveniles are the defendants).
48. **The correct answer is (B).** This is determined by law and/or constitution.
49. **The correct answer is (A).** The court of appeals is the layer of the courts just below the Supreme Court.
50. **The correct answer is (D).** Questions of claims are civil questions.
51. **The correct answer is (B).** Jurisdiction is established by constitution.
52. **The correct answer is (B).** Family courts hear cases involving juveniles.
53. **The correct answer is (A).** Usually appointments are made by the executive branch (e.g., governor or mayor).
54. **The correct answer is (C).** This is the rule-making body that establishes how the courts and those who appear therein will operate.

**PART FOUR**

# Model Examinations

# MODEL EXAMINATION 1: ANSWER SHEET

| | | | |
|---|---|---|---|
| 1. Ⓐ Ⓑ Ⓒ Ⓓ | 21. Ⓐ Ⓑ Ⓒ Ⓓ | 41. Ⓐ Ⓑ Ⓒ Ⓓ | 61. Ⓐ Ⓑ Ⓒ Ⓓ |
| 2. Ⓐ Ⓑ Ⓒ Ⓓ | 22. Ⓐ Ⓑ Ⓒ Ⓓ | 42. Ⓐ Ⓑ Ⓒ Ⓓ | 62. Ⓐ Ⓑ Ⓒ Ⓓ |
| 3. Ⓐ Ⓑ Ⓒ Ⓓ | 23. Ⓐ Ⓑ Ⓒ Ⓓ | 43. Ⓐ Ⓑ Ⓒ Ⓓ | 63. Ⓐ Ⓑ Ⓒ Ⓓ |
| 4. Ⓐ Ⓑ Ⓒ Ⓓ | 24. Ⓐ Ⓑ Ⓒ Ⓓ | 44. Ⓐ Ⓑ Ⓒ Ⓓ | 64. Ⓐ Ⓑ Ⓒ Ⓓ |
| 5. Ⓐ Ⓑ Ⓒ Ⓓ | 25. Ⓐ Ⓑ Ⓒ Ⓓ | 45. Ⓐ Ⓑ Ⓒ Ⓓ | 65. Ⓐ Ⓑ Ⓒ Ⓓ |
| 6. Ⓐ Ⓑ Ⓒ Ⓓ | 26. Ⓐ Ⓑ Ⓒ Ⓓ | 46. Ⓐ Ⓑ Ⓒ Ⓓ | |
| 7. Ⓐ Ⓑ Ⓒ Ⓓ | 27. Ⓐ Ⓑ Ⓒ Ⓓ | 47. Ⓐ Ⓑ Ⓒ Ⓓ | |
| 8. Ⓐ Ⓑ Ⓒ Ⓓ | 28. Ⓐ Ⓑ Ⓒ Ⓓ | 48. Ⓐ Ⓑ Ⓒ Ⓓ | |
| 9. Ⓐ Ⓑ Ⓒ Ⓓ | 29. Ⓐ Ⓑ Ⓒ Ⓓ | 49. Ⓐ Ⓑ Ⓒ Ⓓ | |
| 10. Ⓐ Ⓑ Ⓒ Ⓓ | 30. Ⓐ Ⓑ Ⓒ Ⓓ | 50. Ⓐ Ⓑ Ⓒ Ⓓ | |
| 11. Ⓐ Ⓑ Ⓒ Ⓓ | 31. Ⓐ Ⓑ Ⓒ Ⓓ | 51. Ⓐ Ⓑ Ⓒ Ⓓ | |
| 12. Ⓐ Ⓑ Ⓒ Ⓓ | 32. Ⓐ Ⓑ Ⓒ Ⓓ | 52. Ⓐ Ⓑ Ⓒ Ⓓ | |
| 13. Ⓐ Ⓑ Ⓒ Ⓓ | 33. Ⓐ Ⓑ Ⓒ Ⓓ | 53. Ⓐ Ⓑ Ⓒ Ⓓ | |
| 14. Ⓐ Ⓑ Ⓒ Ⓓ | 34. Ⓐ Ⓑ Ⓒ Ⓓ | 54. Ⓐ Ⓑ Ⓒ Ⓓ | |
| 15. Ⓐ Ⓑ Ⓒ Ⓓ | 35. Ⓐ Ⓑ Ⓒ Ⓓ | 55. Ⓐ Ⓑ Ⓒ Ⓓ | |
| 16. Ⓐ Ⓑ Ⓒ Ⓓ | 36. Ⓐ Ⓑ Ⓒ Ⓓ | 56. Ⓐ Ⓑ Ⓒ Ⓓ | |
| 17. Ⓐ Ⓑ Ⓒ Ⓓ | 37. Ⓐ Ⓑ Ⓒ Ⓓ | 57. Ⓐ Ⓑ Ⓒ Ⓓ | |
| 18. Ⓐ Ⓑ Ⓒ Ⓓ | 38. Ⓐ Ⓑ Ⓒ Ⓓ | 58. Ⓐ Ⓑ Ⓒ Ⓓ | |
| 19. Ⓐ Ⓑ Ⓒ Ⓓ | 39. Ⓐ Ⓑ Ⓒ Ⓓ | 59. Ⓐ Ⓑ Ⓒ Ⓓ | |
| 20. Ⓐ Ⓑ Ⓒ Ⓓ | 40. Ⓐ Ⓑ Ⓒ Ⓓ | 60. Ⓐ Ⓑ Ⓒ Ⓓ | |

# MODEL EXAMINATION 1: PAROLE OFFICER TRAINEE

## 4 HOURS; 65 QUESTIONS

> **Directions:** For questions 1–20, read each question or incomplete statement and choose the best answer. On your answer sheet, darken the letter that corresponds with your answer choice.

1. The best results of parole are achieved when

   (A) prison itself has been a brutalizing experience.
   (B) the parole officer is a friend of the family.
   (C) the parolee has been carefully prepared before parole.
   (D) a very large percentage of the sentence was served before parole.

2. Release of a convicted offender into the community under conditions imposed by the court is called

   (A) parole.
   (B) probation.
   (C) deferred prosecution.
   (D) pretrial diversion.

3. Probation is granted by

   (A) the jury.
   (B) the probation officer.
   (C) the judge.
   (D) the district attorney.

4. In releasing a prisoner into parole, the correction system is taking a certain risk with that prisoner. In recognition of the risks involved, the parolee may be placed under a number of restrictions. Which of the following is an example of a valid, enforceable restriction placed upon a parolee?

   (A) He may not attend any party at which beer is being served.
   (B) He must notify his parole officer whenever he plans to leave the state.
   (C) Under no circumstances may he quit his job.
   (D) If he decides to spend the night with his girlfriend, he must ask his parole officer for permission.

5. The parole officer fulfills a number of simultaneous roles. Which of the following is NOT a role of the parole officer?

   (A) Social case worker
   (B) Investigator
   (C) Confidant
   (D) Resource broker

6. Reintegration of a parolee into society is best accomplished if the parolee can be released into

   (A) the home of his or her own parents.
   (B) the armed forces.
   (C) a licensed vocational school.
   (D) a supervised halfway house.

7. After many months of scheduled reporting, a parolee begins to skip appointments with the parole officer. The parole officer contacts the parolee's family and learns that the parolee has been staying out all night, returning home clearly "spaced out" on drugs, and bringing home expensive gifts for family members. The parolee's mother shows a videocassette recorder (VCR) to the officer, who notices the serial number on the VCR. A quick check with the police department indicates that this is a stolen item. The parole officer notifies the parole board and the parolee is remanded to prison. The parole officer

   (A) has failed because the parolee violated parole while under the officer's supervision.
   (B) is successful because the parolee was intercepted before committing a crime.
   (C) has failed because a parolee should never need to be sent back to prison.
   (D) is successful because society is being protected from a parolee who was not yet fully rehabilitated.

8. The greatest destabilizing influence upon a recently paroled 19-year-old unmarried male is likely to be

   (A) his group of prearrest friends.
   (B) his girlfriend.
   (C) the police officer who arrested him.
   (D) his mother.

9. The preparole report on a recently paroled young man notes that while in prison he was generally a loner but tagged along with the priest whenever the priest visited. As an inmate, he would offer to serve as an altar boy and would attend mass regularly. For the parole officer to suggest to this parolee that he get involved in various activities in his local parish church would be

   (A) good; religion teaches good values.
   (B) good; the parolee would find activity for idle time and might make wholesome friends.
   (C) bad; the parole officer must not be in the position of promoting religion.
   (D) bad; the collection box and silver vessels may offer too many temptations to a recent prisoner.

10. Probation is a(n)

   (A) right.
   (B) good idea.
   (C) privilege.
   (D) incredibly ridiculous idea.

11. A parole officer is most likely to achieve success with the greatest number of cases if he

   (A) always adheres to the same carefully organized plan for supervising parolees.
   (B) plays it "by ear" with each individual assignment.
   (C) draws upon experience with previous successes and failures and redesigns the treatment plan with each new case.
   (D) researches the personal history of each new assignment and tailors a supervision plan to the specific individual.

12. A very busy, overburdened parole officer with a fully scheduled day learns that a parolee under her supervision is at the door of the office and wishes to speak with her right away. For the parole officer to refuse to see the parolee at this time would be

   (A) proper; parolees must learn the value of schedules and appointments as part of their adjustment to the outside world.
   (B) improper; the parolee might have a serious problem that can be defused if it is dealt with right away.

    (C)   proper; a hurried consultation can have no good results, and other clients would be shortchanged as well.

    (D)   improper; a parole officer should encourage total dependency.

**13.** The parolee is hostile and antagonistic toward the parole officer, refusing to answer questions, follow suggestions, or cooperate in any way other than by appearing regularly at the appointed time. Under these circumstances, the parole officer would be well advised to

    (A)   respond to the parolee with coldness and authoritarian demands.

    (B)   recommend that parole be revoked and the parolee be remanded to prison.

    (C)   request that the parolee be immediately reassigned to another parole officer.

    (D)   independently research the parolee's history and current problems to devise the best approach for reaching and working with the individual.

**14.** A parole officer learns that a new parolee has returned to the same living arrangements as those prior to his incarceration. He is "hanging out" in the same places with the same friends as previously and appears to have nothing to do. The best approach for the parole officer to take is to

    (A)   insist that the parolee move away from the old neighborhood at once.

    (B)   discuss the parolee's interests with him and together develop some plan toward his finding a job, getting job training, or choosing some useful way to occupy his time.

    (C)   threaten the parolee with revocation of parole unless he stops his idle ways at once.

    (D)   enroll the parolee in a group therapy program.

**15.** A few unacquainted parolees under the supervision of a certain parole officer have reported difficulty in refusing drugs when in the company of their old friends. The parole officer invites these parolees to come together at her office on a weekly basis for a support session. This initiative on the part of the parole officer is

    (A)   wise; the parolees can share their concerns and strategies and can give each other encouragement, support, and applause.

    (B)   unwise; this type of initiative is not within the mandate of the parole officer.

    (C)   wise; these parolees obviously need new friends.

    (D)   unwise; introducing a group of former prisoners to each other can lead to no good.

**16.** The formal judgment of the court imposing punishment is known as

    (A)   parole.

    (B)   deferred prosecution.

    (C)   a good idea.

    (D)   the sentence.

**17.** A parole officer has convinced a union local to open its apprenticeship training program to a promising but unskilled parolee. The parolee lacks self-confidence and is reluctant to commit himself to a long-term program. The parole officer should

    (A)   permit the parolee to back down rather than be embarrassed by personal failure.

    (B)   convince the parolee that he has the ability to succeed and impress upon him the long-term benefits of union training.

    (C)   plead with the parolee to enter the program so as not to embarrass the parole officer who worked out the arrangement with the union.

    (D)   insist that the parolee give it a try under threat of a report back to the parole board.

18. A parolee reports to the parole officer that her boyfriend has thrown her out, her parents will not let her come home, and she has no place to live. For the parole officer to temporarily take the parolee home would be

    (A) advisable; the parole officer's home is a safe place for a young woman.
    (B) advisable; a parole officer is responsible for seeing to the shelter needs of all parolees assigned to him or her.
    (C) inadvisable; the relationship between parole officer and parolee must remain professional and at arm's length.
    (D) inadvisable; the parole officer may be open to charges of sex abuse or harassment.

19. Effective supervision of a parolee requires frequent personal contact, during which the parole officer may provide assistance with housing and vocational problems, guidance with personal decision making, and suggestions for dealing with interpersonal relationships within the household and among the parolee's peers. Which of the following should NOT be an aspect of the parole officer-parolee relationship?

    (A) Discussion of the locations of crack houses
    (B) Introduction to community leaders who might be able to steer the parolee toward prospective employers
    (C) Provision of a list of social service agencies that might provide special services of which the parolee would be totally unaware
    (D) Lending money to tide the parolee over in a tight squeeze

20. The first use of probation most probably occurred in

    (A) Los Angeles.
    (B) Boston.
    (C) New York.
    (D) Plymouth Rock, Virginia.

---

**Directions:** In questions 21–45, each question or group of questions is based upon the description of a hypothetical client and his or her individual situation. Read the description, then answer the question or questions on the basis of the description and your own best knowledge and judgment.

---

*Questions 21–27 are based upon the following case description.*

John is a 27-year-old unmarried male recently paroled from the state penitentiary after serving three years of a four-year sentence for armed robbery, illegal possession of a weapon, and possession of a controlled substance. While John has not always been a model citizen, the sentence from which he has just been paroled is the only one that he has served. Any offenses committed by John as a juvenile were disposed of in juvenile court and the records have been sealed. While John has a number of arrests to his credit as an adult, he has never been convicted of any crimes.

John is of above-average intelligence but was an indifferent student in school. He dropped out of high school toward the middle of his junior year, not because he was failing (he had maintained a C average) but because he saw no relevance of high school to his own life. While in prison, John was an enthusiastic shortstop on an intramural baseball team, earned a GED diploma, and worked in the prison printing shop with an eye toward the printing trades. His positive attitude toward activities, education, and vocational training clearly influenced the parole board in John's favor.

John is the fifth child of 7 in an otherwise all-female household. His older sisters have doted on him and have always spoiled him, permitted him extra favors, and covered for him when he misbehaved. His younger sisters resent him as an attention grabber who denied them the privileges of babyhood. John's mother, who has never been married, is a nurturing human being but is an inadequate provider. Male presence in the household has been sporadic and often destabilizing. The various boyfriends of his sisters have frequently served as negative role models, including drug abusers, cat burglars, and women beaters. John is very proud of having fathered 3 small children by 2 women. He occasionally gives money to these women to help them out with supporting the children but is not particularly interested in developing a relationship with the children themselves.

21. You, a female parole officer, have just been handed John's file and have been told to add John to your caseload. You read through the history carefully and, without meeting John, have a distinct feeling that you are the wrong parole officer for him. The first thing you should do is

(A) meet with John to tell him that you would prefer not to be his parole officer and ask him to request that a different parole officer be assigned.
(B) accept the assignment and get to work; if you have judged John's needs correctly, it will soon become evident that a reassignment is called for.
(C) meet with your supervisor and explain that you feel John should be supervised by a man who can serve as a role model.
(D) discuss your feelings with your colleagues and get their input.

22. During preparole planning, an apprentice position was secured for John in a small commercial printing shop a long subway ride from his mother's apartment, to which he was returning to live. At your second meeting with John after his parole release, John tells you that the job is okay but that he is terrified of the subway and fears that he will meet a former buddy who will do him bodily harm because he has turned away from his old friends and his old ways. Under these circumstances, you should

(A) explore with John the possibilities for moving away from the old neighborhood, the old friends, and the old temptations and finding quarters closer to the job, perhaps without a need for carfare.
(B) tell John to grow up and to stop being a sissy.
(C) study a bus map with John to work out a long, circuitous, but safe bus route.
(D) suggest that John quit the job and help him to find work closer to home.

23. At a regularly scheduled meeting with you, John tells you that he is bored with his life and is looking for excitement. Needless to say, you are worried that John's idea of excitement will include drugs, violence, or property crime. The best course of action for you to take is to

(A) forbid John from associating with his preprison group of friends.
(B) order John to enroll in community college courses to take up his time and to better himself.
(C) suggest that John spend more time with his young son and take him to the park to teach him to play ball.
(D) tell John to look for a new girlfriend.

24. Returning to your desk at the end of a long Saturday at work, you find a note that John's mother has phoned you. You return her call to learn that John came in late the previous evening badly bruised and bloodied, intoxicated, and extremely angry. He had left home before she got up in the morning and has not been seen since. She is fearful. Your course of action should be to

(A) do nothing at this time. One day's absence from home is perfectly normal for an adult.
(B) go to the neighborhood and ask questions of shopkeepers, bartenders, and people in the street.
(C) call the printing shop right away to see if John reported to work.
(D) notify the Bureau of Missing Persons.

25. You and John seem to have a good working relationship, and at your last meeting John was very forthcoming about his activities and daily life. At that time, he seemed to be upbeat and optimistic. Today, however, he seems ill at ease with you, shifts in his seat, and has little to say. You suspect that John has become involved with something he'd rather not have you know about. You should

    (A) say nothing to John but make discrete inquiry of his employer, coworkers, family, and friends.
    (B) request police department surveillance of John.
    (C) tell your supervisor of your concerns and ask for guidance on how to proceed.
    (D) ask John directly, in a sympathetic manner, insisting upon a full response to your questions and offering him support and assistance within legal limits.

26. The mother of John's 2 little girls has moved in with a new boyfriend who is a crack user and is often violent. This man has been taking the money John offers for informal child support and beats up the children's mother when she hasn't enough money. John is not earning enough money to support this man's habit, yet he fears for the safety of his children. How should you handle this situation?

    (A) Tell John to take the little girls to live with him and his sisters at his mother's home.
    (B) Warn John that dealing drugs or stealing, even for the benefit of little children, would be a parole violation that would land him back in prison.
    (C) Suggest to John that since one cannot reason with a crack user, he had best look for a second job to come up with more money.
    (D) Accompany John to a child protective services office to help him with filing the necessary papers and to back him up as needed.

27. John has moved out of his mother's home and is now sharing an apartment with 1 old friend, another parolee, and a new acquaintance. You come to visit at the premises and meet the landlord. The landlord assures you that the rent is being paid on time but complains that the men are dirty and noisy and tend to have late-night parties. It would be wise for you first to

    (A) discuss a common approach with the parole officer who is supervising the other parolee.
    (B) meet with the 4 men as a group to discuss the landlord's complaints and to help them in planning to overcome housekeeping and entertaining problems to the landlord's satisfaction.
    (C) tell John to move.
    (D) tell John that the troublemaker within the group must be forced out of the apartment.

28. Mary is a 19-year-old woman who has recently come under your supervision after serving a portion of a sentence for grand larceny. Mary is very pleasant and agreeable but tends to follow her own counsel, not yours. As you are on your way to an appointment with another parolee, you notice Mary standing in a doorway, quite obviously soliciting for prostitution. You should

    (A) pretend not to have seen Mary and go on your way so as to not be late for your appointment.
    (B) hide discreetly, camera in hand, so that you can properly document Mary's illicit activity when she is approached by a prospective client.
    (C) confront Mary and tell her to move on at once to avoid parole violation.
    (D) summon a police officer and report Mary.

29. The sentence from which Lonnie is now on parole resulted from a conviction for arson, but you are aware that Lonnie has a long history of heroin addiction. Since Lonnie did not report for a scheduled meeting with you, you have gone into his neighborhood to find him nodding off in the alley between two buildings. Now that you have found Lonnie, the next thing to do is

    (A) rouse Lonnie and insist that he accompany you as you seek temporary shelter and detoxification for him.
    (B) let him sleep it off; he is doing no harm and is setting no fires.
    (C) take Lonnie into custody.
    (D) wake Lonnie and ask where he got the heroin.

30. Ron, age 41, is divorced from his first wife, with whom he had 2 sons, and is now living with a 22-year-old woman in what appears to be a wholesome household. Ron has now been on parole under your supervision for eight months. He has a steady job at a reasonable living wage, and you are very pleased with his adjustment. Ron's 20-year-old son, Dennis, was just released from prison after serving out an entire one-year sentence. Ron has come to you for help because Dennis has moved into his apartment, is making no financial contribution, and has begun making sexual advances toward Ron's girlfriend. Ron is having trouble keeping his temper and fears he will soon beat up his son. You would be of most help to Ron if you were to

    (A) contact Dennis's parole officer and ask him to intervene.
    (B) tell Ron to throw his son out and change the locks.
    (C) meet with Dennis to hear his side of the story and help Dennis find a job and arrange for alternative living arrangements.
    (D) visit privately with the woman and tell her to choose between the men.

31. Carol, a single parent, was an abused child who as an adult became a child abuser. After serving a portion of a sentence for child abuse, Carol has been released into parole under your supervision. Carol's 3-year-old son and 14-year-old daughter are currently in foster care in the same foster home, and the foster mother has reported no problems. Carol wants her children back. You should

    (A) advise Carol to get married to prove that she plans to provide a stable home for her children.
    (B) tell Carol to go and pick up her children now that she is back.
    (C) request that child protective services return the children to their mother, who is now under your supervision.
    (D) guide Carol in preparing herself to support and make a good home for the children and help her with her presentation to child welfare services.

32. Fred has been in and out of prison for four of the past seven years. Each conviction has been on weapons charges, and each parole has come after exemplary behavior in prison. Fred has been released to parole once again. This is the first time he has been placed under your supervision. At your initial contact with Fred, you sense that he is an immature, insecure individual with few friends and that he tries to impress with bluster and a show of strength. There seems to be no structure to his life outside of prison. As Fred's new parole officer, you should

    (A) tell Fred in no uncertain terms that you will not tolerate weapons possession and demand that he turn over his weapons to you at once.
    (B) ask Fred for an analysis of his own self-destructive behavior.
    (C) work with Fred to plan a daily schedule and find him a therapy group to join.
    (D) suggest to Fred that if he finds prison life to be more satisfactory than life on the outside, he need only commit a minor parole violation to be returned to prison.

**33.** Susan, whose conviction and confinement were based upon the part she had played in a bank robbery, has been on parole under your supervision for more than three years. Throughout this time she has been hostile and unresponsive, though she has reported regularly according to schedule and has remained out of trouble as far as you are aware. Still, you have a nagging suspicion that Susan has not been rehabilitated and might easily be swayed by her companions at any time. Susan's term of parole has two more years to run. It might be wise for you to

(A) report to the parole board that Susan's rehabilitation is not proceeding well.
(B) discuss with your supervisor the possibility of assigning Susan to another parole officer, who might develop better rapport with her and make more progress.
(C) tell Susan that you do not like her attitude and demand that she "shape up."
(D) accelerate Susan's reporting schedule to keep closer tabs on her activities and companions.

**34.** George is an elderly man who was married to his wife for forty-three years. He has just been paroled under your supervision after serving the minimum portion of his sentence for suffocating his wife, who was terminally ill and suffering from a great deal of pain. George is quite obviously depressed and lonely and is clearly no threat to society, but you fear that he might well be suicidal. You would be most helpful and effective if you were to

(A) suggest to George that he join adult singles activities with an eye toward remarriage.
(B) send George to a psychiatrist.
(C) request around-the-clock suicide watch over George.
(D) encourage George to talk to you about his feelings and apprise him of sources and types of professional help that are available.

**35.** Dave has had a long history of drug abuse and has just been paroled from prison after serving a large portion of a long-term sentence for drug dealing. You have been assigned to be Dave's parole officer but have been unable to make contact with Dave, even to set up an initial meeting. You have photographs of Dave in your file, and you are quite certain that you have already seen him out on the streets in the company of drug dealers and quite possibly already in the act of selling. You should

(A) arrange with an undercover police officer to make a purchase and establish good cause for arrest.
(B) walk right up to the person you suspect and ask him if he is Dave.
(C) report your failure to make contact and your suspicions directly to the parole board.
(D) enlist another parole officer to walk past this person with you while you talk loudly about what happens to drug dealers who violate parole.

**36.** Laura, a 25-year-old, married woman who is HIV positive, is a parolee under your supervision. At a regularly scheduled meeting with you, Laura excitedly and happily tells you that she is pregnant. You are distressed at the prospects of the effects of a pregnancy on Laura's own health and at the thought of her giving birth to a baby who could be born HIV positive. You should

(A) keep your misgivings to yourself and congratulate Laura.
(B) insist that Laura have an abortion.
(C) urge Laura to immediately visit a full-service women's health facility.
(D) call Laura's husband and discuss your concerns with him.

**37.** Since his release on parole, Bob has been living with his girlfriend, Jane, who has a clean police record, though she is known to be a prostitute. Bob appears to spend most of his time at the racetrack. Bob attends night school classes, at which he is studying drafting and mechanical drawing. As Bob's parole officer, you would be well advised to

(A)   insist that Bob join Gamblers Anonymous as a condition for remaining on parole.
(B)   help Bob to get a job at the racetrack since he seems to like horses.
(C)   maintain close contact with Bob to be sure that Bob does not develop harmful relationships or habits.
(D)   tell Bob that he is jeopardizing his parole by living with a known prostitute.

**38.**   Richard, a smooth talker and one-time embezzler, has been under your parole supervision for some months. He has been living in the apartment of his older sister, her husband, and their 3 children. Richard is an intelligent young man and has been earning a living as a computer repairperson. He pays his sister for room and board. At his last two visits to your office, Richard has appeared in new, expensive clothing and has been wearing flashy jewelry. You call upon Richard's sister while he is not at home and learn that Richard has been giving lavish gifts to his sister and the children. None of the gifts has any markings that might implicate them as stolen goods, yet they are clearly beyond Richard's means. To learn how Richard is acquiring these items, you should

(A)   ask Richard directly.
(B)   accuse Richard of possession of stolen property and get an explanation.
(C)   check with Richard's employer to learn if Richard is under suspicion for any form of computer fraud.
(D)   tail Richard to see where he goes and what he does in his nonworking hours.

**39.**   Barbara has been living with her large extended family since her release from prison after serving part of a sentence for aggravated assault. She has been working as a short-order cook in a small diner and spending much time with a somewhat questionable, but not criminal, group of friends. Barbara complains to you that everyone in her household picks on her—they criticize her clothing, her manners, the hours she keeps, and her friends. Barbara would very much like to move out of the household, but you are aware that her earnings are not adequate for separate maintenance. Your most helpful act might be to

(A)   assist Barbara with an application for welfare to supplement her earnings.
(B)   call a family meeting to discuss with members of the household how to get along better with Barbara and how to help her to improve herself without being overbearing.
(C)   move Barbara into a women's shelter.
(D)   suggest that Barbara move in with one of her friends.

**40.**   Greg, a confirmed "out" homosexual, has been accused by a neighborhood teenage girl of raping her in an alleyway behind an apartment house. You have been working with Greg for a number of years and are quite certain that the accusation is erroneous. As Greg's parole officer, as guardian of his rights, and as a peace officer, you should

(A)   make a public pronouncement that Greg is gay and is therefore incapable of rape.
(B)   allow an investigation to proceed without your intervention in any way.
(C)   interview Greg to learn of his whereabouts and activities at the time of the alleged rape and to get his input concerning the accusation.
(D)   accuse the girl of bias crime in making a false accusation.

**41.**   The conditions of Bill's parole include a catalog of people with whom he is not permitted to associate, establishments he is prohibited from patronizing, and neighborhoods to which he may not go. Bill has not committed any crimes since his release on parole, but he has been seen with the people he is not allowed to congregate with in places that are off limits. As Bill's parole officer, how will you deal with Bill?

(A)   Immediately report Bill to the parole board as a parole violator.
(B)   Ask Bill why he is engaging in prohibited acts.
(C)   Remind Bill of his parole conditions and warn him that any future violation will land him back in prison.
(D)   Have Bill arrested at once.

**42.** Michael's involvement in organized crime, though in a low-level street position, earned him the prison sentence from which he has just been released on parole. While in prison, Michael cooperated with the authorities, passing on certain information privately. Michael was not privy to any vital secrets, but his cooperativeness did not go unnoticed by fellow prisoners. Michael is not a very bright or perceptive person, and you have reason to fear for his safety now that he is back in the community. It would be a good idea for you to

(A) personally watch Michael carefully.

(B) warn Michael to be careful about his associates and to be wary in his daily activities.

(C) meet with the leadership of the crime family and tell them to keep their hands off Michael.

(D) tell Michael to "disappear" from view until his former fellows in crime forget about him.

**43.** Donna's conviction and subsequent incarceration, from which she is now serving a part of the sentence under supervised parole, was on charges of grand larceny, forgery of negotiable instruments, and bank fraud. With no history of association with criminals or potential criminals, her parole is not conditioned by restriction of friendships. After a period as a model parolee, Donna has begun to avoid you. She frequently calls to postpone her meetings with you, claiming illness or important appointments. Donna's parents do not know her whereabouts, nor can you get any information from her old friends. A fellow parole officer, however, encountered Donna when he discovered a client of his in the garage of a motorcycle gang. Donna had been severely beaten up and her face had been badly slashed. She was clearly embarrassed to be seen. What should you do about Donna?

(A) Maintain telephone contact while discreetly waiting for her face to heal.

(B) Go to the garage and tell Donna that she must go home at once or face going back to prison.

(C) Take Donna to the nearest police station to lodge a complaint against the people who beat her up and slashed her face.

(D) Take Donna to a hospital for treatment of her injuries, then discuss her lifestyle.

**44.** Pete, an accomplished burglar, has now been under your supervision for ten months. He has been employed as a resident building superintendent throughout this time, and his employers have been satisfied with his performance of his assigned duties. But now items of value have begun to disappear from the premises of various tenants in the building. You should first

(A) enter Pete's apartment when he is not there and search for stolen items.

(B) discuss the problem with the building's management.

(C) confront Pete and ask for his analysis and explanation.

(D) turn this matter directly over to the police.

**45.** You have been working with Tom, who served time for armed robbery, for more than two years now. Tom has committed no parole violations or any other criminal acts of which you are aware, but you still do not feel comfortable with him. Tom's time is not fully accounted for, and his standard of living is better than you would expect. When questioned, Tom gives half answers and never looks you straight in the eye. Yet, he has given you no real cause for suspicion and certainly no accusations can be made. Still, you are responsible for protecting society. At this time you should

(A) meet privately with your supervisor to discuss your uneasiness and ask for advice.

(B) meet jointly with Tom and your supervisor to talk out your concerns and plan for Tom's future supervision.

(C) request that Tom's case be assigned to another parole officer.

(D) tell Tom that you do not trust him and that you are watching him with special care.

---

**Directions:** For questions 46–50, decide which of the two sentences presented is grammatically correct and mark its letter, (A) or (B), on your answer sheet.

---

46. (A) The work program planned for a prisoner when he or she enters prison is based on the employment possibilities in the community where they will probably return when released on parole.

    (B) The work program planned for a prisoner when he or she enters prison is based on the employment possibilities in the community to which the prisoner will probably return as a parolee.

47. (A) Reporting by the parolee to the parole officer is essential to good parole work.

    (B) Good parole work is when the parolee reports regularly to the parole officer.

48. (A) Being as how there are legal aspects to parole work, a parole officer must always have been exact as to dates and material recorded in the case records.

    (B) Because of the legal aspects of parole work, a parole officer must keep accurate case records with respect to dates and materials.

49. (A) A parole officer has got to be respectful of the religious convictions of the parolee.

    (B) Respect for the religious convictions of a parolee is necessary on the part of the parole officer.

50. (A) A parole officer who is off duty is not justified in ignoring a parolee engaged in a violation of parole.

    (B) An off-duty parole officer cannot justify himself by ignorance of a parolee which is engaging in the violating of their parole.

---

**Directions:** For questions 51–55, choose the sentence that is better punctuated and mark its letter, (A) or (B), on your answer sheet.

---

51. (A) A parolee who has violated the conditions of parole will be returned to prison at once.

    (B) A parolee, who has violated the conditions of parole, will be returned to prison at once.

52. (A) If police, courts and prisons functioned at the most effective level possible they would not substantially or permanently reduce crime, while conditions that breed crime persist.

    (B) If police, courts and prisons functioned at the most effective level possible, they would not substantially or permanently reduce crime while conditions that breed crime persist.

53. (A) There is a philosophy of law that requires that the individual's knowledge of right and wrong be the sole determinant of guilt.

    (B) There is a philosophy of law, that requires that the individuals' knowledge of right and wrong be the sole determinant of guilt.

54. (A) At a first interview, a parole officer might ask a parolee what kind of person he would like to be?

    (B) At a first interview, a parole officer might ask a parolee, "What kind of person would you like to be?"

55. (A) If a person with a physical addiction is detoxified "cold turkey," he might develop a life-threatening reaction like convulsions or a coma so detoxification should be under medical supervision.

    (B) If a person with physical addiction is detoxified "cold turkey," he might develop a life-threatening reaction, like convulsions or a coma, so detoxification should be under medical supervision.

---

**Directions:** For questions 56–60, choose the statement that expresses the information in the clearest way and mark its letter, (A) or (B), on your answer sheet.

---

56. (A) The personnel officer said that he expected to employ the parolee who had the training enough so that he can do the work.

    (B) The personnel officer said that he might employ the parolee who was trained to do the work.

57. (A) This report concerns the number of cases closed by parole officers in Western County which are more than a year old.

    (B) This report concerns the number of cases more than a year old, which were closed by parole officers in Western County.

58. (A) The person who is waiting in my office has a three o'clock appointment.

    (B) That person is a three o'clock appointment who is waiting in my office for me.

59. (A) We are hoping to expand parole services, so we are looking for a program which will be more economical to operate and which will be easy to administer.

    (B) We are hoping to expand parole services, so we are looking for a program more economical to operate and which will be easy to administer.

60. (A) Alice told her parole officer that her manager, Lisa, said that she was likely to be laid off from her job in the cutbacks due next month.

    (B) Alice told her parole officer that her manager, Lisa, said that Alice was likely to be laid off from her job in the cutbacks due next month.

---

**Directions:** Questions 61–65 consist of a few very short sentences followed by two sentences that combine the information into a single sentence. Choose the single sentence, (A) or (B), that conveys the information most clearly and accurately and mark it on your answer sheet.

---

61. The hit-and-run driver was sorry he had paralyzed the child. He got out of prison. He took money to the family.

    (A) When the hit-and-run driver paralyzed the child he was sorry and so he took money to the family when he got out of prison.

    (B) When the hit-and-run driver got out of prison, he took money to the family of the child who he had paralyzed.

62. The parole officer told Peggy that she was not to leave the state without permission. Peggy went to her cousin's wedding in a neighboring state. The parole officer granted permission.

   (A) Peggy went to her cousin's wedding in a neighboring state after requesting and receiving permission from her parole officer.

   (B) Peggy asked her parole officer for permission to go to her cousin's wedding in a neighboring state and received it and went.

63. The paroled child molester was told to stay away from children. He hung around the schoolyard. He violated his parole. Parole violation leads to a return to prison.

   (A) The child molester violated his parole by hanging around the schoolyard and was returned to prison.

   (B) The parole violator went back to prison after he hung around the schoolyard because he was a child molester who was told to stay away from children.

64. This state has stiff penalties for narcotics violations. There are mandatory prison sentences. Repeat offenders may never be paroled.

   (A) Repeat narcotics offenders may never be paroled because there are stiff penalties and mandatory prison sentences for violations in this state.

   (B) Because of this state's stiff penalties for narcotics violations, repeat offenders may face mandatory prison sentences with no chance for parole.

65. Social service agencies exist to help people in need. No one should feel ashamed to ask for assistance.

   (A) A person who needs assistance should request that assistance from the social service agency that was established to meet that need.

   (B) A person who needs help should ask for it from a social service agency because that is what it is for and the person should not be ashamed.

# MODEL EXAMINATION 1: ANSWERS AND EXPLANATIONS

## ANSWERS

| | | | | | | | | | |
|---|---|---|---|---|---|---|---|---|---|
| 1. | C | 14. | C | 27. | A | 40. | C | 53. | A |
| 2. | B | 15. | A | 28. | D | 41. | C | 54. | B |
| 3. | C | 16. | D | 29. | A | 42. | B | 55. | B |
| 4. | B | 17. | B | 30. | A | 43. | D | 56. | B |
| 5. | D | 18. | C | 31. | D | 44. | C | 57. | B |
| 6. | D | 19. | D | 32. | C | 45. | D | 58. | A |
| 7. | D | 20. | B | 33. | D | 46. | B | 59. | A |
| 8. | A | 21. | C | 34. | D | 47. | A | 60. | B |
| 9. | B | 22. | A | 35. | B | 48. | B | 61. | B |
| 10. | C | 23. | C | 36. | C | 49. | B | 62. | A |
| 11. | D | 24. | B | 37. | C | 50. | A | 63. | A |
| 12. | B | 25. | A | 38. | A | 51. | A | 64. | B |
| 13. | D | 26. | D | 39. | A | 52. | B | 65. | A |

## EXPLANATIONS

1. **The correct answer is (C).** The better the parolee is prepared for parole, the more successful the parole will be.
2. **The correct answer is (B).** Probation is a sentence imposed by the court.
3. **The correct answer is (C).** As with all sentences, the judge decides if probation will be granted.
4. **The correct answer is (B).** The parole officer must know where the parolee is at all times; therefore, should the parolee decide to leave the state, the parole officer must be notified.
5. **The correct answer is (C).** The parole officer cannot be the confidante of the parolee. This could compromise his or her role or lead to corruption.
6. **The correct answer is (D).** A halfway house provides a transition between prison and civilian society. It allows the parolee to ease back into civilian society.
7. **The correct answer is (D).** The parole officer recommended revocation as soon as the new information regarding the criminality of the parolee came to light.
8. **The correct answer is (A).** All too often it is one's peer group that encourages continued acts of crime.
9. **The correct answer is (B).** Any positive activity that the parolee can become involved in is a good suggestion to make.
10. **The correct answer is (C).** Probation is not a right of any convicted defendant, it is a privilege granted by a judge.
11. **The correct answer is (D).** With the exception of some standard conditions, parole can be most successful when it is individualized for the offender.
12. **The correct answer is (B).** Much of what a parole officer does is crisis control. The parole officer must learn to deal with situations as they are presented rather than necessarily following the day's calendar.

13. **The correct answer is (D).** The parole officer should try, at least once, to see if there is any way to engage the parolee.

14. **The correct answer is (C).** Parolees must conform to the conditions of parole and need to be reminded of these conditions on a regular basis.

15. **The correct answer is (A).** Anything that can help parolees maintain a crime-free lifestyle should be tried by the parole officer. Group work often can be beneficial to those with problems.

16. **The correct answer is (D).** The imposition of punishment is the sentence.

17. **The correct answer is (B).** Part of parole work is guiding parolees into areas that may keep them from returning to their criminal lifestyles. The parole officer should do everything he or she can to facilitate this.

18. **The correct answer is (C).** Parole officers must not become too personal with their parolees.

19. **The correct answer is (D).** The lending of money violates the professionalism that must be maintained.

20. **The correct answer is (B).** Boston was the home of John Augustus, who introduced probation.

21. **The correct answer is (C).** For parole to have a greater chance of success, the best possible match between parole officer and parolee should be made. Suggesting this to your supervisor is a good idea.

22. **The correct answer is (A).** This allows John to make some decisions on his own.

23. **The correct answer is (C).** This allows John to be a role model for his child and engage in positive activities that he apparently enjoys.

24. **The correct answer is (B).** You need to do some street work to determine what happened so that you can formulate a plan of action.

25. **The correct answer is (A).** You are gathering information from the street and you can use this information in later discussions with John.

26. **The correct answer is (D).** In this case you are serving as a resource broker, making sure that John is accessing the right agency to assist him. You are also demonstrating to John the correct way to handle such a situation.

27. **The correct answer is (A).** You need to involve the other parole officer so that the men see a unified approach to the problems.

28. **The correct answer is (D).** Mary is committing a violation; she should be arrested.

29. **The correct answer is (A).** Given that many addicts relapse and assuming this is the first time relapse has occurred, taking Lonnie to detoxification is consistent with good parole practice.

30. **The correct answer is (A).** Here again, you need to inform the other parole officer. A conference with the son is in order, and, if necessary, a unified approach should be taken.

31. **The correct answer is (D).** You are guiding Carol into a noncriminal lifestyle and following the proper procedures for her to regain her children.

32. **The correct answer is (C).** This is an attempt to find a plan of action for Fred to keep him from returning to prison.

33. **The correct answer is (D).** This will give you a better idea if, indeed, there is something nefarious going on with Susan.

34. **The correct answer is (D).** In this case you are serving as a resource broker by finding out what's going on and referring George to the proper individual.

35. **The correct answer is (B).** You need to make contact with Dave and announce yourself. Remember officer safety.

36. **The correct answer is (C).** This not only protects the baby but Laura as well.

37. **The correct answer is (C).** This is a case where you need to remain aware and informed so you can intervene in a timely manner if necessary.

38. **The correct answer is (A).** The direct approach is almost always the best approach.

39. **The correct answer is (A).** In this case you are serving as a resource broker by getting Barbara in touch with those who might be able to help her in her quest for a crime-free lifestyle.
40. **The correct answer is (C).** Based on your knowledge of the parolee, the direct approach is the best.
41. **The correct answer is (C).** Parolees must be constantly reminded of their conditions.
42. **The correct answer is (B).** It is important to make sure that you protect Michael as best you can.
43. **The correct answer is (D).** This allows you to let Donna know you're on her side, but you will not tolerate her current dangerous lifestyle.
44. **The correct answer is (C).** The direct approach is usually best.
45. **The correct answer is (D).** Again, the direct approach here is best. Tom must know he is being watched.
46. **The correct answer is (B).** The antecedent is "he or she," which is singular. Thus the pronoun "they" is incorrect.
47. **The correct answer is (A).** "Is when" in choice (B) is an illogical construction.
48. **The correct answer is (B).** "Being as how" in choice (A) is wordy and inexact.
49. **The correct answer is (B).** "Has got" in choice (A) is substandard usage.
50. **The correct answer is (A).** "Which is" in choice (B) cannot refer to a person.
51. **The correct answer is (A).** Restrictive clauses are not set off by commas.
52. **The correct answer is (B).** An introductory dependent clause must be followed by a comma.
53. **The correct answer is (A).** No comma is needed to introduce an adjectival modifying clause.
54. **The correct answer is (B).** In choice (A), a question mark is used incorrectly to punctuate an indirect question. The entire sentence is not a question.
55. **The correct answer is (B).** A comma is needed before a coordinating conjunction introducing an independent clause.
56. **The correct answer is (B).** This choice is clearer and less wordy than choice (A).
57. **The correct answer is (B).** In choice (A), the modifier "which are more than a year old" is separated from the word it modifies ("cases").
58. **The correct answer is (A).** Choice (B) is illogical. A person cannot be an appointment.
59. **The correct answer is (B).** Choice (A) is unnecessarily wordy.
60. **The correct answer is (B).** In choice (A), "she" is ambiguous, as "she" could refer to Alice or Lisa.
61. **The correct answer is (B).** Choice (A) confuses the time sequence.
62. **The correct answer is (A).** Choice (B) is unnecessarily wordy.
63. **The correct answer is (A).** This choice is more concrete and clearly states the logical relationship of ideas in the sentence.
64. **The correct answer is (B).** This choice is more concise and places the main idea in an independent clause to emphasize it.
65. **The correct answer is (A).** This choice is more concise.

# MODEL EXAMINATION 2: ANSWER SHEET

1. Ⓐ Ⓑ Ⓒ Ⓓ    21. Ⓐ Ⓑ Ⓒ Ⓓ    41. Ⓐ Ⓑ Ⓒ Ⓓ    61. Ⓐ Ⓑ Ⓒ Ⓓ

2. Ⓐ Ⓑ Ⓒ Ⓓ    22. Ⓐ Ⓑ Ⓒ Ⓓ    42. Ⓐ Ⓑ Ⓒ Ⓓ    62. Ⓐ Ⓑ Ⓒ Ⓓ

3. Ⓐ Ⓑ Ⓒ Ⓓ    23. Ⓐ Ⓑ Ⓒ Ⓓ    43. Ⓐ Ⓑ Ⓒ Ⓓ    63. Ⓐ Ⓑ Ⓒ Ⓓ

4. Ⓐ Ⓑ Ⓒ Ⓓ    24. Ⓐ Ⓑ Ⓒ Ⓓ    44. Ⓐ Ⓑ Ⓒ Ⓓ    64. Ⓐ Ⓑ Ⓒ Ⓓ

5. Ⓐ Ⓑ Ⓒ Ⓓ    25. Ⓐ Ⓑ Ⓒ Ⓓ    45. Ⓐ Ⓑ Ⓒ Ⓓ    65. Ⓐ Ⓑ Ⓒ Ⓓ

6. Ⓐ Ⓑ Ⓒ Ⓓ    26. Ⓐ Ⓑ Ⓒ Ⓓ    46. Ⓐ Ⓑ Ⓒ Ⓓ    66. Ⓐ Ⓑ Ⓒ Ⓓ

7. Ⓐ Ⓑ Ⓒ Ⓓ    27. Ⓐ Ⓑ Ⓒ Ⓓ    47. Ⓐ Ⓑ Ⓒ Ⓓ    67. Ⓐ Ⓑ Ⓒ Ⓓ

8. Ⓐ Ⓑ Ⓒ Ⓓ    28. Ⓐ Ⓑ Ⓒ Ⓓ    48. Ⓐ Ⓑ Ⓒ Ⓓ    68. Ⓐ Ⓑ Ⓒ Ⓓ

9. Ⓐ Ⓑ Ⓒ Ⓓ    29. Ⓐ Ⓑ Ⓒ Ⓓ    49. Ⓐ Ⓑ Ⓒ Ⓓ    69. Ⓐ Ⓑ Ⓒ Ⓓ

10. Ⓐ Ⓑ Ⓒ Ⓓ    30. Ⓐ Ⓑ Ⓒ Ⓓ    50. Ⓐ Ⓑ Ⓒ Ⓓ    70. Ⓐ Ⓑ Ⓒ Ⓓ

11. Ⓐ Ⓑ Ⓒ Ⓓ    31. Ⓐ Ⓑ Ⓒ Ⓓ    51. Ⓐ Ⓑ Ⓒ Ⓓ

12. Ⓐ Ⓑ Ⓒ Ⓓ    32. Ⓐ Ⓑ Ⓒ Ⓓ    52. Ⓐ Ⓑ Ⓒ Ⓓ

13. Ⓐ Ⓑ Ⓒ Ⓓ    33. Ⓐ Ⓑ Ⓒ Ⓓ    53. Ⓐ Ⓑ Ⓒ Ⓓ

14. Ⓐ Ⓑ Ⓒ Ⓓ    34. Ⓐ Ⓑ Ⓒ Ⓓ    54. Ⓐ Ⓑ Ⓒ Ⓓ

15. Ⓐ Ⓑ Ⓒ Ⓓ    35. Ⓐ Ⓑ Ⓒ Ⓓ    55. Ⓐ Ⓑ Ⓒ Ⓓ

16. Ⓐ Ⓑ Ⓒ Ⓓ    36. Ⓐ Ⓑ Ⓒ Ⓓ    56. Ⓐ Ⓑ Ⓒ Ⓓ

17. Ⓐ Ⓑ Ⓒ Ⓓ    37. Ⓐ Ⓑ Ⓒ Ⓓ    57. Ⓐ Ⓑ Ⓒ Ⓓ

18. Ⓐ Ⓑ Ⓒ Ⓓ    38. Ⓐ Ⓑ Ⓒ Ⓓ    58. Ⓐ Ⓑ Ⓒ Ⓓ

19. Ⓐ Ⓑ Ⓒ Ⓓ    39. Ⓐ Ⓑ Ⓒ Ⓓ    59. Ⓐ Ⓑ Ⓒ Ⓓ

20. Ⓐ Ⓑ Ⓒ Ⓓ    40. Ⓐ Ⓑ Ⓒ Ⓓ    60. Ⓐ Ⓑ Ⓒ Ⓓ

# MODEL EXAMINATION 2: PROBATION OFFICER

## 4 HOURS; 70 QUESTIONS

**Directions:** Each question has four suggested answers, lettered (A), (B), (C), and (D). Decide which one is the best answer and darken on your answer sheet the space that corresponds with your answer choice.

1. The "Father of Probation" is
   - (A) Z.R. Brockway.
   - (B) Alexander Maconochie.
   - (C) John Augustus.
   - (D) Sir Walter Crofton.

2. Of the following, the fundamental theory of probation rests most nearly on
   - (A) the fear of punishment.
   - (B) exercise by the court of its power of compulsion.
   - (C) a promise by the offender to better his or her ways.
   - (D) the frequency of recidivism.

3. Which of the following is *not* a purpose of probation?
   - (A) Keeping offenders out of jail and prison
   - (B) Reducing overcrowding
   - (C) Labeling offenders
   - (D) Reintegration of the offender into society

4. Of the following statements, the one that is most accurate with respect to the surveillance of a probationer by a probation officer is that
   - (A) some degree of surveillance lies behind many probation supervision contacts.
   - (B) surveillance is unnecessary if the probation officer is a skilled social case worker.
   - (C) surveillance and the social case work method are mutually exclusive.
   - (D) it is axiomatic that a fully trained probation staff will find the use of surveillance practically unnecessary.

5. A probation officer encountering a reference to "prognosis" in a case report would most accurately associate the term with
   - (A) a causal relationship.
   - (B) psychosis.
   - (C) a congenital disease.
   - (D) a forecast.

6. Probation is most likely to be granted to
   - (A) violent offenders.
   - (B) first-time offenders.
   - (C) chronic offenders.
   - (D) whoever the judge so deems.

7. In reporting on a person who thinks he sees objects that are not present and may not be real, the probation officer should describe such an individual as having
   - (A) claustrophobia.
   - (B) hypochondria.
   - (C) hallucinations.
   - (D) paranoia.

8. The report most valuable in assessing whether an offender will be granted probation is

    (A) the Pre-sentence Investigation.
    (B) the Victim Impact Statement.
    (C) the Parole Revocation Report.
    (D) the Probation Officer's Report.

9. When interviewing an individual with a reputation for being a conciliatory person, the probation officer should most reasonably expect to find that the individual

    (A) is flippantly smooth.
    (B) has an appeasing manner.
    (C) is fickle.
    (D) has an uncontrollable temper.

10. A juvenile whose veracity is frequently doubted is best described as

    (A) a fabricator.
    (B) an alien.
    (C) born out of wedlock.
    (D) underprivileged.

11. An adolescent who is habitually discontented could best be described as

    (A) invidious.
    (B) plaintive.
    (C) quibbling.
    (D) captious.

12. The suspension of all legal proceedings contingent on the accused fulfilling certain terms and conditions is called

    (A) intensive supervised probation.
    (B) parole.
    (C) diversion.
    (D) aftercare.

13. A more structured form of probation with fewer cases per probation officer and more frequent contact between the probation officer and the probationer is known as

    (A) intensive supervised probation.
    (B) parole.
    (C) diversion.
    (D) aftercare.

14. The type of recording that promotes "gestalt" rather than piecemeal thinking is

    (A) chronological recording.
    (B) summarized recording.
    (C) periodic recording.
    (D) topical recording.

15. The person whose duty it is to manage the estate of a minor or of an incompetent is called the

    (A) executor.
    (B) probate officer.
    (C) *amicus curiae.*
    (D) guardian.

16. An order for a witness to appear in court is called

    (A) a subpoena.
    (B) an injunction.

(C)   a mandamus.

(D)   *res judicata.*

17. The rules and regulations the offender must follow while on probation are referred to as

    (A)   the rules and regulations.

    (B)   the pains of probation.

    (C)   the terms and conditions of probation.

    (D)   none of the above.

18. The impact of mental disease upon society is most adequately indicated by

    (A)   its responsibility for sex crimes and delinquency.

    (B)   the phenomenal growth of developmental disability in the United States.

    (C)   the increasing number of deaths resulting from it.

    (D)   the burden of its disabling effects on the community.

19. A deficiency disease is a disorder caused by

    (A)   a deficiency of medical aid.

    (B)   a diet lacking certain vitamins or minerals.

    (C)   a lack of proper rest and relaxation.

    (D)   an insufficient quantity of sugar in the diet.

20. Delinquency on the part of a child is believed to result primarily from

    (A)   emotional and personality maladjustments.

    (B)   environmental handicaps.

    (C)   physical disability.

    (D)   sociological factors.

21. In determining whether or not an offender should be placed on probation, the most important factor for the probation officer to consider is the

    (A)   attitude of the community.

    (B)   personality of the offender.

    (C)   offense.

    (D)   attitude of the court.

22. A probation officer who has an objective attitude in social research would

    (A)   deal only with concrete reality rather than with abstract ideas.

    (B)   use only evidence favorable to the objective.

    (C)   object to all new hypotheses.

    (D)   follow the evidence regardless of personal interests.

23. In collecting social evidence from personnel in the public school system of the city of New York, a probation officer would expect to find that which of the following would make the best social witness?

    (A)   Principal of the school at which the offender was a pupil

    (B)   Superintendent of schools

    (C)   Teacher who is able to individualize pupils

    (D)   Truant officer

24. Some researchers have found that probation is often more strict and requires more of the offender than does

    (A)   diversion.

    (B)   imprisonment.

    (C)   parole.

    (D)   the judge.

25. Progressively minded probation officers agree that the type of social treatment given a delinquent should be determined primarily by the
    (A) nature of the offense committed.
    (B) type and variety of social problems causing the delinquency.
    (C) size of the probation officer's caseload.
    (D) plan recommended by the judge.

26. From a psychological point of view, delinquency can most accurately be considered as
    (A) a definite congenital trait that causes inability to adjust to society.
    (B) overt acts that come into conflict with natural instincts.
    (C) a symptom of a deeper maladjustment that manifests itself in an inability to adjust to society.
    (D) none of the above.

27. The pre-sentence investigation report should be
    (A) factual.
    (B) relative.
    (C) objective.
    (D) all of the above.

28. The belief that crime can be prevented best by enforcing laws rigidly is based on the theory that
    (A) people cannot continue criminal careers as freely during periods of incarceration.
    (B) suppression leads to sublimation.
    (C) punishment is the most effective deterrent known against lawbreakers.
    (D) multiplicity of laws causes confusion in their attempted enforcement.

29. Studies of penology reveal that punishment has
    (A) seldom served as a crime deterrent.
    (B) successfully served as a crime deterrent.
    (C) served as a crime deterrent only in cases of larceny.
    (D) not served as a crime deterrent because the penalties inflicted have been too moderate.

30. In the classifications of crime listed below, the one in which the probation officer would expect to find the highest proportion of arrests of females would be recorded in uniform crime reports under the heading of
    (A) assault.
    (B) automobile theft.
    (C) burglary.
    (D) rape.

31. A national magazine conducting a long-term feature devoted to techniques of crime prevention regularly prints editorial contributions from such people as ex-U.S. presidents, mayors, congressmen, governors, and civil court judges. A probation officer would most logically conclude from this example that
    (A) there is as yet a great deal of inconclusive thinking on the causes of crime and the treatment of those causes.
    (B) public officials are better judges of the effectiveness of crime prevention techniques than people not in the public service.
    (C) the experiences of sociologists and psychiatrists have been wholly negative in the field of crime prevention.
    (D) the best approach to crime prevention is that which encompasses the activities of local, state, and federal officials of every type.

32. The primary reason for recording the results of a probation investigation is that
    (A) it will impress the probation officer with its importance.
    (B) the written record is more impressive and credible than an oral report.
    (C) the reader exerts a minimum of effort in comprehending and digesting the information.
    (D) the data obtained may be made uniformly and permanently available.

33. According to studies conducted on methods of questioning during intake procedure by interviewers such as probation officers, a truthful statement of fact is least easily obtained from the person being questioned if he or she is
    (A) allowed to use an uninterrupted narrative form of expression.
    (B) cross-examined frequently by the person doing the interviewing.
    (C) encouraged to present facts in chronological order.
    (D) interrupted as seldom as possible.

34. The chief concern of the pre-sentence investigation in a criminal court should be, according to the views expressed by the most noted researchers in the field of probation,
    (A) to speed up the court procedures so that more cases can be handled expeditiously.
    (B) to discover the immediate cause of the offender's being brought before the court.
    (C) to determine whether the person brought before the court is innocent or guilty of the charges lodged against him or her.
    (D) to explore all the social factors that have a bearing on the personality and behavior of the offender.

35. To a probation officer, the ultimate objective of a pre-sentence investigation is
    (A) knowledge that will ensure the punishment of the offender if a crime has been committed.
    (B) knowledge that will protect society from the criminal.
    (C) understanding of the offender from the point of view of possible reintegration as a self-sufficient and permanently useful member of society.
    (D) understanding of the offender that will explain why he or she committed the crime and will enable society to guard against that sort of criminal activity.

36. Case study procedure differs from statistical procedure most markedly in that
    (A) the basis for statistical study is observation.
    (B) statistical procedure can be divided into inventory, analysis, and inference.
    (C) incorrect data in statistical procedure may result in an incomplete analysis.
    (D) statistical procedure has a broad numerical base, making restriction of subjects necessary.

37. Suppose that a good probation department is identified by each of the features listed below. If you, a probation officer, were studying the organization of such an agency, you would expect to find its correctional program least affected by the removal of its
    (A) enlightened policies.
    (B) trained and competent personnel.
    (C) suitable equipment and supplies with which to have its work done.
    (D) advisory board of the most notable penologists in the country.

38. Which of the following best expresses one of the fundamental foundations of the probation system?
    (A) A desire to reward the first offender in order to encourage good conduct
    (B) A desire to protect society by facilitating the readjustment of the probationer
    (C) An economy measure designed to save the government the cost of supporting prisoners in institutions
    (D) A growing attitude of leniency toward offenders

39. From the point of view of the probation officer, to integrate children presenting symptoms of mild behavior disorder into normal groups would be

   (A) too radical a proposal; it has never been tried successfully.
   (B) impracticable; participation of problem children would jeopardize the program of the other children in the group.
   (C) undesirable; children otherwise emotionally stable would tend to become corrupted.
   (D) beneficial; it would expose the problem children to the advantageous effect of group activity with children possessing conforming behavior patterns.

40. The pretrial detention of juveniles has been upheld by the U.S. Supreme Court in

   (A) *In Re Gault.*
   (B) *Schall v. Martin.*
   (C) *Fare v. Michael C.*
   (D) It has not been upheld.

41. The case records of a social agency, such as a probation department, should be kept confidential chiefly because

   (A) they record an intimate, personal relationship in which the client may have yielded innermost thoughts to the probation office.
   (B) the agency must avoid charges of false statements or false accusations.
   (C) the probation officer has given a promise of confidence to sources of information.
   (D) the probation record is often incomplete and scrutiny by outsiders may reveal incompetence.

42. A juvenile delinquent is defined as

   (A) someone under the age of 18 who has committed an act that would be a crime if committed by an adult.
   (B) someone who has committed an act that applies only to juveniles.
   (C) someone who has been abandoned by his or her parent(s) or legal guardian(s).
   (D) habitual disobedience to the reasonable and lawful directives of a parent or guardian.

43. Current interest in child guidance clinics was developed because of an increasing belief that

   (A) at least one tenth of the nation's youth is destined to end up in prison if not given systematic guidance.
   (B) children should be treated as miniature adults.
   (C) many of the emotional and mental disabilities of later life result from unfortunate childhood experiences.
   (D) the best interests of the nation require standardization of each child's education.

44. A broken home may be defined as one marked by the absence of one or both parents as a result of death, divorce, separation, or desertion. In discussing with workers the effects of a broken home, the supervisor should point out that

   (A) practically all broken homes will foster delinquency of one kind or another.
   (B) girls, particularly those under 10 years of age, are less likely to be affected by the loss of a parent than boys.
   (C) such family disintegration is not likely to play an important role for a child if it occurs prior to the age of 10.
   (D) the effects upon the child usually depend upon the general structural characteristics of the home.

*Question 45 is based on the following table.*

| I.Q. | Number of Offenders | Number of Offenses | Offenses Per Offender |
|---|---|---|---|
| 61–80 | 125 | 338 | 2.7 |
| 81–100 | 160 | 448 | 2.8 |
| 101 and over | 75 | 217 | 2.9 |

**45.** During a period of probation in which records were kept for 360 children 14 to 18 years of age, probation officers found that the group committed certain offenses, as shown in the preceding table. According to the data,

(A) the more intelligent offenders are no more law-abiding than, and perhaps not so law-abiding as, the less intelligent offenders.

(B) brighter offenders present no more difficult problems than less intelligent offenders.

(C) the majority of this probation group is found to be above the average in intelligence of a normal group of young persons within this age range.

(D) the relationship between the effectiveness of probation work and the number of offenders is in inverse ratio.

**46.** "The fundamental desires for food, shelter, family, and approval, and their accompanying instinctive forms of behavior, are among the most important forces in human life because they are essential to and directly connected with the preservation and welfare of the individual as well as of the race." According to this statement,

(A) as long as human beings are permitted to act instinctively, they will act wisely.

(B) the instinct for self-preservation makes the individual consider personal welfare rather than that of others.

(C) racial and individual welfare depend upon the fundamental desires.

(D) the preservation of the race demands that instinctive behavior be modified.

**47.** "The growth of our cities, the increasing tendency to move from one part of the country to another, and the existence of people of different cultures in the neighborhood have together made it increasingly difficult to secure group recreation as part of informal family and neighborhood life." According to this statement,

(A) the breaking up of family and neighborhood ties discourages new family and neighborhood group recreation.

(B) neighborhood recreation no longer forms a significant part of the larger community.

(C) the growth of cities crowds out the development of all recreational activities.

(D) non-English-speaking people do not accept new activities easily.

**48.** "Sublimation consists of directing some inner urge, arising from a lower psychological level, into some channel of interest on a higher psychological level. Pugnaciousness, for example, is directed into some athletic activity involving combat, such as football or boxing, where rules of fair play and the ethics of the game lift the destructive urge for combat into a constructive experience and offer opportunities for the development of character and personality." According to this statement,

(A) the manner of self-expression may be directed into constructive activities.

(B) athletic activities such as football and boxing are destructive of character.

(C) all conscious behavior on high psychological levels indicates the process of sublimation.

(D) the rules of fair play are inconsistent with pugnaciousness.

49. The interest and curiosity that a child shows in sex matters and activities should be regarded by the probation officer as

    (A) a normal interest to be dealt with as one deals with interest in other subjects.
    (B) something to be disregarded on the assumption that the child will forget about the problem.
    (C) something to be satisfied by some mythical explanation until the child is old enough to be initiated into the mystery involved.
    (D) something to be suppressed by threat of punishment.

50. When a gang is brought before the court for stealing, the probation officer, in making the pre-sentence investigation, should

    (A) deal unofficially with the younger ones and officially with the older members of the gang.
    (B) organize a group of businesspeople to take an interest in the members of the gang.
    (C) recommend that the ringleaders be committed to a child welfare institution and that the others be placed on probation.
    (D) study each member of the gang and deal with each according to individual situation.

51. Which of the following statements can most conceivably be characterized as true?

    (A) Generally speaking, the younger a person is, the less easily he or she can be influenced by suggestion.
    (B) If a probation officer has sufficient technical knowledge of his or her duties, it is not necessary for him or her to exercise tact in dealing with criminal offenders.
    (C) A probation officer should reject entirely hearsay evidence in making a social diagnosis of a case.
    (D) One of the characteristics of adolescence is a feeling in the child that he or she is misunderstood.

52. "Parental attitudes that offer emotional security to the child are good." This statement best expresses the notion that

    (A) emotionally secure children do not have feelings of aggression.
    (B) children should not be held accountable for their actions.
    (C) inadequate parental attitudes include those that do not give the child feelings of belonging and freedom for experience.
    (D) a family in which there is economic dependence cannot be good for the child.

53. Which of the following statements relating to the case recording function in a probation office is the least accurate?

    (A) Case recording in a probation office places emphasis on areas different from those in a private case work agency.
    (B) Since the probation record may be used in court, it requires a higher degree of accuracy than other social agency records.
    (C) Probation records are an extension of the records of the clerk of the court and are available for perusal by the public.
    (D) A probation case record may be used as evidence.

54. Rehabilitation of an offender who has presented serious problems can probably be effected best by the probation officer who

    (A) believes that the behavior is caused by maladjustment and tries to meet the offender's needs accordingly.
    (B) is kind and just but punishes the offender for every lapse of good conduct.
    (C) keeps the offender under constant observation, making him or her conscious of behavior deviations.
    (D) overlooks minor transgressions and rewards the offender for good behavior.

55. Making an adjustment upon release under probation or parole, as the case may be, is believed by court workers to be easier for the

    (A) probationer because the delayed action awaiting release from probation serves to keep him or her aware of the necessity of continuing normal life patterns.

    (B) parolee because he or she is able to idealize the security of the penitentiary in his or her recent experience.

    (C) probationer because he or she has not been removed from normal surroundings.

    (D) parolee because frequent visits by family members and close friends during imprisonment provide periodic psychologically uplifting experiences.

56. In the granting of probation to a war veteran, the question of leniency

    (A) should not enter because greater leniency to the veteran would give him or her an unfair advantage over the nonveteran facing the bar with equal guilt.

    (B) should enter because the veteran has made a universally acknowledged contribution to the protection of our society and deserves the protection of his or her own interests in return.

    (C) should not enter because other important considerations involved in the probation process are the protection of society and the furthering of the best interests of the individual.

    (D) should enter because the military experiences of the veteran may have contributed to his or her being more irresponsible mentally than the nonveteran.

57. The pre-sentence investigation is concerned basically with

    (A) information regarding the offender.

    (B) information regarding the crime.

    (C) recommendations regarding the conditions of probation.

    (D) all of the above.

*Questions 58–60 are based on the facts given in the following case history.*

**Name:** Tom Jones
**Age:** 13
**IQ:** 111
Boy is in 6th grade, schoolwork poor, citizenship fair. He does not constitute a serious behavior problem in school but is often truant.

**Relatives**

Mother, age 33, divorced father of boy and later remarried. Stepfather and boy did not get along. Stepfather is now out of the home and his whereabouts unknown. Mother is employed in a beauty parlor. No other income in family. Woman's mother, age 70, keeps house and looks after boy and his younger sister. Grandmother has absolutely no control over boy.

Sister is 9 years of age, frail, and because of this fact has been spoiled.

Boy is undersized, thin, nervous, irritable, and emotional. He likes to read and reads well. Likes "Wild West" and adventure stories. Boy seems fond of his mother. Family lives in a very poor neighborhood.

The mother has an older sister, married and living on a ranch in Canada. The couple is reported to be fairly well to do and have no children. Their ranch is located in a remote area. The boy's father is remarried and living in Seattle. He has two children by his last marriage. Mother is weak and easygoing, passionately fond of both of her children, but inclined to scold them one minute and pet them the next.

**Reason Before Court**

Boy has been involved with a group of older boys in a series of petty thefts. Was gone from home for two days at one time and when he returned, told a tale of being kidnapped, which was later found to be entirely imaginary.

**58.** According to the facts given in the preceding case history, the most applicable of the following interpretations for the probation officer to make is

(A) economic factors play a minor part in this case.
(B) the boy's taste in reading may indicate a tendency toward instability.
(C) removal of the family to a better neighborhood may solve this problem.
(D) this is a case for the school authorities to handle because of the truancy involved.

**59.** Which of the following conclusions is least likely to be reached in a probation report on this case?

(A) The boy's love of adventure and excitement probably contributes to his behavior problem.
(B) Since the mother lacks stability of character, it is best to take both children from her.
(C) The kidnapping tale, later found to be false, would indicate the possibility of a serious mental defect in the boy.
(D) The security of the aunt and uncle's home would be a determining factor in any plan to place the boy with them.

**60.** Which of the following findings is least likely to be approved by an experienced probation officer?

(A) The boy can be placed and continued on probation beyond his 18th birthday.
(B) Placement in an "ungraded" class in school might greatly benefit this boy.
(C) This family should be referred to a welfare agency in order that the family budget may be supplemented.
(D) Greater affection bestowed on the little sister and the consequent jealousy of the boy is probably one of the causes of delinquency.

**61.** "Professional relationships are not just friendly associations. Contact is not for the sake of contact." The essential purpose of relationship in case work is to

(A) create an atmosphere in which the client feels accepted and believes that his or her needs are recognized.
(B) develop a transference situation that will establish rapport between the client and the worker.
(C) help the client recognize that all people have problems, including the worker, and that the problems are not as serious as he or she believes.
(D) make the client feel that he or she has a friend to whom he or she can speak freely about problems.

**62.** Which of the following statements concerning the characteristics of probation case records is the least accurate?

(A) The best records not only contain objective facts, but also are designed to bring out diagnostic thinking and treatment as well.
(B) Records may be short or long, but they must be easily understood.
(C) In a professional record, interpretation of the meaning of the facts is as important as reporting the facts.
(D) Case records must adhere to a fixed format in order to secure uniformity of service.

**63.** Which of the following should not be included in a diagnostic summary of a probationer?

(A) A listing of the causal factors so far as known
(B) A definition of the difficulties
(C) A final diagnosis
(D) An enumeration of assets and liabilities to be considered in treatment

64. Of the following, the most common weakness in many pre-sentence investigation reports is the probation officer's failure to

    (A)  discuss the crime more fully.

    (B)  verify data.

    (C)  develop a complete marital history.

    (D)  present dynamic interrelationships.

65. Which of the following is the best policy to adopt with regard to the handling of probation violations?

    (A)  Revocation of probation for technical violations should be used to relieve the probation department of difficult, time-consuming cases so that attention may be focused on probationers whose cases show greater promise of success.

    (B)  Revocation of probation for technical violations that do not endanger the community should be contingent upon the feasibility of opening more effective avenues of treatment for the probationer.

    (C)  Technical violations of probation cannot be condoned without jeopardizing the entire structure of work with probationers.

    (D)  The fewer the rules and regulations that are imposed on probationers, the more readily is rehabilitation effected.

66. Assume that a youthful probationer has failed to follow instructions of the court about his recreational activities and church attendance. The probation officer knows he has been frequenting a candy store that has a bad reputation and that he has not attended church. The best action for the probation officer to take at the next interview would be to

    (A)  immediately accuse the probationer of violating probation in order to throw him off guard.

    (B)  ask him point blank how he spends his leisure time.

    (C)  advise him that you have arranged for a "Big Brother" to take him to church every Sunday in order to make sure that he complies with the court direction.

    (D)  try to get him to verbalize his interests, companions, and activities and his feelings toward these.

67. In considering the use of religion as a community resource with possibilities for assisting adult probationers, it would be advisable for the probation officer to

    (A)  consider religion outside the scope of treatment planning since it is a matter of personal belief.

    (B)  determine the probationer's attitude toward religion and plan in accordance with the probationer's belief and needs.

    (C)  explore the probationer's ideas on religion and counsel him or her on needed basic religious concepts and attitudes.

    (D)  make attendance at a church of the probationer's choice a basic prerequisite in the treatment plan.

68. The Interstate Compact, developed to facilitate cooperation among various signatory states,

    (A)  provides the legal means and the administrative machinery for maintaining supervision of parolees and probationers.

    (B)  is primarily focused toward effecting economy in returning violators.

    (C)  aims for the establishment of uniform minimal standards for persons planning to enter the field of correction.

    (D)  is a publication of the National Probation and Parole Association.

69. Which of the following statements is least accurate with respect to statistics in the field of criminology?

    (A) The statistical method is an essential tool in research.
    (B) Statistics in criminology are notoriously untrustworthy.
    (C) Criminal behavior is resolvable to statistical formulae.
    (D) It is very difficult to obtain a representative sampling in criminology.

70. For probation to be properly and successfully administered,

    (A) judges should be entrusted with broad discretionary powers with respect to granting probation.
    (B) statutes should be enacted limiting probation to specific offenses.
    (C) it should be restricted to first offenders.
    (D) the court should in each instance fix a set period of probation.

# MODEL EXAMINATION 2: ANSWERS AND EXPLANATIONS

## ANSWERS

| | | | | | | | | | |
|---|---|---|---|---|---|---|---|---|---|
| 1. | C | 16. | A | 31. | D | 46. | C | 61. | A |
| 2. | C | 17. | C | 32. | D | 47. | A | 62. | D |
| 3. | C | 18. | D | 33. | B | 48. | A | 63. | C |
| 4. | A | 19. | B | 34. | D | 49. | A | 64. | B |
| 5. | D | 20. | A | 35. | C | 50. | D | 65. | B |
| 6. | B | 21. | B | 36. | D | 51. | D | 66. | D |
| 7. | C | 22. | D | 37. | D | 52. | C | 67. | B |
| 8. | A | 23. | C | 38. | B | 53. | C | 68. | A |
| 9. | B | 24. | B | 39. | D | 54. | B | 69. | C |
| 10. | A | 25. | A | 40. | B | 55. | C | 70. | A |
| 11. | B | 26. | C | 41. | A | 56. | C | | |
| 12. | C | 27. | D | 42. | A | 57. | C | | |
| 13. | A | 28. | C | 43. | C | 58. | C | | |
| 14. | B | 29. | A | 44. | D | 59. | C | | |
| 15. | D | 30. | A | 45. | A | 60. | A | | |

## EXPLANATIONS

1. **The correct answer is (C).** Augustus was the first person to supervise people in lieu of them going to prison.
2. **The correct answer is (C).** Probation is a privilege that allows the defendant to stay in the community based on his or her actions or promise thereof.
3. **The correct answer is (C).** Probation keeps offenders from being labeled as "ex-cons."
4. **The correct answer is (A).** Surveillance is a part of all of our contacts with probationers and parolees.
5. **The correct answer is (D).** Prognosis and forecast are "looks into the future."
6. **The correct answer is (B).** This is an attempt to keep first offenders from becoming more hardened criminals.
7. **The correct answer is (C).** Hallucination is the condition of seeing things that are not there.
8. **The correct answer is (A).** The probation officer prepares the Pre-sentence Investigation document for the court.
9. **The correct answer is (B).** One who is conciliatory is appeasing and friendly.
10. **The correct answer is (A).** This refers to a juvenile who lies frequently.
11. **The correct answer is (B).** Plaintive refers to people who are sullen.
12. **The correct answer is (C).** Diversion is an attempt to rehabilitate people without them having to go to court.
13. **The correct answer is (A).** Fewer cases allow for more frequent contact.
14. **The correct answer is (B).** Summarizing enables everyone to understand what has been said.

15. **The correct answer is (D).** Children cannot manage their own affairs; thus, they are assigned a guardian to watch over them.

16. **The correct answer is (A).** A subpoena is a written document requiring one's presence in court.

17. **The correct answer is (C).** The probationer receives and must follow the terms and conditions of probation.

18. **The correct answer is (D).** Approximately 10 percent of people suffer from some kind of mental disability.

19. **The correct answer is (B).** People without proper nutrition can acquire a deficiency disease.

20. **The correct answer is (A).** A child's individual maladjustments can lead to delinquent behavior.

21. **The correct answer is (B).** The offender's personality goes a long way in determining his or her success with probation.

22. **The correct answer is (D).** Being objective means going where the evidence leads.

23. **The correct answer is (C).** Teachers know more about their students due to their regular contact with them.

24. **The correct answer is (B).** Prison requires relatively little from the offender; probation requires the offender to be an active participant.

25. **The correct answer is (A).** The nature of the offense should determine the level of punishment/treatment.

26. **The correct answer is (C).** Psychology focuses on the individual and what is happening with him or her.

27. **The correct answer is (D).** All of these are necessary components of the pre-sentence investigation (PSI).

28. **The correct answer is (C).** This is the classical explanation of criminality.

29. **The correct answer is (A).** It is difficult to measure something that hasn't occurred.

30. **The correct answer is (A).** Females traditionally do not commit the other crimes, although that is changing.

31. **The correct answer is (D).** Crime prevention is a community-wide endeavor.

32. **The correct answer is (D).** Given the slowness of the system, it is important to maintain records.

33. **The correct answer is (B).** This frequent cross-examination technique should be used sparingly.

34. **The correct answer is (D).** The PSI should reflect all information about the defendant and the crime.

35. **The correct answer is (C).** The most important part of the PSI is the officer's punishment recommendation.

36. **The correct answer is (D).** Statistics relies on numbers, whereas case studies focus on individualized information.

37. **The correct answer is (D).** Most probation agencies do not have advisory boards.

38. **The correct answer is (B).** Even with probation, the protection of society is the paramount consideration.

39. **The correct answer is (D).** This refers to mainstreaming.

40. **The correct answer is (B).** *Schall v. Martin* was an important case, allowing for pretrial detention.

41. **The correct answer is (A).** Confidentiality of records is very important.

42. **The correct answer is (A).** This age is consistent among the states.

43. **The correct answer is (C).** The children need help to understand and learn from their past.

44. **The correct answer is (D).** Not all children react the same way to a broken home or to the reasons the home is broken.

45. **The correct answer is (A).** Juvenile crime cuts across IQ lines.

46. **The correct answer is (C).** Basic human desires must be met first.

47. **The correct answer is (A).** Our society has moved from a homogeneous to a heterogeneous society.

48. **The correct answer is (A).** This refers to directing the individual's behavior into socially acceptable areas.

49. **The correct answer is (A).** Normal, depending on the age and type of behavior of the child.

50. **The correct answer is (D).** The juvenile court and probation are based on individualization of the offender.

51. **The correct answer is (D).** Adolescents are maturing and finding their way in life.

52. **The correct answer is (C).** Children need to feel they belong.

53. **The correct answer is (C).** Probation records are confidential.

54. **The correct answer is (B).** The probationer must understand that actions have consequences.

55. **The correct answer is (C).** The probationer remains in the community, making adjustment easier.

56. **The correct answer is (C).** All factors need to be taken into account, with protection of society being the most important.

57. **The correct answer is (C).** The most important part of the PSI is the officer's recommendations.

58. **The correct answer is (C).** This is always a reasonable possibility.

59. **The correct answer is (C).** It is probably not a defect, but it is something to be looked at.

60. **The correct answer is (A).** In most cases, juvenile jurisdiction ends at age 18.

61. **The correct answer is (A).** In many cases, for probation to be successful, the probationer must have a relationship with the officer.

62. **The correct answer is (D).** The case record must follow a logical format that makes sense.

63. **The correct answer is (C).** The final diagnosis should be made by the professional doing the diagnosis. If the professional makes the diagnosis, it should be included.

64. **The correct answer is (B).** All information in the PSI must be verified or not presented (unless done so as an opinion).

65. **The correct answer is (B).** The decision to revoke probation should be part of the overall plan for the probationer, especially with technical violations.

66. **The correct answer is (D).** The officer should know why these conditions are not being followed and should remind the probationer that he is in violation.

67. **The correct answer is (B).** This is consistent with faith-based initiatives.

68. **The correct answer is (A).** Given the mobility of people, the Interstate Compact allows for transfer of supervision between states.

69. **The correct answer is (C).** Social science research is often difficult to "capture" simply with numbers.

70. **The correct answer is (A).** Judicial discretion is important in deciding who should and should not get probation.

# MODEL EXAMINATION 3: ANSWER SHEET

1. Ⓐ Ⓑ Ⓒ Ⓓ
2. Ⓐ Ⓑ Ⓒ Ⓓ
3. Ⓐ Ⓑ Ⓒ Ⓓ
4. Ⓐ Ⓑ Ⓒ Ⓓ
5. Ⓐ Ⓑ Ⓒ Ⓓ
6. Ⓐ Ⓑ Ⓒ Ⓓ
7. Ⓐ Ⓑ Ⓒ Ⓓ
8. Ⓐ Ⓑ Ⓒ Ⓓ
9. Ⓐ Ⓑ Ⓒ Ⓓ
10. Ⓐ Ⓑ Ⓒ Ⓓ
11. Ⓐ Ⓑ Ⓒ Ⓓ
12. Ⓐ Ⓑ Ⓒ Ⓓ
13. Ⓐ Ⓑ Ⓒ Ⓓ
14. Ⓐ Ⓑ Ⓒ Ⓓ
15. Ⓐ Ⓑ Ⓒ Ⓓ
16. Ⓐ Ⓑ Ⓒ Ⓓ
17. Ⓐ Ⓑ Ⓒ Ⓓ
18. Ⓐ Ⓑ Ⓒ Ⓓ
19. Ⓐ Ⓑ Ⓒ Ⓓ
20. Ⓐ Ⓑ Ⓒ Ⓓ

21. Ⓐ Ⓑ Ⓒ Ⓓ
22. Ⓐ Ⓑ Ⓒ Ⓓ
23. Ⓐ Ⓑ Ⓒ Ⓓ
24. Ⓐ Ⓑ Ⓒ Ⓓ
25. Ⓐ Ⓑ Ⓒ Ⓓ
26. Ⓐ Ⓑ Ⓒ Ⓓ
27. Ⓐ Ⓑ Ⓒ Ⓓ
28. Ⓐ Ⓑ Ⓒ Ⓓ
29. Ⓐ Ⓑ Ⓒ Ⓓ
30. Ⓐ Ⓑ Ⓒ Ⓓ
31. Ⓐ Ⓑ Ⓒ Ⓓ
32. Ⓐ Ⓑ Ⓒ Ⓓ
33. _____
34. _____
35. _____
36. _____
37. _____
38. _____
39. _____
40. Ⓐ Ⓑ Ⓒ Ⓓ

41. Ⓐ Ⓑ Ⓒ Ⓓ
42. Ⓐ Ⓑ Ⓒ Ⓓ
43. Ⓐ Ⓑ Ⓒ Ⓓ
44. Ⓐ Ⓑ Ⓒ Ⓓ
45. Ⓐ Ⓑ Ⓒ Ⓓ
46. Ⓐ Ⓑ Ⓒ Ⓓ
47. Ⓐ Ⓑ Ⓒ Ⓓ
48. Ⓐ Ⓑ Ⓒ Ⓓ
49. Ⓐ Ⓑ Ⓒ Ⓓ
50. Ⓐ Ⓑ Ⓒ Ⓓ
51. Ⓐ Ⓑ Ⓒ Ⓓ
52. Ⓐ Ⓑ Ⓒ Ⓓ
53. Ⓐ Ⓑ Ⓒ Ⓓ
54. Ⓐ Ⓑ Ⓒ Ⓓ
55. Ⓐ Ⓑ Ⓒ Ⓓ
56. Ⓐ Ⓑ Ⓒ Ⓓ
57. Ⓐ Ⓑ Ⓒ Ⓓ
58. Ⓐ Ⓑ Ⓒ Ⓓ
59. Ⓐ Ⓑ Ⓒ Ⓓ
60. Ⓐ Ⓑ Ⓒ Ⓓ

61. Ⓐ Ⓑ Ⓒ Ⓓ
62. Ⓐ Ⓑ Ⓒ Ⓓ
63. Ⓐ Ⓑ Ⓒ Ⓓ
64. Ⓐ Ⓑ Ⓒ Ⓓ
65. Ⓐ Ⓑ Ⓒ Ⓓ
66. Ⓐ Ⓑ Ⓒ Ⓓ
67. Ⓐ Ⓑ Ⓒ Ⓓ
68. Ⓐ Ⓑ Ⓒ Ⓓ
69. Ⓐ Ⓑ Ⓒ Ⓓ
70. Ⓐ Ⓑ Ⓒ Ⓓ

# MODEL EXAMINATION 3: PROBATION OFFICER

## 3 HOURS, 30 MINUTES; 70 QUESTIONS

> **Directions:** Each question has four suggested answers, lettered (A), (B), (C), and (D). Decide which one is the best answer and darken on your answer sheet the space that corresponds with your answer choice.

1. The philosophy of case work is based on the
   - (A) recognition of the dignity of the human person.
   - (B) place of the agency in the community.
   - (C) importance of planning realistically with clients.
   - (D) role of the worker in case work treatment.

2. Many pre-sentence investigation reports now contain information about/from the victim. This is known as a
   - (A) victim impact statement.
   - (B) offense impact statement.
   - (C) offender impact statement.
   - (D) full disclosure statement.

3. The interview in case work is used chiefly
   - (A) to get proof of data required for evaluating the client's problems and resources.
   - (B) as a tool to explore with the client his or her feelings about the problem, as well as the problem itself, to arrive at a plan of treatment.
   - (C) because it is less expensive than other methods of work.
   - (D) for statistical purposes on the basis of the worker's record.

4. The offender is required to wear an ankle or wrist bracelet and generally remain at home. This is known as
   - (A) useless.
   - (B) electronic monitoring.
   - (C) keeping the offender "in check."
   - (D) none of the above.

5. The case worker, to be most effective in helping another person, must
   - (A) be free from prejudice of any kind.
   - (B) have a wide knowledge of the individual's cultural background.
   - (C) have received help in order to better understand the client's feelings.
   - (D) be aware of personal feelings regarding the client.

6. One of the best-known marks of a mature person is the ability to
   - (A) control feelings in difficult situations.
   - (B) seek personal pleasure regardless of the consequences.
   - (C) take things as they come, trusting in luck.
   - (D) enjoy many outside interests in life.

7. The return of an offender to the community under supervision after a portion of the sentence has been served is known as
   - (A) probation.
   - (B) unconditional release.
   - (C) parole.
   - (D) release on recognizance.

8. Shock probation includes

    (A)  the use of electronic shock treatments.
    (B)  the use of scare tactics.
    (C)  the use of incarceration as a part of the granting of probation.
    (D)  electronic monitoring.

9. Physical conditions that are caused by emotional conflicts are generally referred to as being

    (A)  psychosocial.
    (B)  hypochondriacal.
    (C)  psychosomatic.
    (D)  psychotic.

10. Conditions of probation that every offender receives are known as

    (A)  punitive conditions.
    (B)  rehabilitative conditions.
    (C)  informal conditions.
    (D)  standard conditions.

11. Kleptomania may best be described as a

    (A)  neurotic drive to accumulate personal property through compulsive acts in order to dispose of it to others with whom one wishes friendship.
    (B)  type of neurosis that manifests itself in an uncontrollable impulse to steal without economic motivation.
    (C)  psychopathic trait that is probably hereditary in nature.
    (D)  manifestation of punishment inviting behavior based upon guilt feelings for some other crime or wrongdoing, fantasy or real, committed as a child.

12. Of the following tests, the one that is NOT ordinarily used as a projective technique is the

    (A)  Wechsler Bellevue Scale.
    (B)  Rorschach Test.
    (C)  Thematic Apperception Test.
    (D)  Jung Free Association Test.

13. The Rorschach Test is a commonly used personality test. Which of the following considerations is the greatest value of this test to the psychiatrist and social worker?

    (A)  It provides practical recommendations with reference to further educational and vocational training possibilities for the person tested.
    (B)  It reveals in quick, concise form the hereditary factors affecting the individual personality.
    (C)  It helps in substantiating a diagnosis of juvenile delinquency.
    (D)  It helps in a diagnostic formulation and in determining differential treatment.

14. Conditional release from prison is known as

    (A)  probation.
    (B)  parole.
    (C)  diversion.
    (D)  a "free ride."

15. Records show that most crimes in the United States are committed by people

    (A)  under 18 years of age.
    (B)  aged 18 to 25.
    (C)  aged 30 to 40.
    (D)  more than 40 years of age.

16. According to current theories of criminology, which of the following is regarded as the most important cause of delinquency?

    (A) Personality maladjustment
    (B) Lack of proper housing
    (C) Mental deficiency
    (D) Community indifference to the need for recreational facilities

17. Delinquent behavior is most generally a result of

    (A) living and growing up in an environment that is both socially and financially deprived.
    (B) a lack of educational opportunity for development of individual skills.
    (C) multiple factors: psychological, biosocial, emotional, and environmental.
    (D) low frustration tolerance of many parents toward problems of married life.

18. A recidivist is

    (A) mentally incompetent.
    (B) incapable of committing a crime.
    (C) a psychopath.
    (D) a habitual offender.

19. Requiring the offender to pay the victim for his or her loss is

    (A) community service.
    (B) restitution.
    (C) payback.
    (D) only right.

20. The most distinctive characteristic of the chronic alcoholic is that he or she drinks alcohol

    (A) socially.
    (B) compulsively.
    (C) periodically.
    (D) secretly.

21. "The chronic alcoholic is the person who cannot face reality without alcohol, and yet whose adequate adjustment to reality is impossible so long as he or she uses alcohol." On the basis of this quotation, it is most reasonable to conclude that individuals overindulge in alcohol because alcohol

    (A) deadens the sense of conflict, giving the individual an illusion of social competence and a feeling of well-being and success.
    (B) provides the individual with an outlet to display feelings of good fellowship and cheerfulness, which are characteristic of an extroverted personality.
    (C) affords an escape technique from habitual irrational fears but does not affect rational fears.
    (D) offers an escape from imagery and feelings of superiority, which cause tension and anxiety.

22. Of the following drugs, the one to which a person is least likely to become addicted is

    (A) opium.
    (B) morphine.
    (C) marijuana.
    (D) heroin.

23. Teenagers who become addicted to the use of drugs are most generally
    (A) mentally defective.
    (B) paranoid.
    (C) normally adventurous.
    (D) emotionally disturbed.

24. If a probationer who has been placed in a job through the efforts of the probation officer later finds a better job, the probationer should
    (A) discuss the job offer with the probation officer.
    (B) grab the new job right away if it offers more money or better opportunity.
    (C) tell the current employer of the better offer and ask for a raise.
    (D) turn down the job so as not to embarrass the probation officer.

25. The Social Service Exchange is utilized by probation officers primarily in order to
    (A) facilitate the operation of the Interstate Compact for the transfer of probationers.
    (B) secure a complete criminal record of the defendant awaiting sentence.
    (C) secure a listing of agencies that have known the defendant or his or her family.
    (D) acquire a developmental history of the defendant.

26. The government agency that is entrusted with the supervision of New York City's penal and correctional institutions for adults is the
    (A) New York City Prison Association.
    (B) Department of Correction.
    (C) Department of Social Welfare.
    (D) Municipal Parole Commission.

27. While once rehabilitative in nature, probation has become
    (A) more sensitive.
    (B) even more rehabilitative.
    (C) more punitive.
    (D) less used.

28. In order to achieve the aims of probation, it is most important for the probation officer to whom a new case has been assigned to
    (A) carefully correct any erroneous preconceived ideas about probation that the new probationer may have.
    (B) develop a positive relationship with the new probationer.
    (C) explain the purposes and aims of probation.
    (D) make sure the new probationer understands the extent of the probation officer's authority.

29. Case recording is an important function of a probation department. It may often be necessary, therefore, for a supervisor in this department to explain to a new worker the reasons for keeping case records. Which of the following is the most important reason for case recording?
    (A) It improves the quality of the services rendered to the client.
    (B) It facilitates the transfer of a case from one worker to another.
    (C) It contributes data for research programs to justify the expansion of probation work.
    (D) It helps determine absolute conformance with the conditions of probation.

30. Of the following statements, which is the most accurate with respect to the criminal court in New York City?
    (A) It exercises jurisdiction over all felonies.
    (B) A petit jury always determines guilt or innocence.

    (C)   Three justices may sit as a group to determine guilt or innocence.

    (D)   It cannot impose sentences beyond one year in state prison.

**31.**   A female, age 22, is arrested in Brooklyn and charged with a misdemeanor. She will most likely be arraigned in the

    (A)   Kings County Supreme Court.

    (B)   criminal court.

    (C)   surrogate court.

    (D)   court on the judiciary.

**32.**   The use of authority as a means of helping a probationer toward better social adjustment

    (A)   has little value.

    (B)   can produce positive results if it leads to self-direction.

    (C)   is contrary to sound case work principles.

    (D)   is the most effective method of preventing recidivism.

---

**Directions:** For questions 33–39, select the definition in Column II that best defines the term listed in Column I. Write the letter of the definition on your answer sheet.

---

**Column I**

**33.**  acquittal

**34.**  arrest

**35.**  citation

**36.**  commitment

**37.**  indictment

**38.**  recidivism

**39.**  rendition jury

**Column II**

(A)  surrender by one state of a person found in that state for prosecution in another state having jurisdiction to try the charge

(B)  an official summons or notice to a person to appear before a court

(C)  the act of taking a person into custody by authority of law

(D)  a formal written statement charging one or more persons with an offense as formulated by the prosecutor and found by a grand jury

(E)  bringing the accused before a court to answer a minimal charge

(F)  an accusation of any offense or unlawful state of affairs originating with a grand jury from its own knowledge or observation

(G)  consignment to a place of official confinement of a person found guilty of a crime

(H)  finding the accused not guilty of a crime after trial

(I)  agreement to appear in court upon request, without bond

(J)  reversion or relapse into prior criminal habits even after punishment

**40.**   The family court is best described as a

    (A)   criminal court.

    (B)   court essentially based on a noncriminal jurisdiction.

    (C)   court for the trial of minor offenses.

    (D)   court for the trial of divorce actions.

**41.**   One of the greatest problems encountered by the justices of the family court is the

    (A)   overcrowded condition of places of detention for juvenile delinquents.

    (B)   absence of any psychiatric services for juvenile delinquents.

    (C)   lack of segregation for juvenile delinquents in the city prison.

    (D)   stigma attached to the fingerprinting of juvenile delinquents.

42. A youngster between 15 and 16 years of age who has committed an act that would be considered a crime if committed by an adult may be arraigned in the family court. Under these circumstances, he or she may be adjudged a

    (A) juvenile delinquent.
    (B) wayward minor.
    (C) youthful offender.
    (D) misdemeanant.

43. According to the statutes, a misdemeanor is an offense

    (A) that is punishable by not more than an indeterminate term of two to four years in a state prison.
    (B) not accompanied by physical violence.
    (C) for which reformatory sentence is mandatory unless sentence is suspended.
    (D) punishable by not more than one year of imprisonment.

44. The concept of sending offenders to another country is referred to as

    (A) transportation.
    (B) diversion.
    (C) a smart thing to do.
    (D) apprenticing.

45. A sentence of one to five years of incarceration is referred to as a(n)

    (A) determinate sentence.
    (B) absolute sentence.
    (C) indeterminate sentence.
    (D) mandatory sentence.

46. The first juvenile court was established in 1899 in

    (A) Los Angeles.
    (B) New York.
    (C) Boston.
    (D) Chicago.

47. In cases of adult offenders, probation differs from parole in that probation involves

    (A) suspension of sentence.
    (B) supervision after imprisonment.
    (C) supervision as a preliminary to parole.
    (D) an unlimited period of surveillance.

48. One of the duties of the probation officer during pre-sentence investigations and the supervision process is the consideration of evidence. Which of the following statements relating to the different types of evidence is least accurate?

    (A) Real evidence consists of any facts that are secured by firsthand experience.
    (B) Testimonial evidence is the assertion of a human being.
    (C) Hearsay evidence has little or no validity in probation practice.
    (D) Expert evidence is the testimony of a person with specialized knowledge of or skill in a particular field.

49. "The effect of rumors may be temporary or lasting. If they are reinforced and if there is no appreciable conflict with other and then with newer impulses, they are likely to persist. The rumor-engendered impression, moreover, is often the first reaction to an event. Subsequent information labors under a psychological handicap even when it is perceived. If a man is ruined by lies that people have the desire to believe, only compelling truths can resurrect him. The truths, though, will not be responded to eagerly, and they most probably will not drive out all the effects from the past." Which of the following statements is most accurate on the basis of the above paragraph?

    (A) Rumor-engendered impressions are readily obliterated if disproved by compelling truths.
    (B) Uninformed rumors should not be spread since they usually ruin people's lives.
    (C) False rumors are disproved with difficulty, and the first impression of uncontested and disproved false rumors is likely to continue.
    (D) Unlike the normal reaction to the rumor proved false, there is a psychological handicap in accepting the uncontested rumor.

50. Which of the following is the main reason for keeping a case record in probation or parole supervision?

    (A) To present a verified picture of all legal aspects of the case
    (B) To provide a complete and objective understanding of the person through knowledge gained from relatives, friends, and other agencies
    (C) To improve the quality of service to the probationer and to help the probation officer understand him or her and his or her situation
    (D) To give a realistic picture of the employment and recreational activities of the person in order to evaluate his or her progress toward rehabilitation

51. Which of the following statements concerning probation case records is the most accurate?

    (A) They are generically different from those in use in the private case work field.
    (B) They differ radically from the procedural records of the court.
    (C) They should out of necessity place less emphasis on the treatment than on the investigation of a person on probation.
    (D) They should emphasize surveillance factors of probation.

52. Which of the following reasons for maintaining records in the probation department has the least significance to the agency and the probation officer?

    (A) Case recording is an essential adjunct to the practice of case work.
    (B) Accurate and current case records facilitate treatment.
    (C) Case records represent the agency's knowledge, insight, experience, efforts, and plans in individual situations.
    (D) Case records represent evidence with which to deny false accusations and derogatory evaluative statements arising in the community.

53. The method of case recording that reflects the interaction between the client and the social worker around the problem as the client sees it and feels about it is known as

    (A) chronological.
    (B) process.
    (C) summary.
    (D) topical.

54. Of the following, which is the most important asset for a probation officer?

    (A) A well-integrated personality
    (B) Expert knowledge of crime causation
    (C) Comprehensive knowledge of community resources
    (D) Good health to enable the office to cope with the hazards of probation work

55. A probation officer newly assigned as a worker in a legalistic agency structure must set goals as a learner in a new experience. Which of the following statements most comprehensively and clearly states the learning goals of the new probation officer?

    (A) To gain a comprehensive knowledge of the basic structure of the agency and the laws under which it operates

    (B) To gain a clear understanding of the objectives of the agency's programs and underlying philosophy that governs the manner in which these programs are administered

    (C) To integrate the knowledge, development of skills in practice, and growth in personal emotional structure that are necessary to enable the officer to help others most effectively

    (D) To gain the ability to recognize distress and signs of emotional disturbance in people and to treat symptomatic behavior while working within the agency framework

56. Which of the following statements is the least accurate?

    (A) The type of evidence available in making a diagnosis of a person under investigation by a probation officer generally is not of a probative value equal to that of facts found in the exact sciences.

    (B) The rehabilitative treatment of a probationer lacks the precision used in treating physical diseases.

    (C) The vast background of experience in probation work today makes it possible for the probation officer to diagnose with certainty the personality and character of the probationer.

    (D) In considering evidence during an investigation, the probation officer can never be sure whether some fact that might alter the entire analysis has been overlooked.

57. Which of the following statements is the most accurate with respect to reciprocal state legislation to compel the support of dependent wives and children, better known as the Uniform Support of Dependents Law?

    (A) The amount of support allotted to women and children has been made uniform throughout the United States.

    (B) Provision has been made for the deserted wife to make the complaint in the state of residence and for the order of support against her husband to be made in the state where her husband now resides.

    (C) Sufficient federal funds have been provided to make it possible for the deserted wife to travel to the state where the deserting husband has been located and make the proper complaint for support there.

    (D) The legal requirements of extradition concerning deserting husbands have been eased, thereby facilitating their return to the state where the spouse resides to face appropriate criminal action.

58. Which of the following statements contains the basic principle upon which "aggressive case work" generally operates?

    (A) When a client applies for help with a delinquent child, the worker, following a complete study of the problem, forcefully defines the solution of the problem to the client.

    (B) The social worker waits until the neglect of a child by parents reaches a point where the court should take action and then proceeds to remove the child from the home.

    (C) New social work techniques are used to arouse the client's interest so that he or she voluntarily requests aid.

    (D) The social worker goes out to meet the client in his or her own setting.

**59.** Treatment of the delinquent child must be based on the child's individual needs primarily because

(A) the child's needs are usually for adequate recreational facilities and better home conditions.

(B) social treatment depends upon social diagnosis, and sound diagnosis requires knowledge of the person.

(C) behavior is usually determined by environment, which is unique for each person.

(D) the child's needs are usually less complicated than those of an adult.

**60.** It has been said that the probation officer working with a delinquent child "becomes for the child a symbol of the authority against which the child rebels." The task of the probation officer is to convert what appears to be a handicap into an asset. Of the following approaches to this problem, which one serves the probation officer most advantageously?

(A) Disguise the role of authority by becoming a friend to the child, who will then respond in a more personal way by talking freely about personal matters and experiences.

(B) Strengthen the parents so that they will relax their parental authoritative role and be more permissive in their discipline of the child.

(C) Maintain authority while offering guidance and counsel on the basis of disciplined concern for the child, genuine warmth, and willingness and capacity to enter into feelings and thinking about persons, situations, and things.

(D) Refer the case to an agency in the community where the nonauthoritative setting will permit reaching the child on a social and psychological basis through the use of treatment techniques for emotionally disturbed children.

**61.** Of the following statements relating to probation of known alcoholics, which is the most accurate?

(A) In order to help an alcoholic person under supervision, a probation officer should consider it important for the family to understand something of the probationer's problem.

(B) Referral of alcoholic probationers to medical facilities for the administration of certain drugs has proven successful in practically all cases.

(C) Research to date demonstrates that, in general, alcoholics on probation make an easy and adequate adjustment.

(D) Most domestic relations problems are caused by alcoholics or heavy drinkers.

**62.** Probation officers frequently encounter problems of young adults—either single or married—with deep, unresolved dependency conflicts and the inability to make mature adjustments in their work, living arrangements, or handling of their marital and parent-child relationships. Of the following, which one is the most appropriate in case work with individuals or families presenting problems of this type?

(A) Environmental service, affording immediate adjustments of an external character

(B) Specific advice and concrete suggestions given directly by the case worker upon his or her own initiative

(C) Case work treatment through which the person learns to handle a situation realistically with lessened anxiety as a result of a clearer understanding of deep-seated, repressed emotional material

(D) Supportive counseling in helping the person gain some insight into the basic problem so that he or she can be helped, if need is indicated, to move on to psychiatric treatment

63. In supervising an unemployed probationer, which of the following actions ordinarily represents good probation practice?

    (A) Refer the probationer immediately to the State Unemployment Bureau.
    (B) Encourage the probationer and give supportive help in using his or her own initiative to secure employment.
    (C) Refer the probationer to personal employer contacts known to the probation officer.
    (D) Fix a time limit for the probationer to get a job before returning him or her to court for violation of parole.

64. The majority of cases going to court because of marital discord are presented at a time of crisis. Which of the following approaches is most essential to the probation officer in offering help to a family in this situation?

    (A) Early analysis of his or her own attitudes and reactions in differentiating between factors already present in the personalities of the husband and wife and of situational factors
    (B) Immediate determination of the legal aspects of the marriage problem and recognition and handling of transference and countertransference in the case work relationship
    (C) Establishing a relationship that will enable the client to express feelings and present the problem as he or she sees it, thus enabling the probation officer to arrive at a sound diagnostic judgment
    (D) Offering a relationship at a level that will provide a vent to the husband and wife, endeavoring to use psychological support to direct them toward reconciliation

65. Mr. Brady, while on probation on a charge of desertion, again absconds, leaving his family without provision for support. The action to be taken first by the probation officer in apprehending the probationer is to

    (A) file a probation warrant with the local police department.
    (B) prepare a violation of probation report requesting the court to issue a bench warrant.
    (C) request the court to revoke the man's probation and advise his wife to make a new complaint of desertion immediately.
    (D) interview the deserted wife in order to understand her feelings about her husband's desertion and to discuss with her, if she wishes, the possible whereabouts of the probationer.

66. A boy of 15, on probation for one year in the family court on an original petition of delinquency made by his inadequate mother, has shown no improvement in his behavior, is beyond his mother's control, and is associating with a gang consisting of other seriously delinquent boys. Which of the following courses of action is most advisable for the probation officer to pursue?

    (A) Refer the boy for psychiatric evaluation or recommendation to determine whether he should be committed to an institution where he might receive treatment in a controlled environment.
    (B) Refer the family to a social agency for counseling to improve the home situation.
    (C) Arrange to have more frequent interviews with the mother.
    (D) Caution the boy that unless he improves his behavior and disassociates himself from the gang, you will be forced to recommend commitment to an institution.

67. An adolescent girl held as a material witness in a case of rape expresses strong hostility toward her mother, whom she claims always favored her younger brother. The mother says in an interview that she was always devoted to her own mother, now deceased, but that she was never able to confide in her or feel that she was understood by her.

This knowledge of the mother's earlier experiences may provide a clue to the probation officer in understanding causative factors in the girl's behavior. Of the following explanations, which one most likely accounts for the poor relationship between mother and daughter?

(A) The mother's greater interest in and warmth for her son would indicate that she had a better relationship with her own father than with her mother.

(B) The mother of the girl had lacked a warm, trusting relationship with her own mother and therefore provided an overpermissive atmosphere in her home for her daughter, believing that this would create a closer relationship between them.

(C) The girl's behavior springs from a fantasized maturity that is a spurious and unreal assumption of an adult status, often a temporary phase in adolescent growth.

(D) The mother of the girl probably had not worked through problems in relationship with her own mother and was unable therefore to establish a sound relationship with her daughter.

68. A girl of 19, adjudicated as a wayward minor and placed on probation, is discovered by the probation officer to be a prostitute, although this has not yet come to the attention of the authorities. Of the following courses of action, which is most advisable for the probation officer to pursue in these circumstances?

(A) Recommend that probation be revoked and that the girl be committed to an institution.

(B) Advise the girl that unless she discontinues this behavior the probation officer will have to report it to the court.

(C) Give the girl an opportunity to work out the problem for herself.

(D) Reevaluate the case, discussing the matter with your supervisor and determining appropriate action to take for the best interests of the community and the probationer.

69. Mrs. Atkins comes to a social agency asking for help with her 8-year-old son, who is a truant from school and is generally willful and disobedient. Mr. Atkins travels a good deal and is seldom at home. He has had very little part in the rearing of the child. Of the following actions, which should the case worker take first?

(A) See the child in order to learn from him why he is misbehaving.

(B) Arrange to see the father in order to advise him to change his job.

(C) Explore with Mrs. Atkins her feelings about the child as well as her feelings about her husband's part in the family picture.

(D) Visit the school to discover the cause of the difficulty there.

70. A 17-year-old male on probation in the family court tells his probation officer that he resents reporting to him because he was innocent of the crime for which he was placed on probation. In addition, he states he dislikes the probation officer. In this situation, the course of action that the probation officer should pursue is to

(A) encourage the probationer to seek legal assistance to reopen the case.

(B) adopt a firm attitude indicating that you are not interested in the probationer's guilt or innocence and insist that he comply with the probation conditions.

(C) seek to understand the reasons why the probationer dislikes you, at the same time indicating to him that he is free to explore legal assistance regarding his original offense.

(D) consider the probationer as rebellious and a potential community threat, recommending that probation be revoked.

# MODEL EXAMINATION 3: ANSWERS AND EXPLANATIONS

## ANSWERS

| | | | | | | | | | |
|---|---|---|---|---|---|---|---|---|---|
| 1. | A | 16. | A | 31. | B | 46. | C | 61. | A |
| 2. | A | 17. | C | 32. | B | 47. | D | 62. | D |
| 3. | B | 18. | D | 33. | H | 48. | C | 63. | B |
| 4. | B | 19. | B | 34. | C | 49. | C | 64. | C |
| 5. | A | 20. | B | 35. | B | 50. | C | 65. | B |
| 6. | A | 21. | A | 36. | G | 51. | B | 66. | D |
| 7. | C | 22. | C | 37. | D | 52. | D | 67. | D |
| 8. | C | 23. | D | 38. | J | 53. | B | 68. | A |
| 9. | C | 24. | A | 39. | A | 54. | A | 69. | C |
| 10. | D | 25. | C | 40. | B | 55. | C | 70. | C |
| 11. | B | 26. | B | 41. | A | 56. | C | | |
| 12. | A | 27. | C | 42. | A | 57. | B | | |
| 13. | D | 28. | B | 43. | D | 58. | D | | |
| 14. | B | 29. | A | 44. | A | 59. | B | | |
| 15. | B | 30. | C | 45. | A | 60. | C | | |

## EXPLANATIONS

1. **The correct answer is (A).** In order for the client to be rehabilitated, it is important that the probation officer help the client preserve what dignity is left after serving a prison term.
2. **The correct answer is (A).** This is an attempt to include the victim in decision making.
3. **The correct answer is (B).** Decisions can't be made without talking to the client.
4. **The correct answer is (B).** Electronic monitoring (EM) is a way to keep some offenders out of jail or prison.
5. **The correct answer is (A).** The case worker cannot be biased, as it will affect how he or she does his or her job.
6. **The correct answer is (A).** Controlling one's feelings in difficult situations is a sign of maturity.
7. **The correct answer is (C).** Early release from prison is called parole.
8. **The correct answer is (C).** This introduces the probationer to the realities of imprisonment and hence makes probation more successful.
9. **The correct answer is (C).** The term psychosomatic is concerned with bodily symptoms caused by mental or emotional disturbance.
10. **The correct answer is (D).** Every probationer must adhere to some of the same conditions.
11. **The correct answer is (B).** Kleptomania is a psychiatric disorder.

12. **The correct answer is (A).** The Wechsler Bellevue Scale is an intelligence test. It is not used for psychological testing.
13. **The correct answer is (D).** The Rorschach Test is often known as the "ink blot" test.
14. **The correct answer is (B).** Parole is release from prison before the completion of a sentence.
15. **The correct answer is (B).** Ages 18 to 25 are referred to as the crime-prone years.
16. **The correct answer is (A).** The delinquent's personality is thought to be the driving force.
17. **The correct answer is (C).** There is no one factor responsible for delinquency.
18. **The correct answer is (D).** Recidivists are people who continue to commit crime.
19. **The correct answer is (B).** It is believed that, when possible, the victim needs to be compensated.
20. **The correct answer is (B).** The alcoholic drinks beyond his or her ability to control it.
21. **The correct answer is (A).** Alcohol often makes people think that things are better than they are—that their problems have disappeared.
22. **The correct answer is (C).** Marijuana has not been shown to be physically or psychologically addictive.
23. **The correct answer is (D).** Addiction is usually the result of emotional problems.
24. **The correct answer is (A).** Any change made by the probationer needs to be discussed with the probation officer first or as soon after as practical.
25. **The correct answer is (C).** It is important to know how many and which social agencies are also involved with the probationer.
26. **The correct answer is (B).** Each city/county identifies its own agency name.
27. **The correct answer is (C).** A philosophical shift has occurred in the purpose of probation.
28. **The correct answer is (B).** A positive relationship facilitates probation practice better than a negative one.
29. **The correct answer is (A).** A good record helps in identifying what did and did not work.
30. **The correct answer is (C).** This is unique to New York State.
31. **The correct answer is (B).** Criminal court handles criminal cases.
32. **The correct answer is (B).** Probationers must learn to respond to authority.
33. **The correct answer is (H).**
34. **The correct answer is (C).**
35. **The correct answer is (B).**
36. **The correct answer is (G).**
37. **The correct answer is (D).**
38. **The correct answer is (J).**
39. **The correct answer is (A).**
40. **The correct answer is (B).** Most family courts are civil courts.
41. **The correct answer is (A).** Overcrowdedness is a problem in the juvenile justice system as well as the adult system.
42. **The correct answer is (A).** Delinquency is crime committed by a juvenile.
43. **The correct answer is (D).** A misdemeanor is a minor offense with less imprisonment.
44. **The correct answer is (A).** For example, England sent criminals to the United States and to Australia.
45. **The correct answer is (A).** Determining when an offender completes his or her sentence is the responsibility of the parole board and/or the Department of Corrections.
46. **The correct answer is (C).** This occurred in response to the concerns of the Child Savers.
47. **The correct answer is (D).** Probationers have not been sent to prison and are subjected to community surveillance.
48. **The correct answer is (C).** Hearsay is one way the probation officer has of knowing what is happening with the probationer.

49. **The correct answer is (C).** People tend to believe what they first see or hear.

50. **The correct answer is (C).** A good case record helps identify what is and is not working.

51. **The correct answer is (B).** Case records belong to the probation office and reflect a variety of information that cannot exist in the official court records.

52. **The correct answer is (D).** Case records should not be used to negate community comments.

53. **The correct answer is (B).** This involves understanding the client from his or her perspective, knowing what he or she thinks and feels about his or her situation.

54. **The correct answer is (A).** Although all of the choices are important, a probation officer must have a well-integrated personality in order to deal with the different types of offenders.

55. **The correct answer is (C).** The new probation officer must be able to integrate professional skills with emotional growth in order to function competently in this new environment and serve clients effectively.

56. **The correct answer is (C).** Diagnosis is an art at best—we simply do not know exactly why people do what they do.

57. **The correct answer is (B).** Compelling support is still difficult to enforce.

58. **The correct answer is (D).** It is important to understand the client in relation to his or her own environment.

59. **The correct answer is (B).** Again, it is important to know as much about the individual as possible.

60. **The correct answer is (C).** This is the definition of discipline.

61. **The correct answer is (A).** The family of the alcoholic plays an important role in understanding the alcoholic's problem and helping with his or her rehabilitation.

62. **The correct answer is (D).** Helping the person help himself or herself is a great way of facilitating probation.

63. **The correct answer is (B).** This helps the probationer take responsibility.

64. **The correct answer is (C).** It is important to establish a relationship with the offender to help him or her take responsibility.

65. **The correct answer is (B).** When a probationer absconds, a revocation must be filed so that when he or she is found he or she will be arrested.

66. **The correct answer is (D).** The boy must take some responsibility for his action and needs to know that his actions have consequences.

67. **The correct answer is (D).** The mother should be referred to therapy so she can ultimately help her daughter.

68. **The correct answer is (A).** The probation should be revoked even if commitment is the consequence.

69. **The correct answer is (C).** The officer should talk with the mother in order to have a better understanding of her role in the family dynamics. The officer should talk to the father, child, and school officials as well.

70. **The correct answer is (C).** Whether the offender likes the probation officer or not is generally irrelevant. The offender needs to know the conditions he must obey and how to pursue any concerns legally.

# MODEL EXAMINATION 4: ANSWER SHEET

1. Ⓐ Ⓑ Ⓒ Ⓓ    21. Ⓐ Ⓑ Ⓒ Ⓓ    41. Ⓐ Ⓑ Ⓒ Ⓓ    61. Ⓐ Ⓑ Ⓒ Ⓓ
2. Ⓐ Ⓑ Ⓒ Ⓓ    22. Ⓐ Ⓑ Ⓒ Ⓓ    42. Ⓐ Ⓑ Ⓒ Ⓓ    62. Ⓐ Ⓑ Ⓒ Ⓓ
3. Ⓐ Ⓑ Ⓒ Ⓓ    23. Ⓐ Ⓑ Ⓒ Ⓓ    43. Ⓐ Ⓑ Ⓒ Ⓓ    63. Ⓐ Ⓑ Ⓒ Ⓓ
4. Ⓐ Ⓑ Ⓒ Ⓓ    24. Ⓐ Ⓑ Ⓒ Ⓓ    44. Ⓐ Ⓑ Ⓒ Ⓓ    64. Ⓐ Ⓑ Ⓒ Ⓓ
5. Ⓐ Ⓑ Ⓒ Ⓓ    25. Ⓐ Ⓑ Ⓒ Ⓓ    45. Ⓐ Ⓑ Ⓒ Ⓓ    65. Ⓐ Ⓑ Ⓒ Ⓓ
6. Ⓐ Ⓑ Ⓒ Ⓓ    26. Ⓐ Ⓑ Ⓒ Ⓓ    46. Ⓐ Ⓑ Ⓒ Ⓓ    66. Ⓐ Ⓑ Ⓒ Ⓓ
7. Ⓐ Ⓑ Ⓒ Ⓓ    27. Ⓐ Ⓑ Ⓒ Ⓓ    47. Ⓐ Ⓑ Ⓒ Ⓓ    67. Ⓐ Ⓑ Ⓒ Ⓓ
8. Ⓐ Ⓑ Ⓒ Ⓓ    28. Ⓐ Ⓑ Ⓒ Ⓓ    48. Ⓐ Ⓑ Ⓒ Ⓓ    68. Ⓐ Ⓑ Ⓒ Ⓓ
9. Ⓐ Ⓑ Ⓒ Ⓓ    29. Ⓐ Ⓑ Ⓒ Ⓓ    49. Ⓐ Ⓑ Ⓒ Ⓓ    69. Ⓐ Ⓑ Ⓒ Ⓓ
10. Ⓐ Ⓑ Ⓒ Ⓓ   30. Ⓐ Ⓑ Ⓒ Ⓓ    50. Ⓐ Ⓑ Ⓒ Ⓓ    70. Ⓐ Ⓑ Ⓒ Ⓓ
11. Ⓐ Ⓑ Ⓒ Ⓓ   31. Ⓐ Ⓑ Ⓒ Ⓓ    51. Ⓐ Ⓑ Ⓒ Ⓓ    71. Ⓐ Ⓑ Ⓒ Ⓓ
12. Ⓐ Ⓑ Ⓒ Ⓓ   32. Ⓐ Ⓑ Ⓒ Ⓓ    52. Ⓐ Ⓑ Ⓒ Ⓓ    72. Ⓐ Ⓑ Ⓒ Ⓓ
13. Ⓐ Ⓑ Ⓒ Ⓓ   33. Ⓐ Ⓑ Ⓒ Ⓓ    53. Ⓐ Ⓑ Ⓒ Ⓓ    73. Ⓐ Ⓑ Ⓒ Ⓓ
14. Ⓐ Ⓑ Ⓒ Ⓓ   34. Ⓐ Ⓑ Ⓒ Ⓓ    54. Ⓐ Ⓑ Ⓒ Ⓓ    74. Ⓐ Ⓑ Ⓒ Ⓓ
15. Ⓐ Ⓑ Ⓒ Ⓓ   35. Ⓐ Ⓑ Ⓒ Ⓓ    55. Ⓐ Ⓑ Ⓒ Ⓓ    75. Ⓐ Ⓑ Ⓒ Ⓓ
16. Ⓐ Ⓑ Ⓒ Ⓓ   36. Ⓐ Ⓑ Ⓒ Ⓓ    56. Ⓐ Ⓑ Ⓒ Ⓓ
17. Ⓐ Ⓑ Ⓒ Ⓓ   37. Ⓐ Ⓑ Ⓒ Ⓓ    57. Ⓐ Ⓑ Ⓒ Ⓓ
18. Ⓐ Ⓑ Ⓒ Ⓓ   38. Ⓐ Ⓑ Ⓒ Ⓓ    58. Ⓐ Ⓑ Ⓒ Ⓓ
19. Ⓐ Ⓑ Ⓒ Ⓓ   39. Ⓐ Ⓑ Ⓒ Ⓓ    59. Ⓐ Ⓑ Ⓒ Ⓓ
20. Ⓐ Ⓑ Ⓒ Ⓓ   40. Ⓐ Ⓑ Ⓒ Ⓓ    60. Ⓐ Ⓑ Ⓒ Ⓓ

(C)    Substantial interpersonal relationship between the teacher and the student

(D)    Reinforcement of learning through recognition

15.    There are several advantages in using videotape as a means of instruction. Which of the following is NOT an advantage of this method of teaching?

(A)    A great number of viewers spread over a large geographical area can be reached.

(B)    A variety of instructional materials can be integrated within a single lesson.

(C)    It is a completely one-way process, with the instructor separated from the students.

(D)    The information and instruction on tape is available for replay whenever desired.

16.    Which of the following statements concerning educational programs in correctional institutions is correct?

(A)    The costs of educational programming in the correctional setting are generally higher than in the regular educational systems.

(B)    The subjects taught in correctional education programs are generally highly innovative.

(C)    The status and priority established for institutional education are commensurate with today's demand for such education.

(D)    Inmate teachers have rarely been used in educational programs in correctional institutions.

17.    Assume that the goal of a training session is to make staff members aware of how it feels to be confined in a correctional institution. The training technique best suited to attain this goal is

(A)    reading relevant literature.

(B)    role-playing.

(C)    panel discussion.

(D)    group discussion.

18.    Following are three statements concerning programmed-learning textbooks.

1.    The subject matter is arranged logically and in small steps.

2.    The texts are structured to demand less concentration than that required for regular methods of instruction.

3.    If the learner has given an incorrect answer, he or she is immediately made aware of it so that he or she may correct it before proceeding with the lesson.

Which of the following correctly classifies the above statements?

(A)    1 and 2 and 3 are correct.

(B)    1 and 2 are correct, but 3 is not.

(C)    1 and 3 are correct, but 2 is not.

(D)    2 and 3 are correct, but 1 is not.

19.    For management by objectives to be successful, all of the following conditions must be fulfilled EXCEPT

(A)    continuous feedback on managerial performance.

(B)    constant supervision of employees by supervisors.

(C)    an intensive training program preceding organizational implementation.

(D)    superior-subordinate relationships characterized by a high degree of cooperation and mutual respect.

20.    Which of the following types of programs is least appropriate in a correctional institution?

(A)    A religious program

(B)    A recreational program

(C)    An individual counseling program

(D)    A methadone maintenance program

21. In a modern "information system," there are two main categories: "standard information," consisting of the data required for operational control, and "demand information," consisting of data that, although not needed regularly or under normal circumstances, must be available when required. Following are four types of data.

    1. Daily count at a prison
    2. Number of correction officers who call in sick each day
    3. Number of prisoners eligible for release within the next six months in certain categories of offenses
    4. Average number of paroles granted: 25 per year

    Which of the following correctly categorizes the above types of data into "standard information" and "demand information?"

    (A) 1 and 2 are standard, but 3 and 4 are demand.
    (B) 1 and 3 are standard, but 2 and 4 are demand.
    (C) 3 is standard, but 1, 2, and 4 are demand.
    (D) 2 is standard, but 1, 3, and 4 are demand.

22. The basic purpose of a detention home for accused juvenile delinquents is to
    (A) serve as a shelter for dependent or neglected children who are temporarily without a home or parental supervision.
    (B) hold delinquent youngsters pending a court hearing or transfer to another jurisdiction or program.
    (C) act as a rehabilitative institution following adjudication.
    (D) act as a rehabilitation institution prior to adjudication.

23. The oversight the probation/parole officer exercises over his or her probationer/parolee is known as
    (A) case work.
    (B) supervision.
    (C) helping.
    (D) rehabilitation.

24. In an effort to assist defendants in obtaining legal counsel, the courts rely most heavily on
    (A) the phone directory.
    (B) bar associations.
    (C) lawyers' guilds.
    (D) legal aid and public defender groups.

25. All of the following statements arc characteristics of minimum-security prisons except which?
    (A) Inmates work under general or intermittent supervision.
    (B) They serve a therapeutic function by creating an environment based upon trust rather than strict controls.
    (C) The inmates at these institutions are often engaged in public works activities.
    (D) The work experiences they provide directly relate to those the prisoner will face in the real world.

26. To better deliver probation and parole services, many times the office will develop
    (A) specialized units.
    (B) specialized surveillance.
    (C) specialized conditions.
    (D) new funding procedures.

27. Of the following, the lowest stratum in prison subculture is occupied by
    (A) bank robbers.
    (B) forgers.

(C)  drug addicts.

(D)  sex offenders.

28.  While on probation or parole, an offender can, as a condition of probation, forfeit his or her

(A)  Fifth Amendment rights.

(B)  Tenth Amendment rights.

(C)  First Amendment rights.

(D)  Fourth Amendment rights.

29.  A correctional program should have measurable objectives so that its success can be evaluated. Of the following, it would be most difficult to measure the

(A)  change in attitude toward work and study resulting from participation in a correctional program.

(B)  percentage of participants who obtain employment after release.

(C)  sum of money earned in a work-release program.

(D)  change in reading level during an educational program.

30.  Of the following, which should be developed first in establishing a successful training program?

(A)  Content of the training program

(B)  Facilities for giving training

(C)  Qualification requirements for staff members

(D)  Agency goals and programs

31.  The role of the courts with respect to rehabilitation in the correctional institutions is best described as

(A)  hands off.

(B)  active.

(C)  nonexistent.

(D)  all of the above, depending on the issues of the case.

32.  All of the following statements concerning the money bail system are correct except which?

(A)  Under the bail system, people may be confined for crimes for which they are later acquitted.

(B)  Members of organized criminal syndicates have little difficulty in posting bail, although they are often dangerous.

(C)  Bail is recognized in the law solely as a method of keeping dangerous persons in jail.

(D)  The bail system discriminates against poor defendants.

33.  In the United States, most dollars, manpower, and attention in the correctional field have been invested in

(A)  traditional institutional services outside the mainstream of urban life.

(B)  innovative correctional programming at large state institutions.

(C)  programs for local jails.

(D)  community-based programs.

34.  Which of the following is the single most important source of statistics on crime in the United States today?

(A)  *FBI Quarterly Review*

(B)  *Uniform Crime Reports of the FBI*

(C)  *Journal of Police Science and Criminal Statistics*

(D)  *Federal Report on Criminal Statistics*

**35.** The chief executive can absolve an offender from the legal consequences of his or her criminality. This is known as

(A) executive clemency.
(B) pardon.
(C) commutation.
(D) executive relief.

*Answer questions 36–41 on the basis of the following selection.*

Man's historical approach to criminals can be conveniently summarized as a succession of three Rs: revenge, restraint, and reformation. Revenge was the primary response prior to the first revolution in penology in the eighteenth and nineteenth centuries. It was replaced during that revolution by an emphasis upon restraint. When the second revolution occurred in the late nineteenth and twentieth centuries, reformation became an important objective. Attention was focused upon the mental and emotional makeup of the offender and efforts were made to alter these as the primary sources of difficulty.

We have now entered yet another revolution in which a fourth concept has been added to the list of Rs: reintegration. This has come about because students of corrections feel that a singular focus upon reforming the offender is inadequate. Successful rehabilitation is a two-sided coin, including reformation on one side and reintegration on the other.

It can be argued that the third revolution is premature. Society itself is still very ambivalent about the offender. It has never really replaced all vestiges of revenge or restraint, simply supplemented them. Thus, while society is unwilling to kill or lock up all offenders permanently, it is also unwilling to give full support to the search for alternatives.

**36.** According to the above passage, revolutions against accepted treatment of criminals have resulted in all of the following approaches to handling criminals EXCEPT

(A) revenge.
(B) restraint.
(C) reformation.
(D) reintegration.

**37.** According to the above passage, society now views the offender with

(A) uncertainty.
(B) hatred.
(C) sympathy.
(D) acceptance.

**38.** According to the above passage, the second revolution directed particular attention to

(A) preparing the offender for return to society.
(B) making the pain of punishment exceed the pleasure of crime.
(C) exploring the inner feelings of the offender.
(D) restraining the offender from continuing a life of crime.

**39.** According to the above passage, students of correction feel that the lack of success of rehabilitation programs is due to

(A) the mental and emotional makeup of the offender.
(B) vestiges of revenge and restraint that linger in correctional programs.
(C) failure to achieve reintegration together with reformation.
(D) premature planning of the third revolution.

**40.** The author of the above passage suggests that the latest revolution will

(A) fail and the cycle will begin again with revenge or restraint.
(B) be the last revolution.
(C) not work unless correctional goals can be defined.
(D) succumb to political and economic pressures.

**41.** Of the following titles, which one best expresses the main idea of the author of the above passage?

(A) Is Criminal Justice Enough?
(B) Approaches in the Treatment of the Criminal Offender
(C) The Three Rs in Criminal Reformation
(D) Mental Disease Factors in the Criminal Correction System

*Answer questions 42–47 on the basis of the following selection.*

In a study by J. E. Cowden, an attempt was made to determine which variables would best predict institutional adjustment and recidivism in recently committed delinquent boys. The results suggested in particular that older boys, who are initially rated as being more mature and more amenable to change when first institutionalized, will most likely adjust better than the manner in which the average boy adjusts to the institution. Prediction of institutional adjustment was rendered slightly more accurate by using the variables of age and personality prognosis in combined form.

With reference to the prediction of recidivism, boys who committed more serious offenses showed less recidivism than average. These boys were also older than average when first committed. The variable of age accounts in part for both their more serious offenses and for their lower subsequent rate of recidivism.

The results also showed some trends suggesting that boys from higher socioeconomic backgrounds tended to commit more serious offenses leading to their institutionalization as delinquents. However, neither the ratings of socioeconomic status nor "home environment" appeared to be significantly related to recidivism in this study.

Cowden also found an essentially linear relationship between personality prognosis and recidivism and between institutional adjustment and recidivism. When these variables were used jointly to predict recidivism, accuracy of prediction was increased only slightly, but in general the ability to predict recidivism fell far below the ability to predict institutional adjustment.

**42.** According to the above passage, which of the following was not found to be a significant factor in predicting recidivism?

(A) Age
(B) Personality
(C) Socioeconomic background
(D) Institutional adjustment

**43.** According to the above passage, institutional adjustment was more accurately predicted when the variables used were

(A) socioeconomic background and recidivism.
(B) recidivism and personality.
(C) personality and age.
(D) age and socioeconomic background.

44. According to the above passage, which of the following were variables in predicting both recidivism and institutional adjustment?

   (A) Age and personality
   (B) Family background and age
   (C) Nature of offense and age
   (D) Personality

45. Which one of the following conclusions is most justified by the above passage?

   (A) Institutional adjustment has a lower level of predictability than recidivism.
   (B) Recidivism and seriousness of offense are negatively correlated to some degree.
   (C) Institutional adjustment and personality prognosis, when considered together, are significantly better predictors of recidivism than either one alone.
   (D) A delinquent boy from a lower-class family background is more likely to have committed a serious first offense than a delinquent boy from a higher socioeconomic background.

46. The study discussed in the passage found that delinquent boys from a higher socioeconomic background tended to

   (A) commit more serious crimes.
   (B) commit less serious crimes.
   (C) show more recidivism than average.
   (D) show less recidivism than average.

47. The most appropriate conclusion to be drawn from the study is that

   (A) delinquent boys from higher socioeconomic backgrounds show less institutional adjustment than average.
   (B) a high positive correlation was found between recidivism and institutional adjustment.
   (C) home environment, although not significantly related to recidivism, did influence institutional adjustment.
   (D) older boys are more likely to commit more serious first offenses and show less recidivism than younger boys.

*Answer questions 48–50 on the basis of the following passage.*

The basic disparity between punitive and correctional crime control should be noted. The first explicitly or implicitly assumes the availability of choice or freedom of the will and asserts the responsibility of the individual for what he or she does. Thus, the concept of punishment has both a moral and practical justification. However, correctional crime control, though also deterministic in outlook, either explicitly or implicitly considers criminal behavior as the result of conditions and factors present in the individual or the environment. It does not think in terms of free choices available to the individual and the resultant responsibility, but rather in terms of the removal of the criminogenic conditions for which the individual may not be responsible and over which he or she may not have any control. Some efforts have been made to achieve a theoretical reconciliation of these two rather diametrically opposed approaches, but this has not been accomplished, and their coexistence in practice remains an unresolved contradiction.

**48.** According to the "correctional" view of crime control mentioned in the above passage, criminal behavior is the result of

(A) environmental factors for which individuals should be held responsible.
(B) harmful environmental factors that should be eliminated.
(C) an individual's choice for which he or she should be held responsible and punished.
(D) an individual's choice and can be corrected in a therapeutic environment.

**49.** According to the above passage, which of the following is a problem in correctional practice?

(A) Identifying emotionally disturbed individuals
(B) Determining effective punishment for criminal behavior
(C) Reconciling the punitive and correctional views of crime control
(D) Assuming that a criminal is the product of his or her environment and has no free will

**50.** According to the above passage, which of the following is an assumption underlying the punitive crime control viewpoint rather than the correctional viewpoint?

(A) Crime is caused by inherited personality traits.
(B) Crime is caused by poor socioeconomic background.
(C) Crime is caused by lack of parental guidance.
(D) Crime is caused by irresponsibility on the part of the individual.

*Answer questions 51–56 solely on the basis of the information contained in the following charts and notes.*

## CHART I: NUMBER OF INMATES ENROLLED IN LIBERTYVILLE'S BASIC OFFICE SKILLS PROGRAM

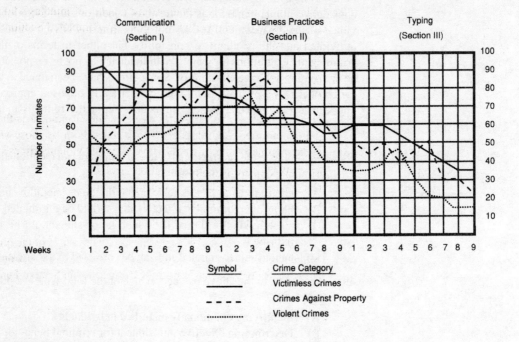

| Symbol | Crime Category |
|---|---|
| ——— | Victimless Crimes |
| – – – – | Crimes Against Property |
| ·············· | Violent Crimes |

**Notes**: Inmates can enter a section of the program at any point. Inmates can complete a section of the program at any point by passing an examination.

Enrollment at the end of a section does not necessarily indicate successful completion of that section.

## CHART II: NUMBER OF INMATES WHO SUCCESSFULLY COMPLETED EACH SECTION OF LIBERTYVILLE'S OFFICE SKILLS PROGRAM

| Crime Category | Completed Section I | Completed Section II | Completed Section III |
|---|---|---|---|
| Victimless Crimes | 78 | 55 | 37 |
| Crimes Against Property | 43 | 57 | 28 |
| Violent Crimes | 80 | 50 | 18 |

## CHART III: PERCENTAGE OF RECIDIVISM WITHIN FIRST YEAR OF PAROLE AMONG INMATES WHO SUCCESSFULLY COMPLETED VARIOUS STAGES OF LIBERTYVILLE'S OFFICE SKILLS PROGRAM

| Crime Category | Completed Section I | Completed Section II | Completed Section III |
|---|---|---|---|
| Victimless Crimes | 40% | 30% | 15% |
| Crimes Against Property | 3% | 15% | 5% |
| Violent Crimes | 35% | 25% | 10% |

51. What (most nearly) is the percentage of inmates who successfully completed Section I and were recidivists?

    (A) 70%
    (B) 78%
    (C) 85%
    (D) 30%

52. What (most nearly) is the ratio of the number of inmates who started Section III the first week to the number who successfully completed Section III?

    (A) 1.5:1
    (B) 1.7:1
    (C) 2.1:1
    (D) 2.5:1

53. During which of the following weeks of the program was the enrollment by those who committed victimless crimes exceeded both by those who committed crimes against property and by those who committed violent crimes?

    (A) Week 1 of the communication section
    (B) Week 3 of the business practices section
    (C) Week 9 of the business practices section
    (D) Week 6 of the typing section

54. If the average number of inmates enrolled in any stage of the program is considered to be the number of inmates enrolled during Week 5 of that section, what is the difference between the average number of inmates enrolled in Section I and in Section III?

    (A) 90
    (B) 125
    (C) 19
    (D) 215

55. Assume that 60 percent of the inmates who completed Section III of the office skills program enrolled the first week of the program and completed all three sections of the program. What (most nearly) is the number of the official initial enrollees who completed the entire office skills program?

    (A) 54
    (B) 125
    (C) 73
    (D) 105

56. Of the following periods, which one exhibits the greatest percentage change in enrollment of inmates in the crimes against property category?

    (A) Weeks 2 to 4 in the communication section
    (B) Weeks 4 to 6 in the communication section
    (C) Weeks 4 to 6 in the business practices section
    (D) Weeks 3 to 4 in the typing section

57. A study of the bail system concluded that of the following factors, the one that has the strongest impact on an accused person's chances of being convicted is

    (A) whether the person is detained or released prior to trial.
    (B) the weight of evidence against the person.
    (C) the type and seriousness of the alleged crime.
    (D) whether the person has a criminal record.

58. Which of the following is the chief disadvantage of using on-the-job training?

   (A) It is initially more costly than using other types of training.
   (B) It is often carried on with little or no planning.
   (C) It requires the worker to remain in the environment in which he or she will be working.
   (D) It prevents the trainee from obtaining the benefits of a professional's experience.

59. A fundamental weakness in the lecture form of training is that it

   (A) does not allow for careful preliminary analysis of significant ideas, their organization, and methods of presentation.
   (B) is basically a one-way form of communication.
   (C) precludes an interesting and challenging presentation.
   (D) is not amenable to use when presentation time limits are stringent.

60. The ultimate criterion of the success or failure of correctional programs has become

   (A) recidivism.
   (B) the number of inmates served by particular correctional programs.
   (C) the cost of treatment per inmate.
   (D) the number of inmates successfully adapting to institutional life.

61. Of the following, which is the best definition of the term "classification" as it is used in a correctional setting?

   (A) The construction of separate facilities for special offenders such as first offenders and suicide risks
   (B) The informal processes that result in a clearly defined subculture among inmates
   (C) The process through which the resources of the correctional institution can be applied effectively to the individual case
   (D) A method of performance evaluation, which, when applied to correctional employees, improves organizational effectiveness and employee morale

62. Of the following, which is the least important factor to consider in determining the ratio of trainees to the individual instructor in a training program?

   (A) The complexity of the skill to be learned
   (B) The method of presentation to be used
   (C) The number of inmates who express interest in the program
   (D) The background of the inmates who express interest in taking the program

63. The primary objective of correctional programs is to

   (A) reduce or eliminate the prisoner's criminal behavior.
   (B) ensure that the prisoner adapts to prison life.
   (C) decrease the cost of correctional administration.
   (D) maximize inmate participation in the community at large.

64. A good discussion group leader does all of the following EXCEPT

   (A) stimulate the sharing of ideas.
   (B) aid the group in exploring alternatives for problems.
   (C) give advice to group members.
   (D) provide materials and help when asked.

65. The largest number of full-time employees in adult correctional institutions in the United States are engaged in

   (A) education and counseling.
   (B) custody and control of inmates.
   (C) health services and correctional administration.
   (D) counseling and social work.

66. Which of the following is generally recognized as the institution that processes the greatest number of persons?

    (A) Juvenile remand shelter
    (B) Jail
    (C) Prerelease guidance center
    (D) Penitentiary

67. The fundamental responsibility of prison management is the

    (A) custody and control of offenders.
    (B) rehabilitation of offenders.
    (C) deterrence of crime.
    (D) punishment of offenders.

68. Changing the focus of the correctional system from the offender to the offense is known as

    (A) the rehabilitative ideal.
    (B) the justice model.
    (C) restorative justice.
    (D) the offense model.

69. Which of the following statements is correct concerning industrial work programs within correctional institutions in the United States?

    (A) Prison-made goods tend to show better workmanship than goods available from private enterprise.
    (B) Prison-made products frequently cost less than similar items that are privately produced.
    (C) The least extensive and successful use of prison industries is found in the federal prisons.
    (D) There are many legal constraints on developing industrial work programs in correctional institutions.

70. Of the following, which is the least effective method of generating community interest in a jail?

    (A) Encouraging the participation of interested citizens in jail programs
    (B) Setting up tours that show the best programs of the jail
    (C) Providing local newspapers with annual reports, budget reports, and feature articles about jail operations and problems
    (D) Establishing jail advisory committees composed of a cross-section of the community

*Answer questions 71–75 on the basis of the following passage.*

The social problems created by the urban delinquent gang member require the attention and resources of the entire community. Recent studies have shown that we are dealing with a boy who early in life has his first official contact with the police and who, shortly afterwards, is bound for juvenile court. The gang member commits several delinquencies before reaching adult status and the earlier his onset of delinquency, the more serious his violations of the law become. There is also evidence of increasingly serious delinquency involvement of a substantial proportion of the gang members. Of major significance are the shorter periods of time between each succeeding offense and the delinquents' employment of or threat to employ force and violence.

All of these findings testify to the urgent need for prevention and treatment to be directed at preadolescents and early adolescents and to be sensitive to the importance of the first signs of youthful disregard for society's legal norms. Follow-up studies on delinquent gang members revealed that 40 percent of the gang members continued into adult crime. For several reasons, this is a minimal figure and should probably be 20 percent higher. It is reasonable to infer that, given more thorough follow-up techniques and a longer follow-up period, an appreciable number of those for whom no criminal records were located will acquire them. In any event, these studies have revealed a strong linkage between delinquency and crime. This linkage has been established by following a group of gang members into adulthood rather than by tracing back a group of adult offenders into delinquency and by utilizing a sample of juveniles dealt with by the police rather than those appearing before a juvenile court or in a clinic.

71. According to the above passage, as delinquents get older, their crimes generally become

    (A) more serious and more frequent.
    (B) more serious but less frequent.
    (C) less serious but more frequent.
    (D) less serious and less frequent.

72. The author of the above passage suggests that delinquents should receive

    (A) severe punishment at the time of their first offense.
    (B) institutional care until such time that they may prove themselves capable of functioning in a free society.
    (C) treatment at preadolescence and early adolescence at the first signs of disregard for societal norms.
    (D) continuous psychological counseling from the time of their first offense until they reach legal age.

73. According to the above passage, delinquent gang members pose a problem that should be the responsibility of the

    (A) community.
    (B) police.
    (C) courts.
    (D) social worker.

74. According to the preceding passage, follow-up studies on delinquent gang members have underestimated the percent of gang members who continued to adult crime because

    (A) their sample was biased: it only involved urban gang members.
    (B) the studies did not follow the "career" of the sample group for a long enough period of time.
    (C) the studies concerned only those juveniles who, as adults, were dealt with by the police and not those who appeared in court or were referred to a clinic.
    (D) the method of following a group of gang members rather than tracing back a group of adult offenders was invalid.

75. According to the preceding passage, what is the actual percent of delinquent gang members who continue into adult crime?

    (A) 20 percent
    (B) 40 percent
    (C) 50 percent
    (D) 60 percent

# MODEL EXAMINATION 4: ANSWERS AND EXPLANATIONS

## ANSWERS

| | | | | |
|---|---|---|---|---|
| 1. A | 16. C | 31. B | 46. A | 61. C |
| 2. B | 17. B | 32. C | 47. D | 62. C |
| 3. D | 18. C | 33. A | 48. B | 63. A |
| 4. C | 19. B | 34. B | 49. C | 64. C |
| 5. B | 20. D | 35. B | 50. D | 65. B |
| 6. B | 21. A | 36. D | 51. B | 66. B |
| 7. B | 22. B | 37. A | 52. C | 67. A |
| 8. C | 23. B | 38. C | 53. B | 68. B |
| 9. D | 24. D | 39. C | 54. A | 69. B |
| 10. C | 25. D | 40. A | 55. D | 70. C |
| 11. D | 26. A | 41. B | 56. B | 71. A |
| 12. B | 27. D | 42. A | 57. D | 72. C |
| 13. C | 28. D | 43. C | 58. B | 73. A |
| 14. C | 29. A | 44. D | 59. B | 74. B |
| 15. C | 30. D | 45. C | 60. A | 75. B |

## EXPLANATIONS

1. **The correct answer is (A).** False praise is never a good motivator.
2. **The correct answer is (B).** Truth in sentencing and determinate sentencing is slowly doing away with parole.
3. **The correct answer is (D).** The use of technology in learning is changing how people learn and is an attempt to become more responsive to the learner.
4. **The correct answer is (C).** Interstate means between states.
5. **The correct answer is (B).** It is difficult to study practical courses by correspondence. They generally require some kind of hands-on work.
6. **The correct answer is (B).** A training program's effectiveness can be measured by its results, not in the feelings it engenders.
7. **The correct answer is (B).** The better the fit between program and participants, the better the results will be.
8. **The correct answer is (C).** The theory behind corrections is (or should be) about protecting the public first; everything else comes second.
9. **The correct answer is (D).** It is the responsibility of the parole board to address the question of parole.
10. **The correct answer is (C).** Halfway houses facilitate a gradual return to civilian life.
11. **The correct answer is (D).** Any skill that cannot be used in civilian life is of little use to the convict.
12. **The correct answer is (B).** A meeting between the trainer and trainee is not necessary for success.

13. **The correct answer is (C).** The general belief is that juveniles are more likely to be changed than adults.
14. **The correct answer is (C).** The quality of the interpersonal relationship is of least importance.
15. **The correct answer is (C).** Videotape does not lend itself to student-teacher interaction.
16. **The correct answer is (C).** Inmate education tries to follow current trends and needs.
17. **The correct answer is (B).** Role-playing puts the staff in the role of convict.
18. **The correct answer is (C).** Programmed learning texts require as much concentration as regular instruction methods.
19. **The correct answer is (B).** Constant supervision makes both employees and supervisors less productive.
20. **The correct answer is (D).** Drug programs are best suited to community corrections.
21. **The correct answer is (A).** One needs to know the daily prisoner count and number of officers on duty that day for planning and security purposes.
22. **The correct answer is (B).** Juvenile detention is the equivalent of adult jail.
23. **The correct answer is (B).** Supervision is the critical watching and directing of the probationer or parolee.
24. **The correct answer is (D).** These groups exist to provide defenses for people accused/convicted of crimes.
25. **The correct answer is (D).** Prison work benefits the institution, not the prisoner's personal needs.
26. **The correct answer is (A).** Specialized units can better serve/supervise specialized types of convicts.
27. **The correct answer is (D).** Sex offenders are held in disdain even by their fellow inmates because of the type of crime they committed.
28. **The correct answer is (D).** Probationers and parolees can be searched at any time by any peace officer.
29. **The correct answer is (A).** Attitudinal change is more subjective than objective.
30. **The correct answer is (D).** Training goals need to reflect department or agency goals.
31. **The correct answer is (B).** The courts have taken a more active role in deciding what types of programs are constitutional.
32. **The correct answer is (C).** Bail is a way of ensuring appearance in court, not necessarily of keeping someone in jail.
33. **The correct answer is (A).** Innovation traditionally garners fewer tax dollars.
34. **The correct answer is (B).** The *Uniform Crime Reports* (UCR) is considered to be the best source of criminal justice statistics.
35. **The correct answer is (B).** Pardon restores a convict's civil rights.
36. **The correct answer is (D).** The idea of a convict returning to civilian life has not yet been fully accepted by society.
37. **The correct answer is (A).** Society never really knows if an offender is rehabilitated or not.
38. **The correct answer is (C).** Reformation involves trying to understand the feelings of the offender.
39. **The correct answer is (C).** In order for reformation to occur, reintegration must be considered.
40. **The correct answer is (A).** Since reintegration has not been accepted, the cycle will begin again.
41. **The correct answer is (B).** The author discusses various historical treatment approaches to criminals.
42. **The correct answer is (A).** According to the passage, most people outgrow criminality.
43. **The correct answer is (C).** According to the passage, personality and age better reflect how one will do in prison.
44. **The correct answer is (D).** According to the passage, one's personality goes a long way toward explaining response to prison and to reoffending.

45. **The correct answer is (C).** According to the passage, the more predictors one has, the better chance there will be for accurate prediction.

46. **The correct answer is (A).** According to the passage, delinquent boys from a higher socioeconomic background tend to commit more serious crimes.

47. **The correct answer is (D).** The later one starts a criminal career, the more likely it will be a serious offense.

48. **The correct answer is (B).** According to the passage, the environment is to blame for one's criminality.

49. **The correct answer is (C).** It is always difficult to reconcile differing philosophies (and this has been a continuing problem for corrections).

50. **The correct answer is (D).** Personal irresponsibility is also the classical explanation for crime.

51. **The correct answer is (B).** See Chart III. Add the percentages under the column "Completed Section I." This includes Victimless Crimes (40%), Crimes Against Property (3%), and Violent Crimes (35%). The total is 78%.

52. **The correct answer is (C).** According to Chart II, 162 inmates completed Section II and therefore went on to Section III. Only 83 inmates completed Section III. That's about one half of the number that completed Section II and therefore is closest to 2.1:1.

53. **The correct answer is (B).** See Chart I. The solid line represents victimless crimes.

54. **The correct answer is (A).** In Week 5 of Section I, there were approximately 215 people who enrolled, and in Section III there were 125 enrolled. The difference is 90 $(215 - 125 = 90)$.

55. **The correct answer is (D).** Approximately 175 inmates enrolled in the first week of the program $(.60 \times 175 = 105)$.

56. **The correct answer is (B).** There was an increase from 50 to 70 people, or almost a 29% increase $\left( \dfrac{20}{70} = .2857 \right)$.

57. **The correct answer is (D).** One's past record is always an important factor in being convicted.

58. **The correct answer is (B).** All too often the convict is just thrown into on-the-job training without any discussion or preplanning.

59. **The correct answer is (B).** Lecturing is one-way communication, but some topics are conducive to this type of information transmittal.

60. **The correct answer is (A).** If an offender fails to return to incarceration, the program is generally considered to be successful.

61. **The correct answer is (C).** Classification attempts to find the best fit for the convict.

62. **The correct answer is (C).** If a program is popular, more instructors can always be found or more sections of the training program offered.

63. **The correct answer is (A).** The whole objective of corrections is to keep the offender from reoffending.

64. **The correct answer is (C).** A discussion leader is a facilitator.

65. **The correct answer is (B).** The primary function of employees in adult correctional institutions is that of custody and control of the inmates. While there are surely other areas of employment, as presented in the other choices, they are ancillary to the primary responsibility of correctional institutions.

66. **The correct answer is (B).** Jails hold individuals convicted, awaiting trial, and awaiting transport to state facilities.

67. **The correct answer is (A).** Prison management is primarily responsible for the custody and control of the prisoners.

68. **The correct answer is (B).** The justice model is an attempt to hold offenders accountable for their behavior.

69. **The correct answer is (B).** The reduced cost of prison goods makes the private sector unhappy.
70. **The correct answer is (C).** Many people either do not read the paper or do not believe what is printed in it.
71. **The correct answer is (A).** This is especially so with gang members.
72. **The correct answer is (C).** The earlier the delinquent get treatment, the better our success with them will be.
73. **The correct answer is (A).** The community has a role to play, but it is a shared responsibility.
74. **The correct answer is (B).** Some gang members stop their criminality and then return to it.
75. **The correct answer is (B).** According to the passage, the answer is 40 percent.

# MODEL EXAMINATION 5: ANSWER SHEET

1. Ⓐ Ⓑ Ⓒ Ⓓ
2. Ⓐ Ⓑ Ⓒ Ⓓ
3. Ⓐ Ⓑ Ⓒ Ⓓ
4. Ⓐ Ⓑ Ⓒ Ⓓ
5. Ⓐ Ⓑ Ⓒ Ⓓ
6. Ⓐ Ⓑ Ⓒ Ⓓ
7. Ⓐ Ⓑ Ⓒ Ⓓ
8. Ⓐ Ⓑ Ⓒ Ⓓ
9. Ⓐ Ⓑ Ⓒ Ⓓ
10. Ⓐ Ⓑ Ⓒ Ⓓ
11. Ⓐ Ⓑ Ⓒ Ⓓ
12. Ⓐ Ⓑ Ⓒ Ⓓ
13. Ⓐ Ⓑ Ⓒ Ⓓ
14. Ⓐ Ⓑ Ⓒ Ⓓ
15. Ⓐ Ⓑ Ⓒ Ⓓ
16. Ⓐ Ⓑ Ⓒ Ⓓ
17. Ⓐ Ⓑ Ⓒ Ⓓ
18. Ⓐ Ⓑ Ⓒ Ⓓ
19. Ⓐ Ⓑ Ⓒ Ⓓ
20. Ⓐ Ⓑ Ⓒ Ⓓ

21. Ⓐ Ⓑ Ⓒ Ⓓ
22. Ⓐ Ⓑ Ⓒ Ⓓ
23. Ⓐ Ⓑ Ⓒ Ⓓ
24. Ⓐ Ⓑ Ⓒ Ⓓ
25. Ⓐ Ⓑ Ⓒ Ⓓ
26. Ⓐ Ⓑ Ⓒ Ⓓ
27. Ⓐ Ⓑ Ⓒ Ⓓ
28. Ⓐ Ⓑ Ⓒ Ⓓ
29. Ⓐ Ⓑ Ⓒ Ⓓ
30. Ⓐ Ⓑ Ⓒ Ⓓ
31. Ⓐ Ⓑ Ⓒ Ⓓ
32. Ⓐ Ⓑ Ⓒ Ⓓ
33. Ⓐ Ⓑ Ⓒ Ⓓ
34. Ⓐ Ⓑ Ⓒ Ⓓ
35. Ⓐ Ⓑ Ⓒ Ⓓ
36. Ⓐ Ⓑ Ⓒ Ⓓ
37. Ⓐ Ⓑ Ⓒ Ⓓ
38. Ⓐ Ⓑ Ⓒ Ⓓ
39. Ⓐ Ⓑ Ⓒ Ⓓ
40. Ⓐ Ⓑ Ⓒ Ⓓ

41. Ⓐ Ⓑ Ⓒ Ⓓ
42. Ⓐ Ⓑ Ⓒ Ⓓ
43. Ⓐ Ⓑ Ⓒ Ⓓ
44. Ⓐ Ⓑ Ⓒ Ⓓ
45. Ⓐ Ⓑ Ⓒ Ⓓ
46. Ⓐ Ⓑ Ⓒ Ⓓ
47. Ⓐ Ⓑ Ⓒ Ⓓ
48. Ⓐ Ⓑ Ⓒ Ⓓ
49. Ⓐ Ⓑ Ⓒ Ⓓ
50. Ⓐ Ⓑ Ⓒ Ⓓ
51. Ⓐ Ⓑ Ⓒ Ⓓ
52. Ⓐ Ⓑ Ⓒ Ⓓ
53. Ⓐ Ⓑ Ⓒ Ⓓ
54. Ⓐ Ⓑ Ⓒ Ⓓ
55. Ⓐ Ⓑ Ⓒ Ⓓ
56. Ⓐ Ⓑ Ⓒ Ⓓ
57. Ⓐ Ⓑ Ⓒ Ⓓ
58. Ⓐ Ⓑ Ⓒ Ⓓ
59. Ⓐ Ⓑ Ⓒ Ⓓ
60. Ⓐ Ⓑ Ⓒ Ⓓ

61. Ⓐ Ⓑ Ⓒ Ⓓ
62. Ⓐ Ⓑ Ⓒ Ⓓ
63. Ⓐ Ⓑ Ⓒ Ⓓ
64. Ⓐ Ⓑ Ⓒ Ⓓ
65. Ⓐ Ⓑ Ⓒ Ⓓ
66. Ⓐ Ⓑ Ⓒ Ⓓ
67. Ⓐ Ⓑ Ⓒ Ⓓ
68. Ⓐ Ⓑ Ⓒ Ⓓ
69. Ⓐ Ⓑ Ⓒ Ⓓ
70. Ⓐ Ⓑ Ⓒ Ⓓ

# MODEL EXAMINATION 5: SUPERVISING PROBATION OFFICER

**4 HOURS; 70 QUESTIONS**

> **Directions:** Each question has four suggested answers, lettered (A), (B), (C), and (D). Decide which one is the best answer and darken on your answer sheet the space that corresponds with your answer choice.

1. During his pre-sentence investigation, a defendant gave information about his participation in the offense that conflicted with the official version. He was placed on probation. Now the district attorney wishes to use him as a witness against a codefendant and asks for permission to use the pre-sentence report as a basis for cross-examination. Of the following, which is the best course of action to take?

    (A) Refuse to turn over the report on the grounds that the report is the property of the court and its contents cannot be revealed without authority of the court.

    (B) Turn over the report to the district attorney, but caution him to hold the source of his information confidential.

    (C) Refer the request to your supervisor.

    (D) Advise the district attorney's office that the entire report cannot be sent to him but portions of it may be discussed with his representative.

2. During the course of a pre-sentence investigation, the defendant reveals certain details of the offense not previously known and involves others who have not been apprehended. Of the following, which is the first action to be taken by the probation officer on the case?

    (A) Discuss this matter with the chief probation officer and ask for guidance on methods of procedure.

    (B) Report the new information to the district attorney's office immediately.

    (C) Withhold the information until it can be disclosed to the court through the pre-sentence report in order to let the court decide how it is to be used.

    (D) Advise the client of the importance of this information and ask him if he is prepared to make the same disclosures to the district attorney.

3. A young man on probation after an offense involving fraudulent checks and impersonation of an officer is given work at a hospital as an attendant. Within three weeks, he marries a nurse's aide. A full investigation discloses that he told her he was wealthy, of good family, and working humbly to "prove" himself. Of the following, which is first action for the probation officer to take in this case?

    (A) Secure a warrant and cause his arrest immediately.

    (B) Check with the hospital to get other details.

    (C) Attempt to analyze the behavior pattern for causative factors.

    (D) Recommend that the young couple get an annulment.

4. A probation officer comes to the supervisor greatly upset about a situation that he believes will result in the breakup of the marriage of one of his clients. He knows that the office has some emergency money and requests that this be advanced to his client so he can travel to Tampa, Florida, to see the wife. She is living there with her parents, who are antagonistic to the probationer. Of the following, which is the most important action for the supervisor to take?

   (A) Approve the request and expedite the loan.
   (B) Tell the probation officer to contact the parents and determine the reason for their antagonism to the probationer.
   (C) Tell the probation officer that his concern may be the result of overidentification with the probationer's problems.
   (D) Discuss with the probation officer the fact that he only has his client's version of the pending breakup and that more facts are necessary.

5. The wife of a former probationer telephones the probation office stating that her husband has disappeared and she is anxious to secure all possible leads in order to aid the police in looking for him. Of the following, which is the best way to reply?

   (A) This is a job for the police, but if there are any developments, she will be informed.
   (B) The case is closed and no help can be given to her.
   (C) She should consult her religious adviser and her attorney.
   (D) The husband has had numerous previous girlfriends to whom he might have returned.

6. A person of foreign birth is placed on probation but understands little English and cannot read or write. Of the following, which is the most appropriate action?

   (A) Order him to attend night classes in English.
   (B) Direct him to find someone who speaks his language to interpret the conditions of probation.
   (C) Encourage him to seek language training and tell him that his probation will be revoked if he shows unwillingness to overcome his language handicap.
   (D) Give him guidance in finding a language class that will fit his needs and situation.

7. The probation officer who made the pre-sentence investigation on a certain case happens to be personally acquainted with the judge who imposed sentence. Some time later, the judge receives a letter from the sentenced prisoner. The judge asks the probation officer to investigate this letter and make a recommendation. Of the following, which is the best action for the probation officer to take?

   (A) Make the investigation and report directly to the judge.
   (B) Ask the judge to speak to a superior about this assignment.
   (C) Complete the report and submit it to a superior for approval without prior consultation with the superior.
   (D) Report to a superior that there has been a request for a supplementary investigation and await decision as to whether it should be assigned to that officer or another officer.

8. A probation officer is given to extensive, detailed chronological entries in all of the cases under his supervision, even though typing service is at a premium. Of the following, which is the best course of action for the supervisor to take?

   (A) Explain that such extensive entries show a lack of understanding of the case and are, therefore, unnecessary.
   (B) Persuade him to trim his lengthy dictation to conserve typing and dictation time.

(C) Encourage him to vary his recording method according to the needs of the case, using periodic summaries or evaluative paragraphs as alternatives wherever possible.

(D) Help him to select one type of case recording that is appropriate to every case work situation.

9. Having read another agency's record for information, it is good case recording practice to

(A) quote the agency worker as the source of information and include any pertinent opinions given in the agency file.

(B) identify the source and report it over your signature as a part of the record.

(C) use the words "it is alleged," or "according to a reliable source," or "we have been informed."

(D) refer to the other agency as Confidential Source No. 1, etc.

10. Structuring judges' sentencing to attempt a more fair sentencing system is known as

(A) Sentencing Guidelines.

(B) the Sentencing Grid.

(C) the Sentencing Project.

(D) the Fairness in Sentencing Law.

11. The least important reason for a probation officer to make a pre-sentence investigation and report is to

(A) assist the judge in making proper disposition of the case.

(B) find conditions within the family that need the services of other agencies.

(C) assist the probation officer who will supervise the defendant if he or she is placed on probation.

(D) provide a case record for the institution if the defendant is committed.

12. Which of the following responsibilities of a supervisor of probation officers is the most important?

(A) Assist a probation officer, on an emergency basis, in the handling of the caseload if he or she is sick or overburdened.

(B) Check the amounts claimed by probation officers in expense accounts as fully as possible by personal visits or telephone.

(C) Require the probation officers under supervision to submit case reports at regular intervals and review these reports to ensure proper progress.

(D) Cooperate with other supervisors so that office policy will be uniform and fairly equal workloads can be maintained.

13. Whether an offender returns to prison is primarily the responsibility of

(A) the probation/parole officer.

(B) the judge.

(C) the parole board.

(D) the warden.

14. Which of the following is most accurate in regard to violation of probation?

(A) A violator should be returned to court only if guilty of a serious violation.

(B) A violator should be returned to court if further use of the authority of the court will have a therapeutic value in the case.

(C) A violator should be returned to court only if detention is necessary for community protection.

(D) A violator should be returned to court if commitment to a correctional institution had been under consideration before placement on probation.

196 Part Four: Model Examinations

15. In dealing with violations of probation that have resulted in arrest, the probation officer should first
    (A) arrange for an immediate hearing before the sentencing judge in the original case.
    (B) discuss and evaluate the new violation with the arresting officer.
    (C) place a detainer against the probationer.
    (D) secure a voluntary statement from the probationer including mention of guilt or innocence.

16. A probation officer sees a man on the street who he believes is being sought under warrant as a probation violator. The probationer is not under his supervision. Of the following, which is the first action the probation officer should take?
    (A) Identify himself to the man and attempt to determine the latter's identity.
    (B) Warn the probationer and report to his office that he has seen the violator.
    (C) Advise the probationer to give himself up.
    (D) Immediately contact the probation officer who has been supervising this probationer.

17. Probation primarily functions at
    (A) the state level.
    (B) the county level.
    (C) the city level.
    (D) the level most closely related to the offender.

18. A probation officer is a professional person who has specialized knowledge and skills in the area of case work in an authoritative setting. When the period of probation is ended, good probation practice suggests that
    (A) the probation officer cease to be interested in the probationer since the case is closed.
    (B) if there has been a good relationship between officer and probationer, contacts may be continued over a period of years.
    (C) the probation officer should remain the only person with whom the probationer can feel completely comfortable and confident.
    (D) the probation officer should maintain continued interest in the probationer so that case files can be built up and possibly used with other probationers.

19. In cases of juvenile delinquency, which of the following is NOT an advantage of probation over commitment to an institution?
    (A) Probation offers an individualized form of treatment.
    (B) Probation is less expensive.
    (C) Probation gives greater protection to the community.
    (D) Probation leaves the offender in normal home surroundings.

20. Which of the following is a problem for home detention?
    (A) Inability to adequately supervise those assigned to home detention
    (B) Failure of the judge to put individuals on home detention
    (C) Call forwarding
    (D) Failure of the family to cooperate

21. Of the following, the chief factor that limits the use of the services of private social case work agencies by probation departments is
    (A) the belief by probation departments that the private agencies are unable to give constructive services to the probationers.
    (B) that the law prohibits use of such services in most types of cases.
    (C) the reluctance of probationers to accept voluntarily the services of these agencies.
    (D) the prohibitive cost of these services to the courts.

ARCO  ■  Probation Officer/Parole Officer Exam

22. Environmental manipulation as an approach to treatment is often required in probation supervision. Of the following, the best illustration of this approach is a case in which the probation officer

   (A) adopts a positive rather than a negative attitude toward the client's future after probation is over.
   (B) suggests physical changes in the probationer's life and makes referrals to various social agencies for assistance.
   (C) applies knowledge of case work techniques in every aspect of probation supervision.
   (D) cautiously makes use of authority in supervision.

23. A probation officer shows the supervisor a letter he received from a committed prisoner on whom he had made a pre-sentence investigation. The prisoner requests information about himself obtained through the investigation. Of the following, which is the best action for the supervisor to take?

   (A) Tell the probation officer to reply to the letter with all the information requested.
   (B) Arrange for appropriate legal counsel with his own superior.
   (C) Return the letter to the warden at the institution, stating that the probation officer should be removed from the inmate's mailing list.
   (D) Advise the prisoner that the information secured is privileged and such details are not given to anyone outside the agency.

24. The disparity in the terms of sentences imposed by different judges in criminal courts for identical crimes has been a cause for serious concern. Of the following, the greatest problem involved in the imposition of a sentence is that

   (A) the judges do not have any basis on which to impose a sentence other than their own judgment.
   (B) a serious crime may be punishable by a shorter sentence than a minor offense.
   (C) some judges will enjoy greater popularity than others.
   (D) the term of sentence a criminal receives is within the limits set for the crime, dependent on varying standards of the judges.

25. In penal administration, "indeterminate sentence" means

   (A) a sentence with a length that depends on the behavior and improvement of the convicted person while in prison.
   (B) a long prison sentence at hard labor.
   (C) a sentence with a minimum and a maximum term determined by the judge within statutory limits.
   (D) a sentence based on circumstantial evidence.

26. "Experience pragmatically suggests that dislocation from cultural roots and customs makes for tension, insecurity, and anxiety. This holds for the child as well as the adolescent, for the new immigrant as well as the second-generation citizen." Of the following, the most important implication of the above statement for a social worker in any setting is that

   (A) anxiety, distress, and incapacity are always personal and can be understood best only through an understanding of the child's present cultural environment.
   (B) in order to resolve the conflicts caused by the displacement of a child from a home with one cultural background to one with another, it is essential that the child fully replace his or her old culture with the new one.
   (C) no treatment goal can be envisaged for a dislocated child that does not involve a value judgment, which is itself culturally determined.
   (D) anxiety and distress result from a child's reaction to culturally oriented treatment goals.

27. Accepting the fact that mentally gifted children represent superior heredity, the United States faces an important eugenic problem chiefly because

    (A)  unless these mentally gifted children mature and reproduce more rapidly than the less intelligent children, the nation is heading for a lowering of the average intelligence of its people.

    (B)  although the mentally gifted children always excel scholastically, such children generally have less physical stamina than the normal child and tend to lower the nation's population physically.

    (C)  the mentally subnormal are increasing more rapidly than the mentally gifted in America, thus affecting the overall level of achievement of gifted children.

    (D)  unless the mental level of the general population is raised to that of gifted children, the mentally gifted will eventually usurp the reigns of government and dominate the mentally weaker.

28. One of the most frequent criticisms of probation and parole is its level of

    (A)  political influence.

    (B)  professionalism.

    (C)  fragmentation.

    (D)  qualifications.

29. In many states, the only requirement to be a probation/parole officer is

    (A)  a high school diploma.

    (B)  a bachelor's degree.

    (C)  a master's degree.

    (D)  experience in social services.

30. In recent years there have been some significant changes in the treatment of patients in state psychiatric hospitals. These changes are primarily caused by the use of

    (A)  electric shock therapy.

    (B)  tranquilizing drugs.

    (C)  steroids.

    (D)  the open ward policy.

31. The psychological test that makes use of a set of twenty pictures each depicting a dramatic scene is known as the

    (A)  Goodenough Test.

    (B)  Thematic Apperception Test.

    (C)  Minnesota Multiphasic Personality Inventory.

    (D)  Healy Picture Completion Test.

32. One of the most effective ways in which experimental psychologists have been able to study the effects on personality of heredity and environment has been through the study of

    (A)  primitive cultures.

    (B)  identical twins.

    (C)  mental defectives.

    (D)  newborn infants.

33. In city hospitals with psychiatric divisions, the psychiatric function is predominantly that of

    (A)  the training of personnel in all psychiatric disciplines.

    (B)  protection of the community against potentially dangerous psychiatric patients.

    (C)  research and study of psychiatric patients so that new knowledge and information can be made generally available.

    (D)  short-term hospitalization designed to determine diagnosis and recommendations for treatment.

**34.** Predictions of human behavior on the basis of past behavior frequently are inaccurate because

(A) basic patterns of human behavior are in a continual state of flux.

(B) human behavior is not susceptible to explanation of a scientific nature.

(C) the underlying psychological mechanisms of behavior are not completely understood.

(D) quantitative techniques for the measurement of stimuli and responses are unavailable.

**35.** Sociocultural factors are being reevaluated in case work practice as they influence both the worker and the client in their participation in the case work process. Of the following factors, which one is currently being studied most widely?

(A) The social class of worker and client and its significance in case work

(B) The difference in native intelligence that can be ascribed to the racial origin of an individual

(C) The cultural values affecting the areas in which an individual functions

(D) The necessity in case work treatment of the client's membership in an organized religious group

**36.** Deviant behavior is a sociological term used to describe behavior that is not in accord with generally accepted standards. This may include juvenile delinquency, adult criminality, and mental or physical illness. Comparison of normal with deviant behavior is useful to case workers because it

(A) makes it possible to establish watertight behavioral descriptions.

(B) provides evidence of differential social behavior that distinguishes deviant from normal behavior.

(C) indicates that deviant behavior is of no concern to case workers.

(D) provides no evidence that social role is a determinant of behavior.

**37.** Alcoholism may affect an individual client's ability to function as a spouse, parent, worker, and citizen. A case worker's main responsibility to a client with a history of alcoholism is to

(A) interpret to the client the causes of alcoholism as a disease syndrome.

(B) work with the alcoholic's family to accept the individual and stop trying to reform him or her.

(C) encourage the family of the alcoholic to accept case work treatment.

(D) determine the origins of the particular drinking problem, establish a diagnosis, and work out a treatment plan for the individual.

**38.** There is a trend to regard narcotic addiction as a form of illness for which the current methods of intervention have not been effective. Research on the combination of social, psychological, and physical causes of addiction would indicate that social workers should

(A) oppose hospitalization of addicts in institutions.

(B) encourage the addict to live normally at home.

(C) recognize that there is no successful treatment for addiction and act accordingly.

(D) use the existing community facilities differentially for each addict.

**39.** A study of social relationships among delinquent and nondelinquent youths has shown that

(A) delinquent youths generally conceal their true feelings and maintain furtive social contacts.

(B) delinquents are more impulsive and vivacious than law-abiding youths.

(C) nondelinquent youths diminish their active social relationships in order to sublimate any antisocial impulses.

(D) delinquent and nondelinquent youths exhibit similar characteristics of impulsiveness and vivaciousness.

**40.** Which of the following is the chief danger of interpreting the delinquent behavior of a child in terms of morality alone when attempting to get at its causes?

(A) One may overlook the likelihood that the causes of the child's actions are more than a negation of morality and involve varied symptoms of disturbance.
(B) A child's moral outlook toward life and society is largely colored by that of the parents, thus encouraging parent-child conflicts.
(C) Too careful a consideration of the moral aspects of the offense and of the child's needs may often negate the demands of justice in a case.
(D) Standards of morality may be of no concern to the delinquent and he or she may not realize the seriousness of the offenses.

**41.** Of the following, the most essential goal of the case work supervisor in the management of a new worker should be to help the new worker

(A) achieve case work competence equal to that of the supervisor.
(B) match the case work standards of performance of other competent staff members.
(C) achieve individual, independent case work competence.
(D) learn new case work concepts.

**42.** Of the following, the most important single condition to be met in order to achieve a professionally sound evaluation of a case worker by the case work supervisor is that the

(A) evaluation process be shared by both the supervisor and the worker.
(B) supervisor have considerable experience in the process of evaluation.
(C) case worker's effectiveness be capable of testing by a follow-up review of closed cases.
(D) agency administrator participate in the evaluation process.

**43.** In planning with a staff worker the agenda for regularly scheduled supervisory conferences, it is expected that

(A) the worker will take some responsibility and initiative for learning needs.
(B) the supervisor would review the worker's records before each conference.
(C) administrative directives would determine the content of the conferences.
(D) over a span of time, an opportunity to review the worker's total caseload can be arranged.

**44.** When a case work student early in fieldwork experience expresses anxiety about the conduct of a forthcoming interview, the best course for the student's agency supervisor to take is to

(A) make a good agency case record available to the student as a sample.
(B) help the student prepare an outline of all the areas that should be covered in the interview.
(C) ascertain the personality factors that have created or contributed to this anxiety.
(D) encourage the student to approach the interview as a test and accept the inevitability of some mistakes.

**45.** Of the following, which case gave basic constitutional rights to juveniles at the adjudication stage?

(A) *Miranda v. Arizona*
(B) *Kent v. United States*
(C) *Stanford v. Kentucky*
(D) *In Re Gault*

**46.** A social worker brings to his case work supervisor a problem in which he disagrees with a firm recommendation of a consultant from another discipline. Of the following, the best course of action for the supervisor to take first is to

(A) analyze the situation with the worker and encourage him to work this problem out directly with the consultant.

(B) attempt to work the problem out directly with the consultant.

(C) discuss the relationship problem directly with the consultant's chief.

(D) bring the problem to the chief of social work services.

47. In handling a particular case, a case worker is using the services of both a consulting psychiatrist and the case work supervisor. The role of the supervisor is one of

(A) no responsibility to the case worker since the psychiatrist does the teaching.

(B) participation in the case worker's conferences with the psychiatrist so that the supervisor can be fully cognizant of the psychiatrist's recommendations.

(C) helping the case worker clarify questions and objectives to be achieved in conferences with the psychiatrist.

(D) making certain that the case worker fully carries out the psychiatrist's recommendation.

48. A supervisor who had been in charge of a certain unit had always orally and informally notified her workers at the start of each day of daily routine functions and operations that needed attention. She was transferred to another unit, and her successor substituted for the system of oral instructions the practice of informing her staff of such matters by means of short, written lists of what was to be done. The chief drawback of the procedure introduced by the new supervisor is that it

(A) reduces the area of interpersonal relations, which is so important to cordial supervisor-worker interaction.

(B) channels the job and creates in the minds of the workers the feeling that they may not exercise their judgment in any situation.

(C) prevents the staff from asking questions to clarify the details of the work to be performed during any particular day.

(D) provides for the establishment of a detailed routine working procedure without prior consultation of the employees who will actually do the work.

49. "Experts in the field of personnel administration generally agree that an employee should not be under the immediate supervision of more than one supervisor." A certain worker, because of an emergency situation, divides his time equally between two limited caseloads on a prearranged time schedule. Each unit has a different supervisor, and the worker performs substantially the same duties in each caseload. The above quotation is pertinent in this situation chiefly because

(A) each supervisor may demand too much of the worker's time, each feeling that the cases in her unit should have priority.

(B) the two supervisors may have different standards of work performance and may prefer different methods of doing the work.

(C) the worker works part-time on each caseload and may not have full knowledge or control of the situation in either caseload.

(D) the task of evaluating the worker's services will be doubled, with two supervisors instead of one having to rate the work.

50. Experts in modern personnel management generally agree that employees on all job levels should be permitted to offer suggestions for improving work methods. Of the following, the chief limitation of such suggestions is that they may at times

(A) be offered primarily for financial reward and not show genuine interest in improvement of work methods.

(B) be directed toward making individual jobs easier.

(C) be restricted by the employees' fear of radically changing the work methods favored by their supervisors.

(D) show little awareness of the effects on the overall objectives and functions of the entire agency.

**51.** Assume that you were recently appointed to the position of a unit supervisor. Since you are interested in doing your best in this new assignment and in learning your job as quickly as possible, you have been continuously supervising the tasks of your workers very closely. One of the experienced workers under your supervision tells you that she finds your constant and very close attention to her job performance both objectionable and unnecessary. The best action for you to take in this situation is to

(A) explain to the worker that, since you have the ultimate responsibility for ensuring the proper functioning of the unit, you are using the most appropriate method to do so.

(B) obtain a more detailed explanation of the worker's objections, tell her that you will think about them, and then critically examine your actions as a supervisor, seeking higher supervisory advice if it seems necessary.

(C) inform this worker that you are carefully scrutinizing the work of all your workers in this manner and that it would be unfair to exempt her from such close observation in spite of her long experience.

(D) suggest to the worker that, inasmuch as she was the only worker who had objected to your work style, she might be in the wrong.

**52.** A case work supervisor becomes aware that a worker has a troubling personal problem that interferes with the worker's efficiency. The appropriate action for the supervisor to take is to

(A) use supervision to resolve the worker's problem so that his level of efficiency can increase.

(B) help the worker to discipline his job functioning until the problem is resolved.

(C) refer the worker immediately to an appropriate service so that he might resolve his problem quickly.

(D) relieve the worker temporarily of difficult job responsibilities until he resolves his problem and increases his efficiency.

**53.** A case work supervisor has learned from the agency administrator that one of his workers has expressed dissatisfaction with him and has requested a transfer to another supervisor. Of the following, the most appropriate action for the supervisor to take is to

(A) be indulgent with the worker and attempt to elicit the worker's positive feelings toward him.

(B) terminate the supervisory relationship and approve the transfer of the worker.

(C) encourage the worker to express his dissatisfaction directly to him.

(D) urge the worker to postpone his request for transfer.

**54.** A case work supervisor becomes aware that one of his unit workers with a caseload comparable to that of other workers in the same unit spends several evenings a week working overtime. The supervisor can best deal with this situation by

(A) helping the worker organize his work more efficiently.

(B) commending the worker for his conscientiousness.

(C) prohibiting the worker from staying in the agency beyond office hours.

(D) reducing the worker's job responsibilities.

**55.** A case worker with a number of cases requiring extensive counseling has revealed in her case records a subtle but consistent rejection of domineering women. When the supervisor becomes aware of this pattern, she should

(A) suggest that the worker seek psychological help for her own problems as reflected in her case work bias.

(B) arrange to have all such cases handled by another worker who has no such pattern.

(C) tell the case worker that she must accept the role of the domineering woman in most family situations.

(D) make the pattern known to the worker and emphasize her availability to give supervisory help with it.

56. Your bureau is considering the establishment of a new bureauwide policy relating to its dealings with private agencies. The top administrative staff of the bureau wishes to obtain staff support in favor of the new policy. Which of the following is the best method of presenting the policy to the experienced rank and file workers in the bureau so that the details and ramifications of the policy under consideration will be clearly understood?

(A) Present each worker with a copy of the proposed policy and ask him or her to read it carefully and to prepare a list of recommendations for or against each major proposal in it.

(B) Divide the staff into two parts, one assuming the role of the bureau staff and the other the role of an agency staff, and have them act out the policy as it would be carried out on the operational level.

(C) Give each worker in the unit individual on-the-job training in the details of the proposed policy and ask each to try it out for a week in the field before forming any opinion concerning its feasibility.

(D) Hold a staff meeting with the workers in the unit to conduct an organized group discussion of the proposed policy and its various aspects.

57. Process recording of a case work interview is a useful supervisory tool because it

(A) makes possible verification of the client's statements about his or her resources.
(B) enables the case worker to formulate a social diagnosis.
(C) reveals the interaction of client and case worker.
(D) can readily be used for demonstration purposes.

58. In evaluating a skilled case worker's potential for becoming a competent case work supervisor, which of the following is the most important asset to have?

(A) The ability to communicate case work concepts dynamically
(B) The ability to conform fully to administrative requirements
(C) The ability to win the approval of people easily
(D) The ability to teach factual material effectively

59. The basic justification for the establishment of staff development seminars for case workers in an agency is that

(A) it promotes better service to the agency's clients.
(B) the shortage of case workers makes it necessary to hire some who are inadequately trained.
(C) it provides the supervisor with an opportunity to observe the function of the workers closely.
(D) the agency thereby becomes more attractive to prospective staff members.

60. In planning staff development seminars, the most valuable topics for discussion are likely to be those selected from

(A) staff suggestions based on the staff's interest and needs.
(B) topics recommended for consideration by professional organizations.
(C) topics selected by the administration based on demonstrated limitations of staff skill and knowledge.
(D) topics selected by the administration based on a combination of staff interest and objectively evaluated staff needs.

61. Staff meetings designed to promote professional staff development are most likely to achieve this goal when

    (A) there is wide participation among staff members who attend the meetings.
    (B) participation by the most skilled and experienced staff members is predominant.
    (C) participation by selected staff members is planned before the meeting sessions.
    (D) supervisory personnel take major responsibility for participation.

62. A unit supervisor is conducting a staff meeting that the division director has called for the purpose of determining how to meet the rising need for service in a certain area. The supervisor has been asked to serve as chairperson of the meeting. Which of the following steps should the chairperson take first at this meeting?

    (A) Assign specific responsibility to each staff member for the execution of some phase of the plan to be adopted in order to solve the problem expeditiously.
    (B) Break the overall problem down into workable units to make for a simpler solution.
    (C) Invite the members of the staff present to voice their opinions on how to solve the problem in light of the proposed plan of action.
    (D) Present a definitive and complete resume of the problem to be resolved.

63. Assume that you are the leader of a conference attended by representatives of various city and private agencies. After the conference has been under way for a considerable time, you realize that the representative of one of these agencies has said nothing. It would generally be best for you to

    (A) ask him if he would like to say anything.
    (B) ask the group a pertinent question that he would be best able to answer.
    (C) make no special effort to include him in the conversation.
    (D) address the next question you planned to ask to him directly.

64. A member of a decision-making conference generally makes his or her best contribution to the conference when he or she

    (A) compromises on his or her own point of view and accepts most of the points of other conference members.
    (B) persuades the conference to accept all or most of his or her points.
    (C) persuades the conference to accept his or her major proposals but yields on the minor ones.
    (D) succeeds in integrating his or her ideas with the ideas of the other conference members.

65. Which of the following is the least accurate statement concerning the compilation and use of statistics in social work?

    (A) Interpretation of statistics is as necessary as their compilation.
    (B) Statistical records of expenditures and services are one of the bases for budget preparation.
    (C) Statistics on the quality of services rendered to the community will clearly delineate the human values achieved.
    (D) The results achieved from collecting and compiling statistics must be in keeping with the cost and effort required.

66. A supervisor with a management load of 5 case workers receives a complaint from Ms. Adams, one of her case workers. Her complaint is that Mr. Brown, another case worker, has a lighter caseload and less demanding duties than his colleagues. Which of the following is the most appropriate action for the supervisor to take?

    (A) Explore the basis of Ms. Adams' complaint.
    (B) Refuse to discuss Mr. Brown's job responsibilities with Ms. Adams.

(C) Discuss the problem at a group conference.

(D) Reduce Ms. Adams' caseload and job responsibilities.

67. A client has complained to the case work supervisor that a worker on his case has been negligent in helping him with his problem. The supervisor reviews the situation, interviews the client, and ascertains that the client's complaint is an outgrowth of his overanxiety. The most appropriate course of action for the supervisor to take is to

(A) handle the case himself.

(B) refer the client back to his worker.

(C) refer the client to another social worker in the agency.

(D) refer the client to an appropriate community agency for help.

68. Assume that a social case worker has been newly assigned to a caseload of about seventy cases. In order for her to be able to meet promptly the needs of the clients in this caseload, she should first

(A) arrange for each client to come to the office for a brief interview.

(B) read the case history of each client to get a general understanding of the problems involved.

(C) concentrate on those cases having the most serious problems.

(D) make a short visit to the home of each client to determine immediate needs.

69. Caseloads are heavy in most social agencies. The most effective way for a case work supervisor to help his or her employees cope with the problem of a heavy caseload is to

(A) set a maximum time limit for all interviews and adhere strictly to this schedule.

(B) schedule clients for office interviews at infrequent intervals so that more interviewing time is available when the interview does take place.

(C) reduce the intake by asking the administrator to order more stringent intake policies.

(D) instruct workers to devote more interviewing time to serious problem cases and less time to clients who are making better adjustments.

70. Of the following, the most valuable contribution the supervisor can make in cases involving the counseling of clients with emotional problems is that of helping the worker on the case to

(A) decide the appropriate areas for consultation with a psychiatrist.

(B) achieve case work objectivity by distinguishing the client's problems from his or her own problems.

(C) determine when to terminate contact with the client.

(D) determine environmental problems involved in the client's situation.

# MODEL EXAMINATION 5: ANSWERS AND EXPLANATIONS

## ANSWERS

| | | | | | | | | |
|---|---|---|---|---|---|---|---|---|
| 1. C | | 16. A | | 31. B | | 46. A | | 61. A |
| 2. B | | 17. B | | 32. B | | 47. C | | 62. D |
| 3. C | | 18. B | | 33. D | | 48. A | | 63. D |
| 4. D | | 19. C | | 34. C | | 49. B | | 64. D |
| 5. A | | 20. C | | 35. C | | 50. D | | 65. C |
| 6. D | | 21. C | | 36. B | | 51. B | | 66. A |
| 7. D | | 22. B | | 37. D | | 52. C | | 67. B |
| 8. C | | 23. B | | 38. D | | 53. C | | 68. B |
| 9. B | | 24. D | | 39. B | | 54. A | | 69. D |
| 10. A | | 25. C | | 40. A | | 55. D | | 70. A |
| 11. D | | 26. C | | 41. C | | 56. D | | |
| 12. C | | 27. A | | 42. A | | 57. C | | |
| 13. C | | 28. C | | 43. A | | 58. A | | |
| 14. B | | 29. A | | 44. D | | 59. A | | |
| 15. B | | 30. B | | 45. D | | 60. D | | |

## EXPLANATIONS

1. **The correct answer is (C).** The release of the pre-sentence report should be approved by the supervisor.
2. **The correct answer is (B).** As an officer of the court, it is the probation officer's responsibility to report new information to the district attorney.
3. **The correct answer is (C).** The officer should try to figure out what the probationer's motivation is.
4. **The correct answer is (D).** All relevant information should be obtained before a decision is made.
5. **The correct answer is (A).** She should be referred to the police.
6. **The correct answer is (D).** You should also find an interpreter to assist you and the probationer.
7. **The correct answer is (D).** The judge received an *ex parte* communication and is acting on it. The supervisor is in charge.
8. **The correct answer is (C).** Not every case requires such extensive recording.
9. **The correct answer is (B).** Proper documentation regarding the source of information is very important.
10. **The correct answer is (A).** Sentencing guidelines are an attempt to standardize sentencing among judges.
11. **The correct answer is (D).** While all are important, the record for the institution is probably the least important. The institution will probably do its own assessment anyway.
12. **The correct answer is (C).** The supervisor must know what his or her probation officers are doing and how well they are doing it.

13. **The correct answer is (C).** Parole officers recommend; the parole board decides.
14. **The correct answer is (B).** The probationer must be made aware of the court's authority.
15. **The correct answer is (B).** Gathering information is important for decision making.
16. **The correct answer is (A).** The probation officer should identify himself and arrest the probationer (keeping officer safety in mind).
17. **The correct answer is (B).** While often a state agency, its practice is at the county level.
18. **The correct answer is (B).** Contacts could be continued, but professionalism should be maintained at all times.
19. **The correct answer is (C).** An offender who is off the streets is no longer a predator.
20. **The correct answer is (C).** New technology makes home detention more difficult.
21. **The correct answer is (C).** Many probationers are reluctant to seek help and often must be forced to do so.
22. **The correct answer is (B).** Getting the probationer to change his or her lifestyle is usually the only way to come close to keeping the individual from becoming an offender again.
23. **The correct answer is (B).** The response should be in keeping with the legal conditions in any given state.
24. **The correct answer is (D).** This is the reason for sentencing guidelines.
25. **The correct answer is (C).** The actual time served is decided by the parole board.
26. **The correct answer is (C).** The social worker's values should not subvert what is intrinsically best for the child.
27. **The correct answer is (A).** If one accepts that fact, finding and nurturing these children, whatever their social strata and economic circumstance, is paramount.
28. **The correct answer is (C).** Probation and parole are often considered to be separate from all aspects of the criminal justice system.
29. **The correct answer is (A).** This is the same standard as is required for other members of the criminal justice community.
30. **The correct answer is (B).** Although there has been an increase in the use of electric shock therapy, patients in state psychiatric hospitals (usually schizophrenic individuals) have benefited greatly from the use of tranquilizers that keep patients calm and enable them to function at a higher level.
31. **The correct answer is (B).** The test-taker reveals himself or herself by using his or her own experiences to explain the scenes.
32. **The correct answer is (B).** Heredity and environment are uniquely matched in identical twins.
33. **The correct answer is (D).** A short term of thirty days or less is the norm.
34. **The correct answer is (C).** People often change their behavior for inexplicable reasons.
35. **The correct answer is (C).** There has been a recent preoccupation with culture and its effects in corrections.
36. **The correct answer is (B).** This works if there is an agreed-upon standard of normalcy.
37. **The correct answer is (D).** The most important of these is the treatment plan for the alcoholic.
38. **The correct answer is (D).** Individualized treatment is always the preferred method.
39. **The correct answer is (B).** Impulsiveness runs counter to self-control.
40. **The correct answer is (A).** Examination by a physician might reveal medical problems or psychological explanations for the behavior.
41. **The correct answer is (C).** The case workers must learn to work on their own.
42. **The correct answer is (A).** The standard for evaluation should be communicated to the worker.
43. **The correct answer is (A).** Workers need to be self-starters and realize that they have a responsibility for their own success, education, and training.
44. **The correct answer is (D).** The best approach is to understand that mistakes will be made but that they are not debilitating.
45. **The correct answer is (D).** *Gault* is the juvenile's *Miranda*.

46. **The correct answer is (A).** The worker and the consultant should meet to determine why there are differences. The final responsibility, however, is the worker's.

47. **The correct answer is (C).** The supervisor should not do the worker's work.

48. **The correct answer is (A).** Interpersonal relations are important, but different supervisors have different styles.

49. **The correct answer is (B).** A person cannot serve "two masters" and should not be required to do so.

50. **The correct answer is (D).** Any suggestions need to be in line with the agency's mission. If the agency does not have a mission (or vision), then it needs to develop one.

51. **The correct answer is (B).** Supervisors should constantly be aware of their techniques and should modify them (when and where appropriate) for the workers who are being supervised.

52. **The correct answer is (C).** Referral to the appropriate agency is the best alternative and demonstrates concern on the part of the supervisor.

53. **The correct answer is (C).** The supervisor needs to understand the employee's reasons for dissatisfaction before any problem solving can occur.

54. **The correct answer is (A).** Balancing conscientiousness and efficiency is a difficult, but teachable, skill.

55. **The correct answer is (D).** The worker may not be aware of the pattern, so telling her and offering any assistance is the best course of action.

56. **The correct answer is (D).** The staff meeting is the quickest and probably the most efficient method of getting feedback, although, in such a setting, many employees will not respond.

57. **The correct answer is (C).** Knowing how the worker interacts with clients helps the supervisor oversee and evaluate the worker.

58. **The correct answer is (A).** The ability to communicate effectively is probably the most important skill for a supervisor.

59. **The correct answer is (A).** Constant training is important for workers to maintain their skills.

60. **The correct answer is (D).** Training topics should bridge the gap between workers' interests and needs and the administration's needs.

61. **The correct answer is (A).** Wide participation of staff members enriches the development of all.

62. **The correct answer is (D).** This is also known as setting the agenda for the meeting.

63. **The correct answer is (D).** Some people will respond only when asked directly.

64. **The correct answer is (D).** Whenever an individual can share ownership in an idea, success will be achieved.

65. **The correct answer is (C).** Statistics cannot serve as the basis for evaluating human values.

66. **The correct answer is (A).** Information must be gathered before a decision can be rendered.

67. **The correct answer is (B).** Generally, the workers should always handle the problems of their caseload.

68. **The correct answer is (B).** This is the most efficient way of obtaining knowledge and information, but the new worker should understand that not all case workers are good at documenting.

69. **The correct answer is (D).** Supervisors need to assist their workers in prioritizing clients' needs.

70. **The correct answer is (A).** No agency can handle all client problems. The case worker needs to know how, when, and to whom to refer the client.

# MODEL EXAMINATION 6: ANSWER SHEET

1. Ⓐ Ⓑ Ⓒ Ⓓ      21. Ⓐ Ⓑ Ⓒ Ⓓ      41. Ⓐ Ⓑ Ⓒ Ⓓ      61. Ⓐ Ⓑ Ⓒ Ⓓ

2. Ⓐ Ⓑ Ⓒ Ⓓ      22. Ⓐ Ⓑ Ⓒ Ⓓ      42. Ⓐ Ⓑ Ⓒ Ⓓ      62. Ⓐ Ⓑ Ⓒ Ⓓ

3. Ⓐ Ⓑ Ⓒ Ⓓ      23. Ⓐ Ⓑ Ⓒ Ⓓ      43. Ⓐ Ⓑ Ⓒ Ⓓ      63. Ⓐ Ⓑ Ⓒ Ⓓ

4. Ⓐ Ⓑ Ⓒ Ⓓ      24. Ⓐ Ⓑ Ⓒ Ⓓ      44. Ⓐ Ⓑ Ⓒ Ⓓ      64. Ⓐ Ⓑ Ⓒ Ⓓ

5. Ⓐ Ⓑ Ⓒ Ⓓ      25. Ⓐ Ⓑ Ⓒ Ⓓ      45. Ⓐ Ⓑ Ⓒ Ⓓ      65. Ⓐ Ⓑ Ⓒ Ⓓ

6. Ⓐ Ⓑ Ⓒ Ⓓ      26. Ⓐ Ⓑ Ⓒ Ⓓ      46. Ⓐ Ⓑ Ⓒ Ⓓ      66. Ⓐ Ⓑ Ⓒ Ⓓ

7. Ⓐ Ⓑ Ⓒ Ⓓ      27. Ⓐ Ⓑ Ⓒ Ⓓ      47. Ⓐ Ⓑ Ⓒ Ⓓ      67. Ⓐ Ⓑ Ⓒ Ⓓ

8. Ⓐ Ⓑ Ⓒ Ⓓ      28. Ⓐ Ⓑ Ⓒ Ⓓ      48. Ⓐ Ⓑ Ⓒ Ⓓ      68. Ⓐ Ⓑ Ⓒ Ⓓ

9. Ⓐ Ⓑ Ⓒ Ⓓ      29. Ⓐ Ⓑ Ⓒ Ⓓ      49. Ⓐ Ⓑ Ⓒ Ⓓ      69. Ⓐ Ⓑ Ⓒ Ⓓ

10. Ⓐ Ⓑ Ⓒ Ⓓ      30. Ⓐ Ⓑ Ⓒ Ⓓ      50. Ⓐ Ⓑ Ⓒ Ⓓ      70. Ⓐ Ⓑ Ⓒ Ⓓ

11. Ⓐ Ⓑ Ⓒ Ⓓ      31. Ⓐ Ⓑ Ⓒ Ⓓ      51. Ⓐ Ⓑ Ⓒ Ⓓ      71. Ⓐ Ⓑ Ⓒ Ⓓ

12. Ⓐ Ⓑ Ⓒ Ⓓ      32. Ⓐ Ⓑ Ⓒ Ⓓ      52. Ⓐ Ⓑ Ⓒ Ⓓ      72. Ⓐ Ⓑ Ⓒ Ⓓ

13. Ⓐ Ⓑ Ⓒ Ⓓ      33. _____      53. Ⓐ Ⓑ Ⓒ Ⓓ      73. Ⓐ Ⓑ Ⓒ Ⓓ

14. Ⓐ Ⓑ Ⓒ Ⓓ      34. _____      54. Ⓐ Ⓑ Ⓒ Ⓓ      74. Ⓐ Ⓑ Ⓒ Ⓓ

15. Ⓐ Ⓑ Ⓒ Ⓓ      35. _____      55. Ⓐ Ⓑ Ⓒ Ⓓ      75. Ⓐ Ⓑ Ⓒ Ⓓ

16. Ⓐ Ⓑ Ⓒ Ⓓ      36. _____      56. Ⓐ Ⓑ Ⓒ Ⓓ

17. Ⓐ Ⓑ Ⓒ Ⓓ      37. _____      57. Ⓐ Ⓑ Ⓒ Ⓓ

18. Ⓐ Ⓑ Ⓒ Ⓓ      38. Ⓐ Ⓑ Ⓒ Ⓓ      58. Ⓐ Ⓑ Ⓒ Ⓓ

19. Ⓐ Ⓑ Ⓒ Ⓓ      39. Ⓐ Ⓑ Ⓒ Ⓓ      59. Ⓐ Ⓑ Ⓒ Ⓓ

20. Ⓐ Ⓑ Ⓒ Ⓓ      40. Ⓐ Ⓑ Ⓒ Ⓓ      60. Ⓐ Ⓑ Ⓒ Ⓓ

# MODEL EXAMINATION 6: SUPERVISING PROBATION OFFICER

**4 HOURS; 75 QUESTIONS**

> **Directions:** Each question has four suggested answers, lettered (A), (B), (C), and (D). Decide which one is the best answer and darken on your answer sheet the space that corresponds with your answer choice.

1. The most important of the following functions of a supervisor of probation officers in relation to the staff is to
   - (A) conduct conferences for staff members with problem situations in their caseload.
   - (B) maintain adequate statistical controls over the work of the staff.
   - (C) observe and evaluate the day-to-day relationships between the probation officers and the probationers.
   - (D) provide leadership and guidance for the staff.

2. Of the following contributions that a supervisor may make to the development of a probation officer under his or her supervision, which would be most helpful in the professional growth of this officer?
   - (A) Providing necessary information regarding the function and structure of the court and the services offered by community agencies
   - (B) Assisting him or her in achieving a nonjudgmental attitude toward his or her probationers
   - (C) Suggesting evening courses in the field for which the probation officer may register
   - (D) Evaluating the probation officer's needs, capacities, and weaknesses and planning work with him or her on them

3. It has been said that supervision of the worker helps to remove the "I" from the worker-client relationship. This statement means most nearly that supervision
   - (A) helps the worker maintain a professional attitude in the treatment process.
   - (B) prevents the worker from making important decisions without consulting a more experienced person.
   - (C) helps the client achieve ego status in the relationship to the worker.
   - (D) presents deviations from the client-centered orientation that is operative in most agencies today.

4. In interpreting the specific qualifications for the correction field to professionally trained new workers, it is most important for the administrator to emphasize that the worker must
   - (A) come to terms with himself or herself and accept the role of authority and the routines prescribed by law.
   - (B) learn methods of investigation and supervision in probation.
   - (C) accept the fact that there will be no supervision by professionally trained personnel.
   - (D) recognize that caseloads will be excessive and therefore opportunities for case work will be virtually nonexistent.

5. In evaluating the work performance of a probation officer under supervision, which of the following factors is the most important for the supervisor to consider?

   (A) The extent to which probationers keep their appointments for reporting
   (B) The size of the caseload the probation officer is able to carry
   (C) The resourcefulness shown by the probation officer in planning for probationers
   (D) The attitude of probationers to the probation officer at the close of their periods of supervision

6. Which of the following is least important to the overall effectiveness of a supervisor of probation officers?

   (A) Rights and welfare of the probationers receive full consideration.
   (B) Staff members perform their duties in accordance with established policy and legal restrictions.
   (C) Staff members perform their duties promptly and efficiently.
   (D) Standards of service to probationers preclude the possibility of criticism by other community agencies.

7. Supervision in social case work is a helping and an educating process. In order for it to be effective with a student trainee, the supervising case worker must

   (A) frequently sacrifice his or her own meaningful relationship with the client and let the student's sometimes awkward relationship intervene.
   (B) never be separated from the client.
   (C) recognize that the student's professional growth is not worth even a temporary inconvenience to the client.
   (D) immediately intervene and take the case out of the student's hands when the latter's approach shows signs of bungling.

8. With respect to making special assignments to members of the staff, a supervisor of probation officers should generally

   (A) avoid making special assignments since they breed favoritism.
   (B) make the special assignments in accordance with the capacities of the probation officers.
   (C) distribute the special assignments equally among the staff.
   (D) train all probation officers so that any one of them is able to handle any special assignment.

9. Suppose that a supervising probation officer, with heavy responsibilities, has a sudden vacancy on the probation staff that cannot be filled for a period of six weeks. In arranging the caseload of the missing worker during the period, the supervisor should

   (A) divide the caseload among the other probation officers and reorganize the assignments completely when the new probation officer reports.
   (B) assign temporarily to other workers those cases requiring immediate action or those in which emergencies develop.
   (C) assume direct responsibility for case work service to the clients of the missing probation officer.
   (D) assign a student trainee to assume temporary responsibility for the caseload.

10. In the planning of an in-service training program for probation officers, the least important of the following goals would be to

   (A) establish the need for group conferences within individual units.
   (B) help the staff develop a better understanding of the dynamics of human behavior.
   (C) give the staff members opportunities to further their professional development.
   (D) learn more about the programs and services of community agencies.

11. If a supervisor is not alert enough to recognize and help resolve confusion on the part of the worker, the latter will ultimately show frustration in some way. Out of such frustration, an improved professional relationship can emerge if

    (A) the supervisor has the strength to make an admission of fault to the worker without giving up the function of supervisor.
    (B) the administrative regulations are sufficiently flexible so as to permit transfers of supervision without incurring antagonisms.
    (C) no injury has been done to any client.
    (D) the supervisor has the integrity and willingness to recognize what has been done and to ask his or her own supervisor for assistance.

12. In discussing the work of a probation officer, a supervisor should be especially careful to refrain from comments touching on the probation officer's

    (A) personal characteristics.
    (B) lateness in submitting reports.
    (C) faulty spelling.
    (D) intelligence.

13. If a worker under your supervision disagrees with your evaluation of his performance, the most desirable way for you to handle the situation is to

    (A) arrange for a conference between the worker, your supervisor, and yourself for case review purposes.
    (B) explain that you are in a better position than he to assess his performance objectively.
    (C) give him the basis of your evaluation and let him talk to you about it freely.
    (D) discuss specific details with him and show where improvement is necessary.

14. For a supervisor who has made an error in judgment or in procedure to accept responsibility openly for this error is

    (A) desirable; such admission will indicate to the staff that it is the policy of supervision to treat errors leniently.
    (B) undesirable; such action will cause the staff to lose confidence in the supervisor.
    (C) desirable; such action will result in improved professional relationships between supervisor and staff.
    (D) undesirable; such admission will reflect unfavorably on the entire staff.

15. From the standpoint of the role of administrator of a probation division, the supervising probation officer is chiefly responsible for

    (A) execution of probation policies and ensuring that the probation officers operate in accordance with the law.
    (B) professional development of new probation officers in the area of case work techniques.
    (C) programs of training designed to stimulate the professional growth of the probation officers, with the ability to operate independently as the eventual goal.
    (D) seeing that the needs of probationers are met on an objective basis, without undue emotionalism on the part of the probation officers.

16. When a supervising probation officer represents the probation department at court sessions, the relationship between the officer and the court is least dependent upon the

    (A) acceptance by the judge of the aims of probation.
    (B) individual judge assigned to the court.
    (C) jurisdiction of the particular court.
    (D) regulations stated or indicated in the probation law.

17. In a probation department with separate investigation and supervision units, a case supervisor assigns a supervision caseload to a probation officer who is equally skilled in investigation and supervision but who has indicated a preference for investigation. The case supervisor's action was

    (A) wise; the probation officer should be discouraged from concentrating on investigation.
    (B) unwise; the case supervisor failed to take account of the human factor.
    (C) wise; the probation officer should not have voiced a preference.
    (D) unwise; the case supervisor's assignment worked to the detriment of the department.

18. A probation officer supervising a probationer believes that the man has been making no effort to find employment. He brings this up in an interview, finds the man resistant to his suggestions for finding or seeking a job, and finally tells the man that unless he finds a job, any job, soon, he will cite him for violation of probation and bring him before the judge. When the man responds by saying that he will not take a job unless he finds one in which he is interested, the probation officer goes to his supervisor and requests permission to cite the man as a probation violator. In this situation, it would be best for the supervisor to

    (A) discuss the matter with the probation officer and advise him to first explore the situation with the probationer in order to determine the basis for the man's attitudes and to help him to face the reality of his situation.
    (B) give the probation officer permission to cite the man for violation immediately.
    (C) see the probationer himself and explore the situation with him in order to determine the basis for his attitudes and to help him face the reality of his situation.
    (D) transfer supervision of the probationer to another probation officer without going into the situation any further.

19. Probation staff meetings should generally not be called for the purpose of

    (A) discussing specific applications of policies.
    (B) evaluating the degree of success that has resulted from the application of newly adopted procedures.
    (C) sharing experiences and problems.
    (D) reaching a decision on a difficult case.

20. Which of the following is the most valuable single supervisory method of evaluating the work of a probation officer?

    (A) An intensive interview at the time of the annual evaluation
    (B) Discussion of the probation officer's work with the case supervisor
    (C) Case reading
    (D) A schedule of weekly group conferences

21. Assume that a probation officer, in working with probationers, is unable to understand and deal with the causative factors underlying various types of symptomatic behavior. As a result, the handling of probationers in the caseload is both superficial and ineffectual. Under these circumstances, the supervising probation officer should

    (A) consider transferring this probation officer to another supervisor.
    (B) suggest that the probation officer read more in the field of mental hygiene.
    (C) supervise this probation officer more intensively, evaluating total functioning and building on strengths.
    (D) in the future assign cases to the probation officer that require only environmental manipulation.

22. When a judge complains to a supervisor that a probation officer's reports on violations of probation are inadequate, the supervisor should
    - (A) discuss the matter with the chief probation officer.
    - (B) review future violation reports with the probation officer before they are submitted.
    - (C) assign another probation officer to prepare future violation of probation reports.
    - (D) supervise the probation officer more closely in all aspects of work.

23. Planning supervision and treatment for probationers is an essential part of the work of the probation department. The most desirable of the following methods of handling this phase of the work is to have the
    - (A) probation officer consult with the supervisor before making any plans.
    - (B) probation officer develop several possible plans and consult with the supervisor before deciding which plan to use.
    - (C) probation officer initiate his or her own plans, subject to the approval of the supervisor.
    - (D) supervisor formulate the plan in each case and turn it over to the probation officer to carry out.

24. Of the following, the major practical reason for dividing a probation staff into two separate divisions—investigation and supervision—is that
    - (A) during periods when pre-sentence investigations are excessively heavy, supervision is bound to suffer.
    - (B) probation officers must learn to specialize if they are to achieve professional status.
    - (C) two different personalities are required, since investigation involves the ability to elicit facts, whereas supervision involves case work skills.
    - (D) workers engaged in supervision, which requires greater professional skill, should receive higher salaries.

25. Assume that a supervisor of probation officers has submitted a report and recommendation in connection with the pre-sentence investigation of a difficult case by one of his probation officers. The judge has decided not to follow the recommendation. The supervisor's knowledge of all the pertinent facts leads him to believe that his recommendation is the only acceptable course of action. It would be most desirable for him to
    - (A) accept the judge's decision since the ultimate responsibility is his.
    - (B) discuss the case and his recommendation with one of the other judges and ask him to interpret the recommendation to the judge handling the case.
    - (C) review the case briefly with the judge and point out the factors upon which the recommendation was based.
    - (D) submit an alternate recommendation in order to get the judge to review the case.

26. A supervisor of probation officers should make every effort to interpret the socio-legal aspects and limitations of a probation department to the public so that the public may appreciate probation objectives as fully as possible. The content and level of explanation and interpretation should be determined chiefly by the
    - (A) nature and extent of the interest of the individual or group.
    - (B) attitude of the case supervisor.
    - (C) attitude of the probation officers under his or her supervision.
    - (D) policies of the agency on the subject of public relations.

**27.** In reviewing a report submitted by a probation officer in preparation for a formal violation hearing, the point that the supervisor should scrutinize most closely is the

(A) extent to which the violation of the terms of probation is also a violation of other laws.

(B) nature of the proof of the violation that is to be submitted to the court.

(C) probationer's general attitude and work adjustment.

(D) regularity of meeting office appointments on the part of the probationer.

**28.** When a supervising probation officer reports to the court on the content of a pre-sentence investigation, it is generally most important for the officer to

(A) be prepared with a major recommendation.

(B) be prepared with a major recommendation and with sufficient alternatives in case the major recommendation is not accepted.

(C) be ready with a full statement of facts.

(D) express an opinion of the case, especially if his or her views disagree with those of the judge.

**29.** The most desirable plan to follow in coping with the problem of understaffing and excessive caseloads in a probation department is to

(A) budget the time of the probation officer in accordance with the seriousness of the offense committed.

(B) classify probationers on the basis of the intensity of supervision required in each case.

(C) discharge probationers from supervision at the first indication that they are adjusted to the community.

(D) recommend to the court that the length of probation periods be reduced.

**30.** The expression "span of control" as used in public administration refers to the

(A) number of individuals one person can supervise effectively.

(B) length of time a person can concentrate on a given task.

(C) necessity of avoiding monotony in order to maintain efficiency.

(D) need for a realistic table of organization.

**31.** In connection with the use of drugs such as chlorpromazine and reserpine in the treatment of mentally ill patients, which of the following statements is least correct on the basis of current knowledge?

(A) These drugs are broadening the horizons of therapy.

(B) Many patients are now able to leave mental hospitals whereas formerly there seemed little hope.

(C) A great deal more needs to be known about the reasons that the drugs have a favorable effect on patients.

(D) These drugs are taking the place of psychotherapy and the shock therapies.

**32.** Projective personality tests such as the Rorschach and the Thematic Apperception tests are

(A) used in place of psychiatric examination.

(B) valuable in confirming or negating the psychiatric diagnosis.

(C) more helpful when used with offenders than with nonoffenders.

(D) so inaccurate even when given by a skilled psychologist that their value is very questionable.

**Directions:** For questions 33–37, select the definition in Column II that best defines the term listed in Column I. Write the letter of the definition on your answer sheet.

| Column I | Column II |
|---|---|
| 33. transference | (A) a plausible explanation invented to account for belief or behavior motivated from unconscious sources |
| 34. sublimation | (B) the transfer of the psychic energy of the libido into socially acceptable channels of endeavor |
| 35. narcissism | (C) the shifting of emotional attachments from one person or object to another |
| 36. sadism | (D) the process by which an emotional trauma, after repression, becomes changed into a hysterical physical symptom |
| 37. compensation | (E) gratification, frequently of an erotic nature, derived from the contemplation of one's body or personality |
| | (F) the mechanism by which an approved or admirable character trait is developed to conceal from the ego the presence of an opposite one |
| | (G) sexual gratification obtained by the infliction of pain upon others |
| | (H) abnormal sexual passion in which one finds pleasure in abuse and cruelty from his or her associate |

38. The court of last resort is generally referred to as

(A) the appeals court.
(B) the district court.
(C) the court of last resort.
(D) the Supreme Court.

39. Which of the following may not bring proceedings to establish the paternity of a natural child and compel its support?

(A) The mother
(B) The district attorney
(C) A representative of a charitable or philanthropic society
(D) The New York City Department of Welfare

40. The principal purpose of explicitly stating the conditions of probation in the Code of Criminal Procedure is to

(A) serve as a supervision and treatment guide for the probation officer.
(B) form the basis of legal action against a probation violator.
(C) show the probationer what can and cannot be done.
(D) warn the probationer that nonadherence to these conditions will result in a return to court.

41. The U.S. Supreme Court allows for the execution of juveniles who are at least

(A) 12 years old.
(B) 15 years old.
(C) 16 years old.
(D) 18 years old.

**42.** Under the law, a physician who treats a drug addict in New York City must report the addict to the

(A) New York City Police Department.
(B) county medical society.
(C) New York City Department of Health.
(D) Federal Narcotics Bureau.

**43.** No person may be held or tried upon a charge of felony unless by

(A) a presentment.
(B) an indictment.
(C) an information.
(D) arrest.

**44.** Which of the following misdemeanors is not within the jurisdiction of the criminal court?

(A) Unlawful entry
(B) Libel
(C) Practicing medicine without a license
(D) Possession of burglar's instruments

**45.** Of the following, which does not have the authority to grant adoptions under any circumstances?

(A) Civil court justice
(B) Surrogate
(C) Justice of the family court
(D) Supreme Court justice

**46.** Which of the following statements is the least accurate with respect to the criminal court?

(A) The criminal court operates without benefit of any new or additional statutory authority.
(B) The criminal court has no power to enter an "order of protection."
(C) The criminal court is strictly limited to a criminal jurisdiction.
(D) The criminal court denies a complainant or a defendant the right to a formal trial and judgment.

**47.** In dealing with gangs and gangsters, the probation officer must keep in mind that

(A) gangsters are criminals.
(B) many gangsters are dangerous.
(C) gangs are a plague on our society.
(D) all of the above.

**48.** Which of the following is the most important reason why merely a change of residence of a probationer to another neighborhood would NOT be likely to prevent that person from committing crimes in the future?

(A) He or she will inevitably return to the old neighborhood.
(B) He or she will continue to be influenced by friends who will visit a new home.
(C) The change leaves fundamental problems untouched.
(D) The change does not necessarily provide a better environment because of the housing shortage.

**49.** Alcoholics who have served even a short prison term have learned to live without alcohol, yet their first impulse following release is frequently to become intoxicated. Of the following, the most likely reason for such an impulse is that

(A) they have not been in prison long enough.

(B) this is a normal reaction for nonalcoholics as well as alcoholics on release.

(C) their powerful psychic drive for drinking has not been curbed.

(D) they lack the determination to give up drink.

50. "Probation and parole are never going to be panaceas for crime and delinquency. These we shall always have with us since conformance to any set of social norms must always be a matter of degree. Even in a millennial society, the inhabitants of the outer ends of the adjustment ellipse would probably be denominated delinquent. And we do not live in a millennial society." On the basis of the above quotation, it is most valid to conclude that

(A) probation and parole will eventually cure crime and delinquency.

(B) the incidence and degree of crime and delinquency are positively correlated with the complexity of the societal organization.

(C) crime and delinquency will not exist in a millennial society.

(D) interpretations of what constitutes crime and delinquency are dynamic and based upon the social norms of the time.

51. Although adequate comparative information on juvenile delinquency is still difficult to obtain, the general trend since 1927 indicates a rise in juvenile delinquency. This trend also reveals

(A) an increase in the proportion of female offenders.

(B) that girls are proportionately more delinquent than boys.

(C) that girls' cases are not concentrated in the same age period as boys' cases.

(D) that no valid estimate of juvenile delinquency in terms of proportion of female to male offenders can be made.

52. According to studies made to determine success or failure of parole, which of the following statements in regard to the rate of recidivism of parolees is least accurate?

(A) Men convicted of burglary have a high rate of recidivism.

(B) The longer the period served in the institution, the lower the rate of recidivism.

(C) Men convicted of fraud or forgery have unusually high rates of recidivism.

(D) The rate of recidivism is much lower for the first and occasional offender than for the habitual and professional criminal.

53. Which of the following statements best indicates the extent to which the probation officer should make use of community resources in carrying out a plan of treatment for a probationer?

(A) In order to lighten the tremendous load of probation departments, all possible cases should be referred to private agencies in the community.

(B) The law places the total responsibility on the probation officer to do the necessary case work, thus excluding any use of other agencies.

(C) The probation officer must retain full responsibility for case work supervision, using community agencies for specialized services.

(D) The probation officer must retain full responsibility for surveillance of probationers, using community agencies for case work services.

54. Preventive detention for juveniles was approved by the U.S. Supreme Court in

(A) *In Re Gault.*

(B) *Stanford v. Kentucky.*

(C) *Schall v. Martin.*

(D) *Fare v. Michael C.*

55. That a (juvenile) probation officer was an agent of the state and did not necessarily operate in the child's best interest was the holding of

    (A) *In Re Gault.*
    (B) *Stanford v. Kentucky.*
    (C) *Schall v. Martin.*
    (D) *Fare v. Michael C.*

56. The *primary* purpose served by probationers reporting to the probation officer is

    (A) the ability of the probation officer to "check out" the probationer's affect and demeanor.
    (B) to provide a framework for discipline and authority.
    (C) to provide an easy way to consult with the probationer.
    (D) because it's the only way to have contact with the probationer.

57. Of the following, the most desirable method of developing the interviewing skills of a probation officer is for the supervisor to

    (A) recommend reading specific recent professional books on accepted principles and methods of interviewing.
    (B) help the officer analyze unconscious motives and thought processes in the interview.
    (C) help the officer consciously evaluate strengths and weaknesses as an interviewer.
    (D) urge the officer to take further courses in interviewing.

58. A new probation officer under your supervision expresses some nervousness when approaching a first interview with a client known to have a quick temper. It would be most desirable for you to advise this officer to

    (A) impress upon the client his or her power of arrest.
    (B) emphasize to the probationer the penalty for probation violation.
    (C) maintain a stern, professional bearing and be prepared to ask a series of pointed questions.
    (D) attempt to find grounds of mutual interest through which a friendly relationship can be established.

59. Interviews are the primary tool of the case work process. In probation work they are used chiefly to

    (A) impress upon the probationer that he or she is under constant surveillance.
    (B) provide counseling and guidance for the person in trouble.
    (C) secure reports on the probationer's activities for case recording.
    (D) carry out the orders of the court.

60. One type of interviewing technique is known as "clarification." This technique is used most appropriately when a probationer

    (A) manifests discouragement and needs reassurance.
    (B) is confused in his or her own mind about either facts or thoughts or their significance.
    (C) needs to be "told off."
    (D) is limited in the ability to express feelings.

61. Signs of ambivalence on the part of a client during an interview generally show that the client

    (A) is deliberately withholding information in order to be misleading.
    (B) wants to please the probation officer.
    (C) resents being interviewed by a probation officer.
    (D) has conflicting feelings about beliefs and personal allegiances.

62. Through case reading, a supervising probation officer discovers that a probation officer under supervision habitually argues with clients. The supervisor should

(A) reprimand the probation officer for emphasis on authority.

(B) confer with the probation officer about his or her philosophy of case work and interviewing practices.

(C) remind the probation officer that the client should be given some opportunity to express himself or herself.

(D) reassign the caseload and give the probation officer clients who require less direction.

63. A delinquent boy under age 15 was committed to a residential treatment institution operated by a voluntary agency. While in court, at the time of his commitment, he threatened to escape as soon as he arrived at the institution. In view of these circumstances, the best course of action for the probation officer to take would be to

(A) accept this information as part of the total behavior picture of the boy but, at the same time, inform the institutional representative of the boy's statement in court.

(B) recommend that the boy go to a state training school instead of a voluntary agency.

(C) impress upon the boy that if he escapes he will be brought before the court for further action.

(D) ignore his wish to escape and permit the institution to deal with the boy as it sees fit.

64. Which of the following policies to follow in requesting psychiatric examinations of children brought into a children's court is the most practical?

(A) Every delinquent child brought into court should be examined psychiatrically.

(B) Only delinquent children who commit serious aggressive acts should be examined psychiatrically.

(C) Psychiatric examinations should be confined to those delinquent children who show signs of emotional disturbance or conflict.

(D) Psychiatric examinations should be confined chiefly to delinquent children committing sex offenses.

65. Assume that a graduate engineer on probation for sending defamatory postcards seriously needs work but consistently fails to keep appointments or follow plans for securing work. Of the following, the most probable explanation for his behavior is that

(A) he is incompetent.

(B) he is schizophrenic.

(C) the trauma of this experience with the law has permanently injured his personality.

(D) he has feelings of uncertainty about his ability to work and become self-supporting.

66. Assume that the probation officer assigned to the case described in question 65 comes to you, his supervising officer, for assistance. On the basis of the facts in the case as presented, the most desirable course of action for you to recommend would be that the probation officer at the next interview should

(A) explain to the probationer his feelings of incompetence and inferiority.

(B) give his client a "pep" talk, explaining that society today is tolerant toward probationers.

(C) get the probationer to verbalize his self-condemnation and feelings of self-pity.

(D) suggest the advisability of psychiatric treatment and make such a referral, if possible.

67. Assume that a new probation officer has had fieldwork experience in a private agency dealing with children's behavior problems. He handled a limited caseload at this agency, with ample time for staff consultation and record review. The first records he dictates as a probation officer are voluminous and contain minute details on the attitudes, expressions, and interests of his client. As his immediate supervisor, it would be most desirable for you, in this situation, to

    (A) impress upon him that lengthy records are neither necessary nor desirable.
    (B) help the probation officer recognize that "process" recording is useful in certain types of case situations but that it is not necessarily valid in all cases.
    (C) advise the probation officer to do more fieldwork and spend less time on office routine.
    (D) help the probation officer evaluate the relative importance of all the phases of his work in terms of the present work situation.

68. Of the following, which factor has the greatest effect on the average length of time required to make a thorough and complete pre-sentence investigation?

    (A) The density of population in the area covered by the probation officer
    (B) The quality of the investigation
    (C) The aptitudes of the probation officer
    (D) The type of transportation used by the probation officer

69. The technique in counseling in social work that encourages positive, self-initiated action on the part of the client has been professionally designated as

    (A) client centered.
    (B) directive.
    (C) dynamic passivity.
    (D) rapport focused.

70. The case worker who is not interested in the history and background of the individual as a means of understanding him or her and the development of problems, but who is concerned almost entirely with the client's immediate relationship to the environment and the attitude toward the immediate problem, is engaged in

    (A) psychiatric case work.
    (B) diagnostic case work.
    (C) supportive case work.
    (D) functional case work.

71. The field of social case work now recognizes a division in its theory and practice into two schools, namely, functional and diagnostic. The former was developed as a result of

    (A) Rankian influence.
    (B) psychoanalytically oriented social case work.
    (C) the mysticism of some of Freud's disciples.
    (D) Adler's theory of birth trauma.

72. In their book, *Unraveling Juvenile Delinquency*, in which 500 delinquents were compared with 500 nondelinquents, Sheldon and Eleanor Glueck show that

    (A) a study of cultural influences, to be sound and fair, should be focused entirely upon the external factors comprising the neighborhood or residential area.
    (B) no significant criminality existed in either paternal or maternal families of delinquents.
    (C) there was little, if any, significant difference between the familial backgrounds of the two groups in terms of emotional disturbance, mental retardation, criminality, and drunkenness.
    (D) emotional disturbance and mental retardation were generally characteristic of the paternal and maternal families of the delinquents.

**73.** Some sociologists postulate a theory that explains criminal behavior on the basis of "discordant culture." This means that an individual may commit a crime because of

(A) the contradictory demands made upon him or her by society.
(B) technological improvements and cultural lag.
(C) the example of dishonesty in public office.
(D) conflict between immigrant parents and Americanized children.

**74.** In administering a treatment program in a juvenile court, one must take into consideration that statistical studies dealing with reading development deficiency and delinquency clearly reflect that

(A) almost all delinquent children manifest a reading development deficiency of two or more years.
(B) reading development deficiency plays no significant role since the development deficiency for the general elementary school population is close to 50 percent.
(C) educational needs play little or no role in rehabilitation.
(D) reading development deficiency is closely correlated with motor disabilities.

**75.** The Cornell Index makes available information concerning psychosomatic and neuropsychiatric tendencies in a subject. Of the following, the most accurate statement in connection with the use of this index is that it

(A) should be used only by a psychiatrist.
(B) can be used by a psychologist but only if he or she has the interpretive assistance of a psychiatrist.
(C) should be used only by a team consisting of a psychiatrist, psychologist, and psychiatric case worker.
(D) can be used and interpreted by a probation officer.

# MODEL EXAMINATION 6: ANSWERS AND EXPLANATIONS

## ANSWERS

| | | | | | | | | |
|---|---|---|---|---|---|---|---|---|
| 1. | D | 16. | C | 31. | D | 46. | D | 61. | D |
| 2. | D | 17. | B | 32. | B | 47. | D | 62. | B |
| 3. | A | 18. | B | 33. | C | 48. | C | 63. | A |
| 4. | A | 19. | D | 34. | B | 49. | C | 64. | C |
| 5. | C | 20. | C | 35. | E | 50. | D | 65. | D |
| 6. | D | 21. | C | 36. | G | 51. | A | 66. | D |
| 7. | A | 22. | B | 37. | F | 52. | B | 67. | D |
| 8. | B | 23. | C | 38. | D | 53. | C | 68. | B |
| 9. | C | 24. | C | 39. | B | 54. | C | 69. | A |
| 10. | A | 25. | C | 40. | B | 55. | D | 70. | D |
| 11. | A | 26. | A | 41. | C | 56. | A | 71. | A |
| 12. | D | 27. | B | 42. | C | 57. | C | 72. | D |
| 13. | C | 28. | A | 43. | B | 58. | C | 73. | A |
| 14. | C | 29. | B | 44. | B | 59. | B | 74. | A |
| 15. | A | 30. | A | 45. | A | 60. | B | 75. | D |

## EXPLANATIONS

1. **The correct answer is (D).** Leadership is what the supervisor should provide.
2. **The correct answer is (D).** Developing a training agenda would direct the supervisor's goals.
3. **The correct answer is (A).** Being professional requires removing your ego, your "I," from the worker-client relationship.
4. **The correct answer is (A).** Knowing yourself is a key to good probation work.
5. **The correct answer is (C).** A good officer understands there are many avenues toward working with his or her probationers and can demonstrate his or her ability to tailor different programs for the range of individuals under supervision.
6. **The correct answer is (D).** Criticism comes with any supervisory territory.
7. **The correct answer is (A).** Being a trainer/teacher often means sacrificing something of yourself so the student can learn.
8. **The correct answer is (B).** Fit the officer to the job.
9. **The correct answer is (C).** The supervisor must personally fill the gap from time to time.
10. **The correct answer is (A).** Group conferences are not necessary.
11. **The correct answer is (A).** Admitting fault and/or apologizing is a sign of character, not weakness.
12. **The correct answer is (D).** Unless it is directly related to the job, intelligence should be left out of the discussion.
13. **The correct answer is (C).** You should also explain the appeal mechanism (if one exists).
14. **The correct answer is (C).** Again, admitting your mistake is a sign of character.
15. **The correct answer is (A).** While all of these are important, it is vital that the supervisor serves as the liaison between the agency and the officers.

16. **The correct answer is (C).** The jurisdiction is irrelevant to the probation department or officer.

17. **The correct answer is (B).** Assuming that preferences can be accommodated, the supervisor should have assigned an investigative caseload to this individual.

18. **The correct answer is (B).** The probationer has made his choice, the officer has given the options, and the supervisor needs to support his officer.

19. **The correct answer is (D).** Case decision making should be the responsibility of the officer assigned.

20. **The correct answer is (C).** Working with the officer is a good idea as well.

21. **The correct answer is (C).** The supervisor also needs to direct the officer toward strengthening his or her weaknesses.

22. **The correct answer is (B).** Part of the review should be to assist the officer in making better reports.

23. **The correct answer is (C).** Individual plans for individual offenders is always the best approach.

24. **The correct answer is (C).** A structure that allows officers to perform what they are best at is most practical.

25. **The correct answer is (C).** Reviewing with the judge is a good idea (if such a relationship exists), but it should be kept in mind that ultimately the officer must do what the judge wants done.

26. **The correct answer is (A).** Presentations (and information) should be tailored to the group.

27. **The correct answer is (B).** It is of primary importance to be able to document the nature of the violation of the probationer to the court's satisfaction.

28. **The correct answer is (A).** The recommendation is an integral part of the report, supported by the information obtained.

29. **The correct answer is (B).** Classification is the best way to deal with this kind of problem.

30. **The correct answer is (A).** This is generally believed to be 5 to 7 people.

31. **The correct answer is (D).** The drugs are an adjunct, not a replacement, to therapy.

32. **The correct answer is (B).** The more information the better, generally, in diagnoses.

33. **The correct answer is (C).**

34. **The correct answer is (B).**

35. **The correct answer is (E).**

36. **The correct answer is (G).**

37. **The correct answer is (F).**

38. **The correct answer is (D).** The Supreme Court may have other names in some other states, but it is the final arbiter of questions and conflict.

39. **The correct answer is (B).** The district attorney is concerned with criminal matters only.

40. **The correct answer is (B).** The probationer must know his or her responsibilities and when he or she fails to meet them.

41. **The correct answer is (C).** This was shown in the case *Stanford v. Kentucky* in the mid-1980s.

42. **The correct answer is (C).** This is state specific and not necessarily the law in other states.

43. **The correct answer is (B).** This comes from the grand jury and may not necessarily be required in every state.

44. **The correct answer is (B).** This requires a civil remedy.

45. **The correct answer is (A).** This is specified in state codes.

46. **The correct answer is (D).** The criminal court does not usually deny a complainant the right to a formal trial, and therefore, based on the question, this is the *least* accurate response.

47. **The correct answer is (D).** Gangsters engage in criminal activity and gangs foster this behavior.

48. **The correct answer is (C).** The problem is the nature of the probationer, not the new neighborhood. Wherever he or she may be, there are always victims available.

49. **The correct answer is (C).** An alcoholic is always an alcoholic. If an alcoholic has not been rehabilitated with regard to his or her drinking problem, he or she will most likely revert to drinking again.

50. **The correct answer is (D).** Laws change based on what society wants.

51. **The correct answer is (A).** The number of female delinquents is clearly on the rise, and they are becoming more violent.

52. **The correct answer is (B).** The length of time incarcerated does not appear to be an influencing factor in recidivism.

53. **The correct answer is (C).** One of the roles of the officer is that of resource broker. He or she, at all times, maintains responsibility for the offender.

54. **The correct answer is (C).** This case allows for juveniles to be held for what they might do.

55. **The correct answer is (D).** This case removed some of the objectivity and helping status of the juvenile probation officer (JPO).

56. **The correct answer is (A).** The officer needs to see the probationer, whether in the office or on the streets, and preferably both.

57. **The correct answer is (C).** Developing interviewer skills is paramount. Taking courses is also a good idea, as is reading relevant materials.

58. **The correct answer is (C).** A professional, no-nonsense approach is absolutely essential.

59. **The correct answer is (B).** The more information gathered, the better the guidance given.

60. **The correct answer is (B).** Paraphrasing, giving the offender back his or her words and thoughts, also helps.

61. **The correct answer is (D).** The source of this conflict would be good to know.

62. **The correct answer is (B).** The supervisor also should observe some interviews to better assess and direct his or her officer.

63. **The correct answer is (A).** The officer and the institution need to know what the offender said.

64. **The correct answer is (C).** Those children who show such signs need to be evaluated by a medical professional. Knowledge is necessary for a proper recommendation to be made.

65. **The correct answer is (D).** These feelings must be explored, but he also needs to know that he must find a job.

66. **The correct answer is (D).** An alternative might be a referral to some type of counselor.

67. **The correct answer is (D).** The private sector is fundamentally different from the public sector, and the adjustment is often difficult.

68. **The correct answer is (B).** The better the quality of investigation is, the better the report will be. Sometimes, however, only a cursory investigation can be undertaken, and the quality of the report will most certainly reflect that.

69. **The correct answer is (A).** The focus is on the client rather than the offense.

70. **The correct answer is (D).** This means starting at the present moment and moving forward.

71. **The correct answer is (A).** Otto Rank was a psychotherapist who believed in the concept of reoccurring patterns in life. As such, diagnosis was not as important as analyzing these patterns of functioning.

72. **The correct answer is (D).** The Gluecks believed their study demonstrated that emotional disturbance and mental retardation were inherited characteristics from both the maternal and paternal families.

73. **The correct answer is (A).** This theory is especially helpful in understanding different cultures. It should also be remembered, however, that people in America are subject to American law and culture, not the law (or culture) from which they came.

74. **The correct answer is (A).** Ineffective school performance is a characteristic of most delinquents. An inability to read well would certainly lead to ineffective school performance.

75. **The correct answer is (D).** The Cornell Medical Index is a psychological test similar to the MMPI that measures a variety of behaviors across several scales. It is, in sum, one of many tests that can be used to assess the "functioning" of an individual.

# PART FIVE

# Career Information
# Resources

# HOW TO FIND A JOB IN PROBATION OR PAROLE

Very often finding a job is a matter of luck. However, we'd like to take some of the luck out of it and make it more directive. Below are a variety of sources you can use in your search for employment in the probation and parole fields.

## THE PRIVATE SECTOR

Most jobs in the private sector can be found in two ways: employment agencies or newspaper classified advertisements. Wherever you live there is certainly a local employment agency. However, you are probably aware that there are only a small number of private probation agencies throughout the country that employ individuals as probation officers. To find a job in the private sector, you should contact the various city probation departments to find out if they use private agencies. If you can get the name and/or number from the city itself, it will help you in your search. Call to make an appointment, and bring your resume. Keep in mind that they are the first interview that you will have in the line for employment, so you should dress appropriately and be somewhat informed about what the job requires. Reading through the section on various careers in this book will help you. You should also run a search for employment agencies on a search engine like Lycos (www.lycos.com) or Yahoo! (www.yahoo.com). Use words like "probation" and "parole." Combining words like "private+probation" or "private+parole" is also useful in narrowing down your search. Once you get an address or phone number of an agency, contact the agency directly to see how positions are filled and for the job requirements. If you know of specific names of private agencies, you can also run an online search for those companies' Web sites.

There are also dozens of career-oriented Web sites that might be helpful to you. One excellent site is America's Job Bank at www.ajb.dni.us/index.html. You can post your resume online, as well as search for jobs on a state-by-state basis. Other job search engines include www.monster.com and www.hotjobs.com.

## FEDERAL JOBS

The Office of Personnel Management (OPM) is the place to start. This department maintains a list of job openings that is updated daily. In addition, the OPM also publishes the *Federal Exam Announcement* each quarter. Although it is not responsible for hiring candidates, the OPM will provide you with access to each hiring agency, and there you can get the specific details about each job. You can reach the OPM's telephone line at 912-757-3000, seven days a week, 24 hours a day.

The Office of Personnel Management can also be found at www.usajobs.opm.gov. You will find here a complete application for federal employment along with instructions on how to fill it out. At this site you can find explanations of federal job categories and specific job descriptions. You can then search geographically and alphabetically to find out which jobs have current openings and exactly where the openings are located. The listings, in turn, refer you to full vacancy announcements, including qualifications, requirements, and application procedures and deadlines. With adequate equipment you can download the announcement. Or you can then take notes from the information on your screen. Likewise, you can download application forms or even apply electronically using your computer. Or you can follow instructions for getting the proper forms by telephone or mail.

Another excellent source is the *Federal Jobs Digest*, a biweekly newspaper that lists thousands of government jobs, both in the United States and in other countries. The Digest also has a Web site that features thousands of job listings. You can visit the Web site at www.jobsfed.com or contact the *Federal Jobs Digest* by e-mail: webmaster@jobsfed.com; voice: 800-824-5000; or fax: 914-366-0059.

Finally, you can apply directly to the Federal Department of Probation. Under this department are ninety-four federal districts. Within each district is a U.S. district court. You can find them under the heading "U.S. Government" in the blue pages of your telephone directory.

## STATE EMPLOYMENT

Almost every state has its own Web site. In most cases, state Web sites follow a typical naming convention: www.state.__.us. In the blank, you would fill the two-letter code for the state you are interested in. For Arizona, for example, you would enter www.state.az.us. For Pennsylvania, enter www.state.pa.us. Note that a few state Web sites deviate from this convention. Following is a list of the latest URLs for the state sites. Be aware, however, that they may change from time to time.

- **Alabama:** www.state.al.us
- **Alaska:** www.state.ak.us
- **Arizona:** www.state.az.us
- **Arkansas:** www.state.ar.us
- **California:** www.state.ca.us
- **Colorado:** www.state.co.us
- **Connecticut:** www.state.ct.us
- **Delaware:** www.state.de.us
- **District of Columbia:** www.dchomepage.net
- **Florida:** www.state.fl.us
- **Georgia:** www.state.ga.us
- **Hawaii:** www.state.hi.us
- **Idaho:** www.state.id.us
- **Illinois:** www.state.il.us
- **Indiana:** www.state.in.us
- **Iowa:** www.state.ia.us
- **Kansas:** www.accesskansas.org
- **Kentucky:** www.kydirect.net
- **Louisiana:** www.state.la.us
- **Maine:** www.state.me.us
- **Maryland:** www.state.md.us
- **Massachusetts:** www.state.ma.us

- **Michigan:** www.state.mi.us
- **Minnesota:** www.state.mn.us
- **Mississippi:** www.state.ms.us
- **Missouri:** www.state.mo.us
- **Montana:** www.discoveringmontana.com
- **Nebraska:** www.state.ne.us
- **Nevada:** www.state.nv.us
- **New Hampshire:** www.state.nh.us
- **New Jersey:** www.state.nj.us
- **New Mexico:** www.state.nm.us
- **New York:** www.state.ny.us
- **North Carolina:** www.ncgov.com
- **North Dakota:** www.discovernd.com
- **Ohio:** www.state.oh.us
- **Oklahoma:** www.state.ok.us
- **Oregon:** www.state.or.us
- **Pennsylvania:** www.state.pa.us
- **Rhode Island:** www.state.ri.us
- **South Carolina:** www.myscgov.com
- **South Dakota:** www.state.sd.us
- **Tennessee:** www.state.tn.us
- **Texas:** www.state.tx.us
- **Utah:** www.state.ut.us
- **Vermont:** www.state.vt.us
- **Virginia:** www.state.va.us
- **Washington:** access.wa.gov
- **West Virginia:** www.state.wv.us
- **Wisconsin:** www.wisconsin.gov
- **Wyoming:** www.state.wy.us

## LOCAL EMPLOYMENT

In many instances, city and county employment information can be found on your state's Web site. However, if you live in a large city, it is likely that the city has its own site. In New York City, for example, you can find information about becoming a probation officer at the following URL: www.ci.nyc.ny.us/html/prob/html/po.html. In other parts of the country, you may have to apply for jobs through the local county. For example, if you wanted to work in Los Angeles you would have to contact the Los Angeles County Department of Probation (562-940-2554) or visit its Web site at probation.co.la.ca.us.

You should also investigate to see if there is a local (large) city civil service publication that lists upcoming job announcements. For example, in New York City, *The Chief-Leader* is the primary source for upcoming civil service jobs. (You can write to them at 277 Broadway, New York, NY 10007 to order a subscription.) You will also find information about state and federal jobs in the paper.

## JUVENILE PROBATION

Many jobs in juvenile probation are not civil service positions. Check your local newspaper and call the local juvenile court (its number should be in the blue pages of your local telephone book) and inquire if there are any juvenile probation officer (JPO) jobs and how positions are filled. Many are filled by sending a resume to the chief juvenile probation officer and/or the judge.

# HOW TO GET A JOB IN PROBATION OR PAROLE

Now that you know where to look for a job, you need to understand the procedure. The procedure you must follow to get a government job varies little from job to job and from one level of government to another. There are variations in details, of course, but certain steps are common to all.

## THE NOTICE OF EXAMINATION OR ANNOUNCEMENT

Once you have found a *Notice of Examination* (it may be called an announcement), read it very carefully. If you can, get a copy for yourself. If not, then take the time to write notes. Make sure you have written down all of the details. The *Notice of Examination* will give a brief job description. It will tell the title of the job and describe some of the job duties and responsibilities. On the basis of the job description, you will decide whether or not you want to apply for this job. If the job appeals to you, you must concentrate on the following:

- **Education and experience requirements.** If you cannot meet these requirements, do not bother to apply. Government service can be very competitive. The government has more than enough applicants from whom to choose. It will not waive its requirements for you.

- **Age requirements.** Discrimination on the basis of age is illegal, but a number of jobs demand so much sustained physical effort that they require retirement at an early age. For these positions there is an entry age limit. If you are already beyond that age, do not apply. If you are still too young, inquire about the time lag until hiring. It may be that you will reach the minimum age by the time the position is to be filled.

- **Citizenship requirements.** Many jobs are open to all people who are eligible to work in the United States, but all law enforcement jobs and most federal jobs are limited to U.S. citizens. If you are well along the way toward citizenship and expect to be naturalized soon, inquire as to your exact status with respect to the job.

- **Residency requirements.** If there is a residency requirement, you must live within the prescribed limits or be willing to move. If you are not willing to live in the area, do not waste time applying.

- **Required forms.** The announcement of the position for which you are applying will specify the form of application requested. For most federal jobs, you may submit either the Optional Application for Federal Employment (OF 612) or a resume that fulfills the requirements set forth in the pamphlet, *Applying for a Federal Job* (OF 510). For other than federal jobs, the *Notice of Examination* may tell you where you must go or write to get the necessary form or forms. Be sure you secure them all. The application might be a simple form asking nothing more than name, address, citizenship, and social security number, or it may be a complex Experience Paper. An Experience Paper, as its title implies, asks a great deal about education, job training, job experience, and life experience. Typically, the Experience Paper permits no identification by name, sex, or race; the only identifying mark is your social security number. The purpose of this procedure is to avoid permitting bias of any sort to enter into the weighting of responses. The Experience Paper generally follows a short form of application that does include a name. When the rating process is completed, the forms are coordinated by means of the social security number.

■ **Filing date, place, and fee.** There is great variation in this area. For some positions, you can file your application at any time. Others have a first day and last day for filing. If you file too early or too late, your application will not be considered. Sometimes it is sufficient to have your application postmarked by the last day for filing. More often, your application must be received by the last date. If you are mailing your application, allow five full business days for it to get there on time. Place of filing will be stated right on the notice. Most applications may be filed by mail, but occasionally in-person filing is specified. Follow directions. Federal and postal positions require no filing fee. Most, but not all, other government jobs do charge a fee for processing your application. The fee is not always the same. Be sure to check this out. If the notice specifies "money order only," plan to purchase a money order. If you send or present a personal check, your application will be rejected without consideration. Of course, you should never mail cash; but if the announcement specifies "money order only," you cannot submit cash, even in person.

■ **How to qualify.** This portion of the notice will tell you the basis on which the candidate will be chosen. Some examination scores consist of a totaling of weighted education and experience factors. This type of examination is called an "unassembled exam," because you do not come to one place to take the exam and it is based upon your responses on the application and supplementary forms. Obviously, these must be complete for you to get full credit for all you have learned and accomplished. The notice may tell you of a qualifying exam, an exam that you must pass in addition to scoring high on an unassembled, written, or performance test. Or the notice may tell you of a competitive exam—written, performance, or combined. The competitive exam may be described in very general terms or may be described in detail. It is even possible that a few sample questions will be attached. If the date of the exam has been set, that date will appear on the notice. Write it down.

When you have the application forms in hand, photocopy them. Fill out the photocopies first. This way you can correct mistakes or make changes before transferring the information to the original application. Work at fitting what you have to say into the space allowed. Do not exaggerate, but be sure to give yourself credit for responsibilities you took on, for cost-saving ideas you gave your prior employer, or for any accomplishments. Be clear and thorough in communicating what you have learned and what you can do.

When you are satisfied with your draft, copy over the application onto the original form(s). Be sure to include any backup material that is requested; by the same token, do not send more "evidence" than is truly needed to support your claims of qualification. Your application must be complete according to the requirements of the announcement but should not be overwhelming. You want to command hiring attention by exactly conforming to requirements.

Check over all forms for neatness and completeness. Sign wherever indicated. Attach the fee, if required. Then mail or personally file the application on time.

When the civil service commission or personnel office to which you submitted your application receives it, the office will date, stamp, log, and open your file. The office may acknowledge receipt with more forms, with sample exam questions, or with a simple receipt slip. Or you may hear nothing at all for months.

Eventually, you will receive a testing date or an interview appointment. Write these on your calendar in red so that you don't let the dates slip by. If you receive an admission ticket for an exam, be sure to put it in a safe place, but keep it in sight so that you will not forget to take it with you to the exam. Begin to study and prepare right away if you have not already done so.

If you are called for an exam, arrive promptly and dress appropriately. Neatness is always appropriate; however, you do not need to "dress up" for a performance exam or for a written exam. If you will do manual work for your performance exam, wear clean work clothes. For a written exam, neat, casual clothing is fine.

## THE INTERVIEW

If there is no exam and you are called directly to an interview, what you wear is more important. Take special care to look businesslike and professional. A neat dress, slacks and blouse, or skirted suit is fine for women; men should wear a suit or slacks, a jacket, and shirt and tie.

If you are called for an interview, you are most likely under serious consideration. There may still be competition for the job—someone else may be more suited than you—but you are qualified, and your skills and background have appealed to someone in the hiring office. The interview may be aimed at getting information about

- **Your knowledge.** The interviewer wants to know what you know about the area in which you will work. You may also be asked questions probing your knowledge of the agency for which you are interviewing. Do you care enough to have educated yourself about the functions and role of the agency?

- **Your judgment.** You may be faced with hypothetical situations—job-related or interpersonal—and be asked questions like, "What would you do if...." Think carefully before answering. Be decisive and diplomatic. There are no "right answers." The interviewer is aware that you are being put on the spot. How well you can handle this type of question is an indication of your flexibility and maturity.

- **Your personality.** You will have to be trained and supervised. You will have to work with others. What is your attitude? How will you fit in? The interviewer will make judgments in these areas on the basis of general conversation with you and from your responses to specific lines of questioning. Be pleasant, polite, and open with your answers, but do not volunteer a great deal of extra information. Stick to the subjects introduced by the interviewer. Answer fully, but resist the temptation to ramble on.

- **Your attitude toward work conditions.** These are practical concerns. If the job will require frequent travel for extended periods, how will you feel about it? What is your family's attitude? If you will be very unhappy about the travel, you may leave the job and your training will have been a waste of the taxpayers' money. The interviewer also wants to know how you will react to overtime or irregular shifts.

## MEDICAL EXAMINATION

Parole and probation officers are often performing work of varying degrees of difficulty, and as such, they are required to be in good health. Because there are normally eyesight or hearing requirements for these positions, these must be checked against local and state agency standards. Because the job sometimes requires standing, lifting, or running, the applicant must be medically able to withstand the rigors. Since all government employers afford some sort of health coverage, there must be assurance of the general health of the employee or at least full awareness of current or potential problems. Drug testing is often included and is legal if applied routinely and equally to all applicants and if notice of it is given beforehand.

## PHYSICAL EXAMINATION

Physical performance testing is limited to applicants for physically demanding jobs. Probation officers, parole officers, police officers, firefighters, and correction officers, for example, must be able to run, climb, and carry, often under stress of personal danger as well as under the pressures of the immediate situation. They may be forced to work in different types of weather, make field trips, and spend time making visual observations and surveillance at various types of locations. Sometimes, especially where speed may be a crucial element, the physical test is competitively scored and enters into the rating the candidate earns for placement on the certification list. Probation and parole officers are also required to have strong communication skills and, therefore, should have no physical limitations pertaining to speech and hearing.

## PSYCHOLOGICAL INTERVIEW

Finally, there is the psychological interview. This interview differs from the general information interview or the final hiring and placement interview in that it tries to assess your behavior under stress. Not all applicants for government jobs must be subjected to a psychological interview. It is usually limited to persons who will carry guns, to people who must make very quick decisions at moments of danger, and to people who might find themselves under interrogation by hostile forces. In other words, probation and parole officers must be able to do their jobs without "cracking" under the strain. As a probation or parole officer, given the nature of the job and the individuals with whom you will come in contact, you may even be required to take a lie detector test.

Reading all the applications and weeding out the unqualified ones takes time. Weighing education and experience factors takes time. Administering and scoring of exams takes time. Interviews, medical exams, and physical performance tests take time. Verifying references takes time. And, finally, the vacancies must occur, and the government agency must have the funds to fill the vacancies.

All of this clarifies why you must not leave a job or a job search at any step along the way. Wait until you are offered your government job before you cut other ties. But when you finally do get that job, you will have a good income, many benefits, and job security.

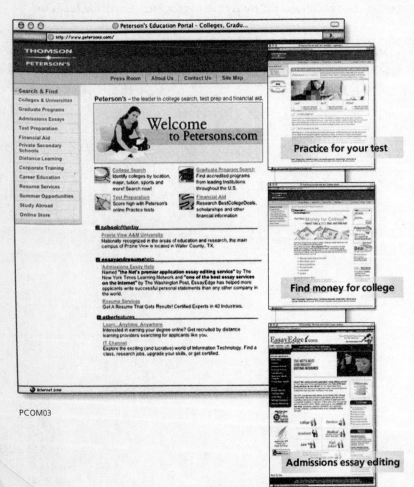